Cold War in South Florida

Historic Resource Study

October 2004

Written by Steve Hach

Edited by Jennifer Dickey

This historic resource study exists in two formats. A printed version is available for study at Everglades National Park, Big Cypress National Preserve, Biscayne National Park, Dry Tortugas National Park, the Southeast Regional Office of the National Park Service, and at a variety of other repositories. For more widespread access, this historic resource study also exists in a web- based format through the web site of the National Park Service. Please visit www.nps.gov for more information.

Cultural Resources Division
Southeast Regional Office
National Park Service
100 Alabama Street, SW
Atlanta, GA 30303
404-562-3117

Big Cypress National Preserve
Biscayne National Park
Dry Tortugas National Park
Everglades National Park

http://www.nps.gov

Cold War in South Florida
Historic Resource Study (2004)

Recommended by: _____   4-1-04
                Chief, Cultural Resources Division   Date
                Southeast Region

Recommended by: _____   4/6/04
                Associate Regional Director, Cultural Resources   Date
                Stewardship and Partnership, Southeast Region

Approved by: _____   7-14-2004
                Superintendent, Everglades National Park   Date

Approved by: _____   9-27-04
                Regional Director, Southeast Region   Date

Contents

Figures

Figure Credits

Foreword

We are pleased to make available this historic resource study, covering the Cold War and historic resources related to it located in south Florida. The study deals with Cold War- related activities and resources in four units of the National Park Services as well as nearby areas. Historians and preservationists are increasingly devoting their attention to the Cold War, which was the defining event in the history of the second half of the twentieth century. This study is a first step in understanding the unique role played by Florida and Florida National Parks in the history of the Cold War. Our hope is that it will serve as a catalyst for the preservation of Cold War- related resources throughout the State of Florida. The study has already resulted in a National Register of Historic Places nomination for the HM- 69 Nike Missile Base within Everglades National Park.

This study was written by historian Steve Hach under a cooperative agreement between the National Park Service and the Georgia Trust for Historic Preservation. We wish to thank the superintendents and staffs of Everglades National Park, Big Cypress National Preserve, Biscayne National Park, and Dry Tortugas National Park for their assistance in preparing this study.

Daniel Scheidt
Chief, Cultural Resources Division
Southeast Regional Office
October 2004

Introduction

South Florida was the location of many important events during the Cold War period 1945- 1989. Indeed, the region served as a forward command center for the projection of U.S. power into the Western Hemisphere throughout the conflict. The region's proximity to Latin America made it an operational center for both covert and overt activities as the United States pursued its policy of containing communism. From the 1950s until the end of the Cold War, government officials directed operations from south Florida military installations such as Homestead Air Force Base, Opa Locka Marine Air Station, and the various U.S. Navy facilities in Key West that affected events in Guatemala, Cuba, Nicaragua, and other nations throughout Latin America. From Miami to Key West, quiet residential neighborhoods were havens for undercover operatives while the swamps and forests served as training grounds. From south Florida the United States launched numerous operations: the overthrow of the Arbenz government of Guatemala in 1954; the unsuccessful Bay of Pigs invasion of 1961; the military buildup necessitated by the Cuban missile crisis of 1962; surveillance, intelligence, and espionage activities against Cuba, Nicaragua, and other nations; and radio and television propaganda broadcasting to Cuba. All activities were justified under the U.S. foreign policy of containment. As the south Florida region helped shape these events, the events helped shape the region. In many cases, physical traces of these operations are still visible on the south Florida landscape.

This Historic Resource Study (HRS) provides a historic context for, and identifies, sites in south Florida related to the Cold War and U.S. relations with Latin America. The report focuses on resources in and near the four national parks located in the region: Everglades National Park (Everglades NP), Biscayne National Park (Biscayne NP), Big Cypress National Preserve (Big Cypress NP), and Dry Tortugas National Park (Dry Tortugas NP). The study identifies structures, remains of structures, and landscapes where activities associated with the Cold War are reported to have taken place. This HRS pays particular attention to sites related to the events mentioned above as well as resources associated with the large Cuban exile population of south Florida. The historic context provides the basis for future nominations to the National Register of Historic Places. The HM- 69 Nike base within Everglades National Park was listed in the National Register in 2004.

This report consists of four main sections. Section One includes a brief introduction to the Cold War and provides historical context for resources identified later in the report. This section is general in nature and is intended to provide the reader with a basic summary of major Cold War events and trends in order to understand better the relevance of resources discovered during the course of this research. The Cold War is a controversial topic for historians. History written on this topic sometimes strays into the realm of political polemic rather than reasoned scholarship. The first section of this report attempts to avoid the pitfalls of both orthodoxy and revisionism while still providing a useful introduction to Cold War history. The United States fought the Cold War for a variety of reasons and utilized a variety of methods in the battle. U.S. motivations for waging the Cold War were multifaceted and cannot be solely explained as a purely altruistic desire to save the "free" world. Such rhetoric is challenged by the reality of the methods used to wage the Cold War. Some of these methods and their effects compromised the ideals and principles of the United States and undermined the oft- stated U.S. goals of supporting freedom and democracy. U.S. Cold War ideological assumptions often resulted in questionable policies and ambiguous outcomes while U.S. policies impacted the nation's politics, society, culture, environment, and demographics in ways that are only now beginning to be examined by historians. The first section of this report illuminates at least some of these broader issues.

Section Two identifies historic resources within the boundaries of Everglades NP, Biscayne NP, Big Cypress NP, and Dry Tortugas NP. These parks, by virtue of their location and resources, played an important role in the Cold War history of the region. Everglades NP served as a training ground for Central Intelligence Agency (CIA)- sponsored Cuban exile espionage and intelligence teams, a site for an air defense missile installation, an open- air research lab for advanced Cold War- related military sensor technology, and as a recreational area for military personnel. Biscayne NP provided landscapes and structures for the training of Cuban exile demolition teams, weapons cache storage for Cuban exile commandos, and training sites for Cuban exile paramilitary groups. Dry Tortugas NP was the location of various Cold War- related radio installations, signal intelligence (SIGINT) facilities, and a landing point for Cuban exiles fleeing Fidel Castro's Cuba. Very little documentation was found on the role of Big Cypress NP.

The remainder of Section Two focuses on other Cold War- related resources located throughout south Florida. These include local military facilities, Cold War- era defense plants, Cuban exile landmarks, and other resources related to various Cold War events in south Florida. This list is in no way comprehensive. Given time, money, and effort, many more Cold War resources could be identified in the region. For those resources that were identified, this report takes the broadest possible view of their role in the Cold War.

Section Three of this HRS includes a list of various archives, museums, and other facilities visited or contacted in the course of preparing this report. It should be noted that for this study, it was not possible to perform an exhaustive search of all listed facilities. In most cases, materials consulted for this HRS were scattered under a wide variety of subject headings. Simply looking under "Cold War Florida" failed to turn up much information of value. Military archives or other government facilities have no records of activities associated with many of the resources identified within this report. In many cases, government research projects such as the Department of Defense's Legacy Project tend to focus on more "concrete" resources such as buildings and other structures.[1] Such projects lack the scope to include the impact of the Cold War on U.S. society and culture and also tend to downplay the negative impacts of the Cold War. As a result, government archives and records may not be the best place to look for documentation on negative environmental effects, civil rights violations, or the true costs of a foreign policy that often did business with dictators and other questionable characters in the name of anticommunism.

The final section of this report is a bibliography of primary and secondary sources related to the Cold War history of the United States and south Florida. Any follow- ups to this HRS should continue consulting with government document repositories and private archives such as George Washington University's National Security Archive to assess the availability of newly declassified documents. Follow- up is especially important in the areas of CIA Cold War activities in south Florida. As mentioned previously, research should not be restricted to subjects such as "Cold War Florida." Important information for this report was found in the National Archives and Records Administration II (NARA II) about John F. Kennedy's assassination and the controversy surrounding it. Researchers must be creative while attempting to document the history of resources identified in this HRS and should be prepared to examine a wide variety of source materials.

The reader should be aware that in many cases, documentation for resources connected to Cold War- era CIA, Cuban exile, and covert operations activities in south Florida is often untrue or at least not completely reliable. Researchers must be careful to separate conspiracy theory fantasy from historical reality. Materials connected to the Kennedy assassination, allegations of U.S. government involvement in drug smuggling, and similar sources should be viewed very critically, particularly where internet resources are concerned. While the internet is a valuable resource for any historical research, there are numerous web sites with inaccurate or incomplete information. Many hoaxes have been perpetrated where the Central Intelligence Agency, Cuban exiles, and Kennedy are involved.

---

1.   See the U.S. Department of Defense's *Coming in From the Cold: Military Heritage in the Cold War* (Washington, D.C.: Dept. of Defense, 1994) for a discussion of the program.

Section One: Brief Overview of the Cold War and Related Activities in South Florida

World War II, the Bomb, and the Origins of the Cold War

On August 6, 1945, the B-29 *Enola Gay* delivered its atomic payload high above the city of Hiroshima, Japan. The bomb exploded, destroying much of the city within seconds. The explosion and radioactive effects of the bomb killed more than eighty thousand Japanese men, women, and children. The deployment of the atomic bomb by the U.S. military at Hiroshima and two days later at Nagasaki, Japan ended World War II. U.S. troops in all corners of the world could hardly believe their good fortune. Fatalistic sensibilities—developed over four years of brutal combat—led them to believe that many of them would have died in an invasion of the Japanese home islands.[1] Now, thanks to the new atomic weapons, their lives had been spared. They would live to see their families and their homes.[2]

Once Japan surrendered, the troops and the American people clamored for an end to wartime conditions. As it had after all other wars in its history, the United States government quickly complied with these wishes. Troops with enough "points" went home where they could get on with their lives. Corporations involved in wartime production began to produce consumer goods once more. The United States emerged from the most devastating war in history in great shape. Compared to other nations—such as the Soviet Union—its casualties were light. Other than the attacks on Pearl Harbor, the Aleutians, and a few isolated areas in the Pacific Northwest, property suffered no damage, civilians suffered no enemy occupation, and the nation emerged from the war in an enviable economic position. The war finally ended the Great Depression and filled many pockets with the fruits of full employment.

Americans generally retreated into the newfound prosperity. Returning GIs started families, and the baby boom began. While many people favored a quick demobilization and a return to the more isolationist tendencies of the American historical past, some leaders found reason to be concerned. Having just paid for victory at the cost of American lives and resources far beyond that which seemed acceptable, the military and political leaders of the United States tried to learn the lessons of World War II so they could avoid World War III. The atomic bomb made it perfectly clear that any future world conflict could very well result in the destruction of the human race. American leaders faced an uncertain world with very strong reminders of what the price could be if they failed to

---

1. The Japanese home islands constitute the main territory of Japan; they do not include those islands acquired through military action during World War II or earlier engagements.
2. The decision to deploy the atomic bomb has been a subject of a great deal of historical controversy in recent years. Many scholars find the orthodox interpretation—that the use of the bomb was the only way to end the war without a costly invasion of the Japanese home islands—inadequate. For a discussion of the historiography on the use of the bomb and the many different interpretations of that use see J. Samuel Walker's "The Decision to use the Bomb: A Historiographical Update," *Diplomatic History* 14 (Winter 1990): 97-114. For a discussion of the controversy surrounding the historical study of the use of the bomb and the now famous 1994-95 political battle over the display of the *Enola Gay* at the Smithsonian Air and Space Museum see Edward T. Linenthal and Tom Englehardt, eds., *History Wars: The Enola Gay and other Battles for the American Past* (New York: Metropolitan Books, 1996).

FIGURE 1. Immediately upon assuming the presidency in 1945, Harry S. Truman faced momentous decisions on the use of the atomic bomb and policy toward the Soviets.

define the right course for the United States. Their decisions in the era following the war would set the course of American history for the next forty- five years. They would also lead to many unforeseen outcomes for the American people, including the residents of south Florida.

American policy makers believed that World War II sprang from several factors. They believed that appeasement was wrong and that the attempt to placate German leader Adolf Hitler's territorial appetites by giving him the Sudetanland of Czechoslovakia increased his drive for war. Appeasement meant that Hitler avoided a costly battle with the well- equipped and well- trained Czech army. It also meant that Nazi territorial aggression went unchecked and resulted in more territorial aggression. Few could forget the folly of Neville Chamberlain announcing "peace in our time" at the very moment Hitler was inaugurating what he claimed would be a thousand- year Reich. U.S. policy makers believed they knew the lessons of Munich: in the future, any power that sought to take over control of another state would have to be confronted vigorously and firmly from the very beginning. "No more Munichs" became a battle cry of many cold warriors.

Americans also tried to learn the lessons of Pearl Harbor. Throughout its history, the U.S. relied on its status as a continental "fortress" thousands of

miles away from the dangers of European entanglements. By nature of its geostrategic location, the United States seemed untouchable to most powers. Now, with the advent of long- range bombers and the special Nazi weapons such as the V- 1 and V- 2 rockets—the forerunners to today's modern cruise and ballistic missiles—Americans no longer enjoyed the protection of two vast oceans. American policy makers witnessed firsthand the devastation of Europe and could not imagine American cities suffering similar fates. If future wars were fought with atomic weapons, the results would be even more horrifying. Pearl Harbor and the devastation in Europe and Japan caused a change of attitude among many American leaders. The United States traditionally maintained an isolationist stance with regard to foreign policy and entered conflicts only after long deliberation and a slow methodical buildup of military forces. In a nuclear age where long- range bombers could drop atomic weapons on cities with little or no warning, isolationism posed unacceptable risks. In the uncertain postwar political climate, many American leaders argued that it made no sense to dismantle the large fighting force that the United States had paid such a steep price to build.[3]

Even before the end of the war, American leaders took steps to assure that in the future the United States would enter conflicts from a position of strength and readiness. U.S. political and military leaders secured the rights to numerous overseas bases and support facilities. The United States first acquired overseas bases, coaling stations, and other trappings of empire in the latter part of the nineteenth century. Even more overseas bases were acquired in the 1898 war with Spain. Now, the nation truly became a superpower with global reach. During World War II and its aftermath, U.S. military and political officials acquired airfields, naval ports, air transit rights, and other power projection necessities so that the United States could respond to trouble anywhere in the world before it reached its own shores and affected its own way of life.[4]

The only credible threat to U.S. foreign policy interests was the Soviet Union. Only the Red Army could challenge U.S. military might and only the spread of communism could challenge the liberal international economic order. The Soviets, under the leadership of Joseph Stalin, paid a horrible price in World War II. Approximately twenty- five million Soviet citizens died during World War II from a combination of German aggression, the hardships of the war, and Stalin's crimes against his own people. It is often said that World War II was won with American treasure and Russian blood. The U.S. fought the war with technology, industrial capacity, and a genius for logistical planning unmatched by any other power. The Soviets, on the other hand, provided the other Allies with the time to marshal their forces by absorbing the full fury of Hitler's invasion of Russia. The Soviets destroyed the bulk of the German *Wermacht* (army), but they paid a tremendous price in lives for each victory. With the war's end, Stalin took steps to ensure that such a cataclysmic event never happened to his people again. However, Stalin's moves to secure Soviet territory and provide a buffer zone against yet another invasion from Europe—as well as the

regime's pledge of support for an eventual world-wide communist revolution—intensified the mistrust and fears of the capitalist powers.

During the war, at places like Yalta and Potsdam, the Allies met to make arrangements for the reconstitution of the various states overrun by the Nazis and liberated by the Allies. In many cases, Franklin Delano Roosevelt, Stalin, and Winston Churchill made ambiguous agreements that seemed practical in the heat of battle but quickly fell apart once the unifying threat of the Axis disappeared. Whereas FDR tended to trust Stalin and the Soviets, Churchill and FDR successor Harry Truman were deeply suspicious of Soviet motives.[5] Churchill often raged at the American strategy of fighting the war in a manner that consigned the whole of Eastern Europe to the Soviets.

During the war's end game and the early postwar era, the Soviets violated the other Allies' understanding of the wartime agreements. Also, Stalin's speeches and Soviet foreign policy frequently contained an ideological thrust abhorrent to the capitalist nations. The "spectre of communism" threatened many important U.S. interests and ran counter to the U.S. goal of a democratic, capitalist, international free trade system. Economic and political elites in the capitalist nations knew firsthand the appeal of communism and feared the many local communist parties that agitated for change during the Great Depression. They worried that peace might bring a return to depression. This depression might help the communists by once again demonstrating the failures of capitalism. With a strong Soviet Union ideologically committed to effecting a world- wide revolution, however unrealistic that seemed given the Soviet Union's poor economic position at the end of the war, communism could conceivably

3. Thomas G. Paterson's *On Every Front: The Making of the Cold War* (New York: W.W. Norton and Company, 1979, rev. ed. 1992) is a classic study of the birth of the Cold War. Much of the analysis of the onset of the Cold War and the mind-set of U.S. policy makers discussed here is drawn from his account.

4. Melvyn P. Leffler's *A Preponderance of Power: National Security, the Truman Administration, and the Cold War* (Stanford: Stanford University Press, 1992) provides an exhaustive account of the origins of the Cold War as well as a discussion of the importance placed on the acquisition of overseas bases and transit rights for U.S. military forces. Leffler finds that the Cold War originated not because U.S. policy makers believed in a legitimate military threat from the Soviets, but because they were worried about any imposition on the American lifestyle at home. Protection of "core values"—i.e. the capitalist system and American dominance of that system—is what led to the Cold War.

5. Daniel Yergin's *Shattered Peace: The Origins of the Cold War* (New York: Penguin Books, 1990) makes much of what the author terms the "Yalta axioms" and the "Riga axioms" and how expectations of postwar Soviet behavior changed over time. The differences in the diplomatic styles of Truman and FDR, as well as the changing beliefs in what the various agreements meant for the postwar world, were very important to the increasing tensions among the Allies and the onset of the Cold War.

spread across Europe and perhaps to the United States. Freedom, whether defined in terms of individual freedom and liberty, or as the right of capitalists to control the means of production, would not flourish under communism as practiced by Stalin. The Soviet Union possessed a strong and highly paranoid leader, a foreign and dangerous ideology, a large and strong military that had borne the brunt of the fighting against Germany, and a reason to hold on to vast territories it had gained during the war—thus removing their productive capacities from the international capitalist trade system. Soviet actions in the postwar era led American policy makers to the conclusion that the Soviets were untrustworthy and incapable of honest negotiation. In the minds of the most committed cold warriors, the Soviets were capable of almost anything other than peaceful coexistence with their former allies.

In the immediate postwar period, a series of events validated the hard-liners' views vis-a-vis Soviet intentions and capabilities. The Soviets violated Truman's understanding of the Yalta agreements and refused to allow elections in occupied territories like Poland. The Soviets refused to allow open access to their territories and skies and provoked the logical question: "what are they trying to hide?" Stalin continued to oppress his own people as well as those of the Soviet-occupied nations. Communist rebels in nations like Turkey and Greece threatened governments that were much more agreeable to capitalist interests. The Chinese nationalist forces of Jiang Jieshi lost their battle to the communist army of Mao Zedong. The Soviets detonated their own atomic bomb in 1949, considerably sooner than western intelligence estimates had predicted, and thus removed the "security blanket" that the U.S. monopoly on atomic weapons provided. These events created a crisis mentality among many U.S. policy makers. They also allowed Republican politicians to accuse the Democrats and President Truman of being "soft on communism" and to secure impressive gains at the polls. In this manner, anticommunism became a huge domestic political issue in the U.S. The dangers posed by a large and assertive communist

movement, directed by Soviet leaders in Moscow, seemed self-evident to American leaders. Unrest and instability anywhere in the world was increasingly perceived as the work of Stalin and his minions. The inability of the cold warriors to control Soviet behavior abroad led to a fear of subversives within the U.S. and sparked waves of political oppression at home. While Moscow did play a role in some foreign communist organizations—including those within the U.S.— and there were American traitors working for the Soviets in various capacities within the U.S., the Soviets were never as omnipotent or powerful as many in the U.S. government feared.

Soviet intentions toward seizing more European territory and eventually effecting a world-wide communist revolution were of paramount importance for U.S. leaders. Because of Stalin's aggressive nature and because the Soviet system was a closed dictatorship, the U.S. had no real way of knowing the intentions of the Soviets. The political, military, and intelligence leadership of the U.S. formulated worst-case scenarios based largely on faulty estimates of Soviet military capabilities. The Soviet Union did possess a clear superiority in conventional forces in Europe, and the Soviets had a much greater capability of making mischief internationally than any other nation except the United States. The Soviet Union and the United States were the only nations that survived World War II in a position to impact world politics.[6] U.S. policy makers acted in what they believed was the most prudent manner. They slowed postwar demobilization and vowed to keep a close eye on the Soviet Union.

Many policy makers believed that any negotiation with the Soviet Union would most likely lead to even more demands. Compromise meant weakness, and in world politics the weak were quickly destroyed. For this reason, it was thought that no accommodation could be reached with the Soviet Union. With the intellectual legwork of diplomats like George Kennan, the U.S. formulated a new policy to deal with what they perceived to be Soviet imperialist/expansionist aims.[7] The containment

---

6. For studies of the Cold War from a variety of perspectives, see John Lewis Gaddis, *We Now Know: Rethinking Cold War History* (New York: Oxford University Press, 1997); Melvyn P. Leffler, *The Specter of Communism: The United States and the Origins of the Cold War, 1917-1953* (New York: Hill and Wang, 1994); Leffler, *Preponderance of Power*; Paterson *On Every Front*; and Thomas J. McCormick, *America's Half-Century: United States Foreign Policy in the Cold War and After* (Baltimore: Johns Hopkins University Press, 1995).

doctrine, as it came to be known, demanded that the advance of communism in Europe—and eventually the entire world—be halted. Implemented through the Truman Doctrine, the Marshall Plan, and NATO, the containment policy resulted in a world divided by the two competing ideologies of capitalism and communism. Policy makers formulated containment to keep Western Europe free from Soviet domination. This was a primary fear for the U.S. and Britain because in postwar Europe local communist parties were influential entities. During the war, communist partisans in many occupied nations fought the Nazis while the more mainstream politicians and many rich capitalists either fled their countries, stayed and did nothing, or collaborated with the occupying Nazi army. If communists could achieve victories at the polls in western Europe, especially in France and Italy, they could take over without the need for fighting or revolution. In an era when policy makers often made little distinction between communism and fascism, the parallels to events in pre- war Germany, notably that Hitler was elected to power, seemed self- evident.

Of course, it was not an easy task to align the people of the U.S. with ideas like containment and the need for a peacetime military buildup. Historically, many Americans were isolationist. In his farewell address of 1796, George Washington advised citizens to "steer clear of permanent alliances with any portion of the foreign world." Thomas Jefferson echoed this sentiment in his 1801 inaugural address when he proclaimed that the United States would pursue a policy of "peace, commerce, and honest friendship with all nations, entangling alliances with none." This attitude was still strong in the nation after World War II. Wartime propaganda did a marvelous job of convincing U.S. citizens that "Uncle Joe" Stalin and the Soviets were brave and honorable allies. Furthermore, the emerging Cold War containment doctrine demanded that the U.S. make fundamental changes to traditional peacetime lifestyles. The Cold War threat, as formulated by U.S. policy makers, demanded that the nation place itself on a permanent wartime footing in terms of defense expenditures and infrastructure. The developing Cold War demanded that the U.S. reconfigure itself as a "national security state" with a large network of overseas bases and possessions, a

peace- time draft, security agencies bent on ferreting out subversives, and a huge military- industrial complex. In many ways, these developments challenged long- held notions that such "trappings of empire" were inconsistent with the principles of a free and democratic society. Battles between the demands of the developing national security ideology and traditional American conceptions of republican government would be an ongoing feature of Cold War culture.

U.S. policy makers decided it would be imprudent to disarm, disengage from world affairs, and give up their monopoly of atomic weapons. The more internationally engaged cold warriors defeated the rush to peace and disarmament in the aftermath of World War II despite the efforts of disparate groups and institutions such as the midwestern isolationist wing of the Republican Party, the newly formed United Nations (U.N.), many American atomic scientists, and others. The more "modern" internationalist politicians portrayed isolationists as cranks and anachronistic crackpots. The new U.N., originally conceived as a collectivist world- governing body along liberal/internationalist principles espoused by Woodrow Wilson, turned into an ideological battleground with nations choosing sides according to their own ideologies. Conscientious atomic scientists, suffering from guilt over the destructive power of the "genie" they had let out of the bottle, were quickly replaced by more "realistic" thinkers supportive of the U.S. atomic monopoly. However, debate about the direction of U.S. foreign policy continued throughout the Cold War.

Historical events conspired to give credence to commonly held notions about the nature of Soviet and, by extension, world communism. Postwar Soviet repression in the occupied territories of Eastern Europe, the Chinese Communist revolution, the Soviet blockade of Berlin, the discovery of Soviet- directed spies in the U.S. atomic weapons program, and the invasion of South Korea by North Korea led to the subsequent hardening of the containment doctrine along the lines proposed in NSC- 68, a top- secret policy- planning document adopted by Truman in 1950. These events permanently established the contours of the

---

7. See Walter Hixson, *George Kennan: Cold War Iconoclast* (New York: Columbia University Press, 1989) for an in-depth look at Kennan and his role as an architect of containment.

Cold War.[8] Few guessed at the time that it would be a feature of American life for the next forty years.

The United States eventually expanded its policy of containment, originally conceived by Kennan as a policy best suited to Western Europe, all over the globe. U.S. policy makers began to view the nations of the world in terms of "dominoes" which could fall to one side or the other. Expanded containment demanded that the United States take all prudent measures to ensure that the majority of the dominoes fell to the capitalist side. It would be a factor in places such as Iran, Guatemala, Vietnam, Cuba, Chile, Angola, Afghanistan, and Nicaragua. While supporters of the containment policy cited its effectiveness in preventing global war between the United States and the Soviet Union and the ultimate U.S. victory in the Cold War, critics pointed out that the policy resulted in the deaths of millions of people as U.S. and Soviet policy makers shifted their conflicts to various colonies and proxy states. Kennan himself criticized what he saw as the misapplication of his ideas about the Soviet system and its tendencies toward territorial aggrandizement.

The ensuing Cold War also had disturbing implications for democracy in the U.S. Cold War policies and the various new national security state institutions assaulted the Constitution on an all too frequent basis. Dissenters in the U.S. who refused to follow the government line vis-a-vis the threat of international communism were identified and silenced wherever and whenever possible. The "red scare" of the 1950s, promulgated by Wisconsin Republican Senator Joseph McCarthy, Federal Bureau of Investigation (FBI) Director J. Edgar Hoover, Richard M. Nixon, and various right-wing military, patriotic, religious, and business organizations, proved disastrous for many citizens who were suspected of communist sympathies. Under the aegis of fighting communism, the FBI and other government agencies spied on U.S. citizens— including Hollywood actors, writers, and

directors—and famous dissenters such as Martin Luther King, Jr. The FBI did more than just gather intelligence, with its counterintelligence program (COINTELPRO) it also sought to deny employment, recognition, and advancement to all those deemed to be "soft on communism" or otherwise critical of the U.S. The "show trials" of the House Un-American Activities Committee (HUAC) in the late 1940s and early 1950s destroyed the lives and livelihood of many Americans. Red-baiting politicians criticized and ridiculed anyone who dared dissent from the hegemonic anticommunist discourse of the era. Politicians like Richard M. Nixon made anticommunism a hallmark of their careers and they frequently denounced their political opponents as "reds" and "parlor pinks" even when no evidence of communist affiliation existed. The Cold War fight against communism impacted struggles within the U.S. for African-American, gay/lesbian, and women's civil rights. Many states, especially southern states including Florida, used their own versions of the HUAC to thwart calls for racial integration in the 1950s and 1960s.[9] Demagogic politicians tended to paint any attempt to reform or critique U.S. society as an effort by the international communist conspiracy to undermine the social fabric of the nation. Government, business, military, religious, and veterans' group officials formed a wide variety of national and state-level committees designed to investigate and expose the "communist menace."

The Cold War, fought in a quest for freedom, democracy, and global capitalism, changed the cultural, political, and social landscape of the United States.[10] Its effects were also felt in many regions of the country in an unforeseen manner as the nation built a large peacetime military, embarked on a massive weapons-building program, and established military and other facilities designed to further the aims of the national security state. Often, the results of Cold War policies were every bit as radical and far-reaching as those of "hot" wars. One region that was significantly impacted by

8. Ernest R. May, ed., *American Cold War Strategy: Interpreting NSC-68* (New York: St. Martin's, 1993) provides a good summary of the role of NSC-68 in the Cold War.
9. Florida copied HUAC with its own Florida Legislative Investigation Committee (FLIC). This committee played a key role in promoting the idea that civil rights leaders and workers in the state were "subversive" and tools of the "communist conspiracy" during the struggles over civil rights and integration in the state.
10. For studies of the impact of the Cold War on American culture and society, see Margot A. Henriksen, *Dr. Strangelove's America: Society and Culture in the Atomic Age* (Berkeley: University of California Press, 1997); Elaine Tyler May, *Homeward Bound: American Families in the Cold War Era* (New York: Basic Books, 1988); Andre Schiffrin, ed., *The Cold War and the University: Toward an Intellectual History of the Postwar Years* (New York: New Press, 1997); and Stephen J. Whitfield, *The Culture of the Cold War* (Baltimore: Johns Hopkins, 1991).

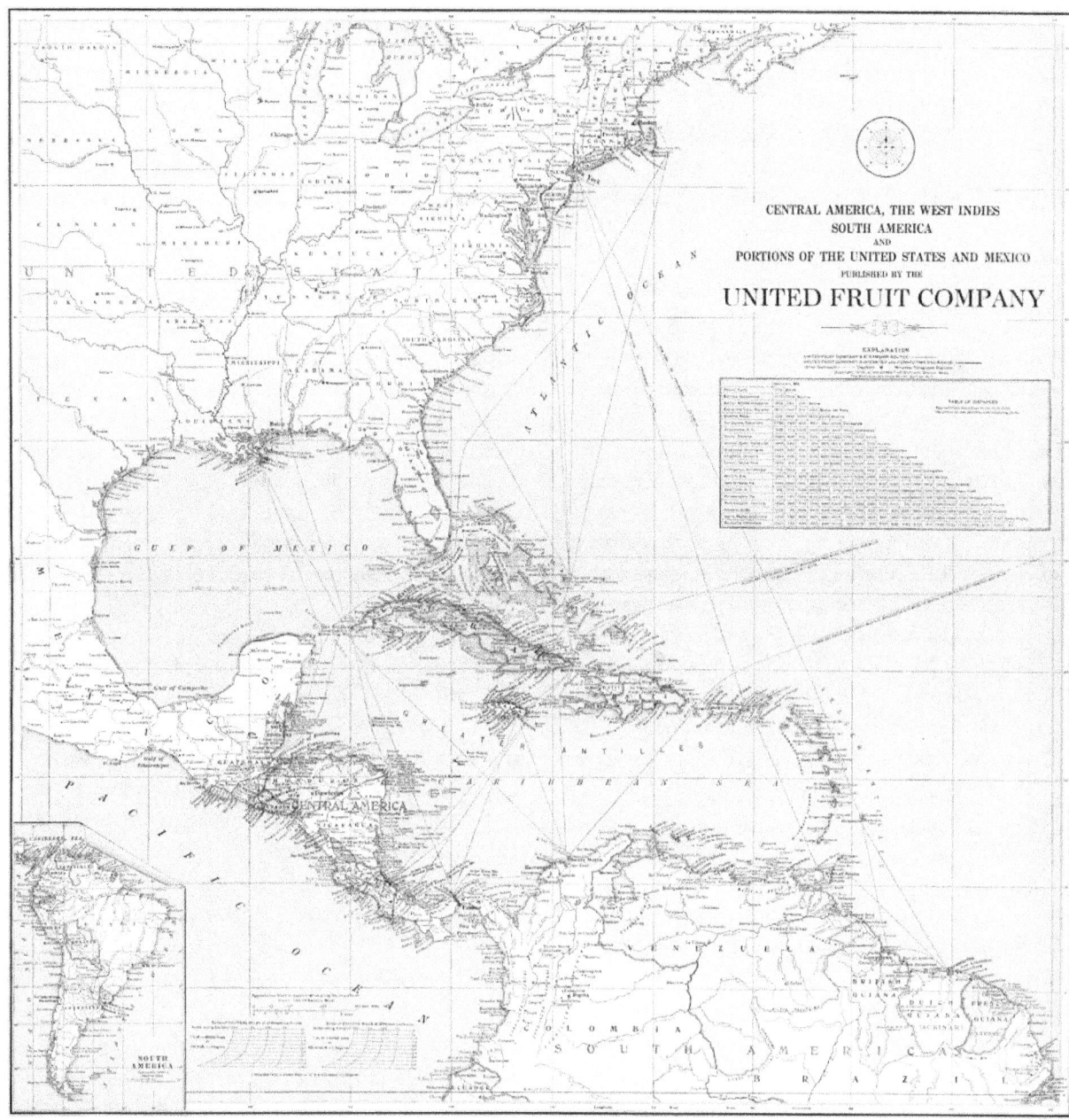

FIGURE 2. Florida and its Latin American neighbors.

the Cold War was the city of Miami and the surrounding south Florida area.

Eisenhower, Latin America, and Cold War Precedents for South Florida History

During the administration of President Dwight D. Eisenhower (1953- 1961), the containment doctrine assumed much of the character it would have for the rest of the Cold War. The assumptions laid out in 1950 by NSC- 68 became the cold warrior's "bible." Soviet gains would be contested wherever they seemed likely to occur. While succeeding administrations differed in their containment tactics, all of them agreed on the need to stop communist territorial gains.[11] All Cold War American presidential administrations tried to insulate themselves from charges that they were "soft on communism." Eisenhower and his high-ranking advisors—men like CIA Director Allen Dulles and Secretary of State John Foster Dulles—

---

11. John Lewis Gaddis makes differing conceptions of containment the centerpiece of his classic work, *Strategies of Containment: A Critical Appraisal of Postwar American National Security Policy* (New York: Oxford University Press, 1982).

relied on overwhelming nuclear superiority to stop the Soviets from any real adventures. In some nations, such as Vietnam in 1954, they refused to commit U.S. forces if the role for those forces was not clearly defined and if no valuable objective could be achieved. In other nations, such as Guatemala and Iran, the Eisenhower administration used covert actions and methods to achieve their desired ends, with the CIA as a major instrument.

In 1954, Guatemala presented the first opportunity for south Florida to take a direct role in the fight against the "international communist conspiracy" presumed to be directed by the Kremlin. The people of Guatemala chose the nationalist leader Jacobo Arbenz in a free and fair election. Arbenz, like many Latin American leaders of the era, wanted to develop his country into something more than a fiefdom for the American United Fruit Company and to eliminate the domination of its economy by American business interests. Guatemala was a stereotypical "banana republic" under United Fruit's economic domination. The company owned 550,000 acres of the nation's arable land and through its policies controlled most of its resources.

Arbenz set off alarm bells in Washington when he proposed a program of land redistribution for the people of Guatemala. United Fruit owned huge tracts of the nation's land but did not use a majority of it because of market concerns. Large tracts of the land lay fallow year after year. Arbenz proposed expropriating the fallow land and paying the company for it over time. United Fruit acted quickly to protect its interests through its connections in Washington—the Dulles brothers were shareholders in the company. U.S. government officials portrayed Arbenz as a communist working for Moscow.[12] "The administration believed that what had started as a middle class reform effort had been transformed into a radical political movement that threatened U.S. strategic and commercial interests both in Guatemala and throughout the hemisphere."[13] Policy makers assumed that if Guatemala came under the influence of communist ideology the other nations of Central America would soon follow. Like "dominoes," the nations of Central and Latin America, and perhaps Mexico too, would fall under the spell of the communists and soon the United States would have "reds" on the border.

For the containment- oriented American cold warriors, this would not do. Eisenhower and the Dulles brothers concocted a plan of covert action against Arbenz and the elected government of Guatemala. They decided to sponsor a coup and replace Arbenz with a leader more supportive of U.S.—and United Fruit—interests. They assigned the CIA the task of eliminating Arbenz and communist influence in Guatemala. The CIA used a variety of methods to effect the change in leadership during Operation PBSUCCESS, including bogus radio broadcasts taped in Miami, air raids, and a few well- trained covert operatives.[14] Arbenz was forced to resign in June 1954 after losing the support of the military. By July, the CIA's handpicked successor, Colonel Carlos Castillo Armas, was made president of the ruling junta. With Armas in power and the threat to United Fruit and other U.S. business interests eliminated, U.S. policy makers considered the Guatemalan operations an unbridled success.

The CIA ran some of its operations in Guatemala from offices in Opa Locka, Florida.[15] The Opa Locka Marine Corps base, along with the airfield adjacent to it, provided easy air access to Guatemala and Latin America. It would later be utilized for similar purposes when the CIA attempted to oust Fidel Castro from Cuba during the early 1960s. Many of the same figures involved in the overthrow of Arbenz—men such as E. Howard Hunt and "Rip" Robertson—would again return to Florida to perform similar roles.[16] Covert CIA operations

---

12. During the Cold War American leaders suspected that nationalist leaders who adopted policies counter to those desired by Washington might be communist. The inability of policy makers to distinguish between genuine nationalist leaders and the oft-postulated "communist dupe" is a central hallmark of the conflict.

13. Stephen G. Rabe, *Eisenhower and Latin America: The Foreign Policy of Anti-Communism* (Chapel Hill: University of North Carolina Press, 1988), 42.

14. See Nicholas Cullather, *Operation PBSUCCESS, The United States and Guatemala 1952-1954* (Langley: U.S. Central Intelligence Agency, 1997); Richard H. Immerman, *The CIA in Guatemala: The Foreign Policy of Intervention* (Austin: University of Texas Press, 1982); John Prados, *Presidents' Secret Wars: CIA and Pentagon Covert Operations Since World War II* (New York: William Morrow, 1986); and Stephen Schlesinger and Stephen Kinzer, *Bitter Fruit: The Untold Story of the American Coup in Guatemala* (Garden City: Doubleday, 1982) for fuller discussions of CIA actions in Guatemala. Similar radio broadcasting efforts would be centered in Miami during efforts to oust Castro in the 1960s.

15. Prados, *Presidents' Secret Wars*, 99.

against Guatemala in 1953 and 1954—and similar activities in Iran during the period—established precedents for the Bay of Pigs, the CIA's covert anti-Castro action plan Operation Mongoose, and most of the other Cold War activities directed at Castro and Cuba. The majority of these operations also relied heavily on south Florida resources.

Eisenhower was fiscally conservative in matters of military and defense spending. He relied on nuclear weapons to deter the Soviets from any major adventures and he tried to fight the Cold War "cheap." He often resorted to covert action to solve his minor containment problems. Eisenhower achieved his goals in Guatemala at a relatively low cost and without revealing the high degree of U.S. involvement in the coup to the U.S. citizenry. It seemed like the best of both worlds for the popular president. He fought the communists as the containment doctrine demanded and he saved money by using unconventional methods. Eisenhower used his victory in Guatemala in the 1956 presidential campaign.[17] Democrats critical of Eisenhower—who, like the Republicans, often used extreme anticommunist rhetoric to criticize the "loss" of whole areas of the world to the communists—were largely silenced.

U.S. policy makers sometimes did not consider the long-term effects of their actions during the Cold War. They frequently made decisions in an atmosphere of crisis. In Guatemala, the U.S. coup against Arbenz inaugurated a bloody civil war that lasted almost until the end of the century. This conflict, exacerbated by U.S. Cold War policies, wrecked the country and hurt the Guatemalan people. Hundreds of thousands of them were killed, tortured, and maimed as a local conflict became enmeshed in the greater world power

struggle between the U.S. and the Soviet Union. Despite this reality, one historian has concluded that "the overthrow of a democratic regime for the establishment of a military dictatorship was applauded as a victory for freedom."[18]

In the battle against suspected international communism, the U.S. government usually preferred right-wing authoritarian dictators over any leader that gave a hint of left-leaning socialist tendencies.[19] The mind-set of the Cold War, with its focus on containment as a zero-sum game between the U.S.S.R. and the U.S., resulted in the installation of a succession of dictatorial leaders who were supported by the U.S. government throughout the world. One historian has written:

> In the mid-1950s, neither democracy nor decency characterized governments throughout Latin America. Dictators, like Trujillo [in the Dominican Republic], Fulgencio Batista of Cuba, and Marcos Perez Jimenez of Venezuela, controlled thirteen of the twenty Latin American republics. The Eisenhower administration found no fault with these tyrants, judging them dependable Cold War allies.[20]

U.S. policies did prevent direct conflict between the United States and the Soviet Union, and eventually led to the collapse of the brutal communist regimes in the Soviet Union and Eastern Europe, these policies also led to the deaths of millions of people and forced countless more to suffer under the iron hand of oppressive dictatorial rule. The downside of U.S. Cold War policies was the "denial of human rights, political repression of opposition voices, [support for] economic policies that kept people in poverty, and providing the means for governments to use violence against their own people."[21] The U.S. government deployed economic pressure,

16. See Hunt's memoir *Give Us this Day* (New Rochelle, NY: Arlington House, 1973), for a summary of his activities in Guatemala in 1954 and south Florida in the early 1960s.
17. Rabe, *Eisenhower and Latin America*, 61.
18. David F. Schmitz, *Thank God They're On Our Side: The United States and Right Wing Dictatorships, 1921-1965* (Chapel Hill: University of North Carolina Press, 1999), 196.
19. For perhaps the most famous attempt at rationalizing this policy see Jeane J. Kirkpatrick, *Dictatorships and Double Standards: Rationalism and Reason in Politics* (New York: Simon and Schuster, 1982). Kirkpatrick draws a moral distinction between supporting "authoritarian" dictators—which the U.S. did frequently throughout the Cold War—and fighting against "totalitarian" dictators—which Kirkpatrick argues were the type present in Soviet-style communist nations. See also Schmitz, *Thank God They're On Our Side*.
20. Stephen G. Rabe, "The Caribbean Triangle: Betancourt, Castro, and Trujillo and U.S. Foreign Policy, 1958-1963," *Diplomatic History* volume 20 (Winter 1996): 55-78, 56. Rafael Trujillo (1891-1961) ruled the Dominican Republic from 1930 until his assassination in 1961. Fulgencio Batista y Zaldivar (1901-1973) was a U.S.-supported dictator who was later forced out of power during the Cuban Revolution. Marcos Pérez Jiménez, born in 1914, became provisional president of Venezuela in 1952 by designation of the armed forces; he was forced out of office in 1958.
21. Schmitz, *Thank God They're On Our Side*, 308.

propaganda, the CIA, and a host of dirty tricks to ensure that the leaders of foreign governments shared its views about the threat of communism. As historian John Prados noted, "In the Cold War vision of a two- camp world, there was apparently little room for indigenous nationalisms."[22]

Building a Strategic Cold War Defense Infrastructure

In order to meet the Soviet threat and advance their national security aims, U.S. policy makers embarked on a massive peacetime military buildup in the aftermath of World War II. In 1948, in response to a communist coup in Czechoslovakia and a feeling that war with the Soviets might be imminent, President Truman argued for and won congressional approval of a peacetime draft and requested funding for universal military training. The Berlin crisis and other events in the late 1940s led to even more calls for fundamental changes to the traditional U.S. peacetime defense posture.

During the 1950s, the U.S. built a massive defense infrastructure to protect the country from any Soviet attack. The main strategic threat at this time was the long- range, nuclear- capable bomber. Of course, details about the actual threat posed by Soviet bombers were sketchy. Some warned of a "bomber gap" between U.S. and Soviet forces and pushed for more defense expenditures and an increase in U.S. strategic forces. The so- called bomber gap, however, proved to be an illusion. The Soviets never built strategic bombers in large numbers. Nevertheless, defense officials constructed radar defense lines and deployed surface- to- air missiles (SAMs)—such as the various Nike systems—to protect the nation from the

bomber threat. The military and political leadership of the U.S., the only nation to ever employ nuclear weapons in combat, studied in minute detail their destructive potential. To protect the nation from a Pearl Harbor- type attack from Soviet bombers, they installed rings of radars, SAMs, and other air defense systems. They defended almost every large city as well as those with critical strategic industries.[23] They designed, funded, and commenced construction of the nation's interstate highway system in order to provide emergency evacuation routes. Schoolchildren practiced "duck and cover" drills designed to protect them from the effects of a nuclear attack, and the fledgling fallout shelter industry grew bigger throughout the decade.[24] United States' citizens directly participated in the defense efforts through programs such as the Ground Observer Corps (GOC). The Ground Observer Corps assigned volunteers to watch the skies in the hopes of detecting any low- flying Soviet aircraft penetrating the radar defenses.

The U.S. built and deployed its own fleet of strategic bombers designed to carry atomic weapons to the Soviet Union. These bombers—including the B- 36, B- 47, and eventually the B- 52—were the direct descendants of the B- 29s that dropped atom bombs on Hiroshima and Nagasaki. The new bombers were assigned to the U.S. Air Force's Strategic Air Command (SAC). SAC bombers sometimes flew airborne alert missions with a full nuclear payload in order to avoid destruction on the ground if the Soviets launched a surprise attack. The "godfather" of SAC, Air Force General Curtis LeMay, developed much of the nation's strategic bombing doctrine and had been responsible for the devastating firebombing raids delivered by U.S. bombers on Japan during World War II.[25] Although LeMay never did, in fact, utter the oft- cited quote

---

22. Prados, *Presidents' Secret Wars*, 107.
23. See John C. Lonnquest, *To Defend and Deter: The Legacy of the United States Cold War Missile Program* (Champaign: U.S. Army Construction Engineering Research Laboratories, 1996); Stephen Moeller, "Vigilant and Invincible," *ADA Magazine* (May-June 1995) available on the web at <http://www.redstone.army.mil/history/vigilant/chap2.html>; Mark Morgan and Mark Berhow, *Rings of Supersonic Steel: The Air Defenses of the United States* (San Pedro, California: Ft. MacArthur Military Press, 1996); Mark Morgan, *Nike Quick Look III: Bomarc/AF Talos* (Ft. Worth: Aeromk, 1990); and David F. Winkler, *Searching the Skies: The Legacy of the United States Cold War Defense Radar Program* (Langley AFB, Virginia: Headquarters Air Combat Command, 1997) for a history of air defenses and air defense missiles in the Cold War.
24. Some historians claim that U.S. civil defense measures were a sham designed as propaganda for public consumption more than a serious effort to protect the population from nuclear war. Indeed, one must question the efficacy of "duck and cover" drills, backyard brick "barbecue" fallout shelters, and other similar measures in the face of multi-megaton, city-busting hydrogen bombs. Guy Oakes, *The Imaginary War: Civil Defense and American Cold War Culture* (New York: Oxford University Press, 1994).
25. See Michael S. Sherry, *The Rise of American Air Power: The Creation of Armageddon* (New Haven: Yale University Press, 1987) for a discussion of LeMay and his role in the war and the creation of modern U.S. air power.

attributed to him about threatening to bomb Vietnam "back into the Stone Age," he developed a reputation as one of the Cold War's fiercest warriors by advocating the use of "overwhelming military force" in cases where military force was employed.[26]

Eisenhower relied heavily on the strategic nuclear forces and the threat of nuclear destruction to contain the Soviet Union. He used the threat of massive retaliation—a nuclear "reign of terror" among the superpowers whereby any overt aggression towards U.S. interests by the Soviets would be met by a massive U.S. nuclear counter-strike—to keep the peace. By relying on nuclear deterrence, he hoped to avoid a direct military conflict with the Soviets. Eisenhower refused to develop conventional military forces to the level demanded by some defense officials and other politicians. To the disappointment of many politicians, military leaders, and defense contractors, Eisenhower emphasized nuclear forces for deterrence and relied on diplomacy and covert actions to wage the Cold War. This allowed him to provide an adequate defense and practice fiscal responsibility. Eisenhower tried to negotiate with the Soviets to end the arms race. Unlike many leaders in the U.S., he believed that the Cold War could be ended through peaceful means. Some criticized Eisenhower, despite his status as the general who had led the Allies to victory in Europe during World War II, as a remote leader content to play golf while larger Cold War concerns went unaddressed. Confident in his own credentials as a warrior and leader, Eisenhower defended his policies and warned the nation of the military-industrial complex's voracious appetite for tax dollars. In 1953, shortly after the death of Joseph Stalin, Eisenhower argued that

> Every gun that is fired, every warship launched, every rocket fired signifies, in the final sense, a *theft* from those who hunger and are not fed, those who are cold and not clothed. This world in arms is not spending money alone. It is spending the sweat of its laborers, the genius of its scientists, the hopes of its children. . . . We pay for a single fighter plane with a half a million bushels of wheat. We pay for a single destroyer with new homes that could have housed more

than eight thousand people. . . . This is not a way of life at all, in any true sense. Under the cloud of threatening war, it is humanity hanging from a cross of iron.[27]

The Cuban Revolution: South Florida Becomes "Ground Zero" in the Cold War

Eisenhower's methods and success at preventing a "hot" war did not please those who demanded a more aggressive posture towards the Soviets. Critics seized on events like Soviet repression in Eastern Europe and the launch of the Sputnik satellite in 1957 as evidence of the shortcomings of Eisenhower's Cold War diplomacy and defense policies. Sputnik fostered the popular belief that the Soviets were ahead in research and technological development. During the 1950s, the U.S. began to develop and deploy other strategic weapons such as the intercontinental ballistic missile (ICBM). These weapons, designed with the help of captured Nazi scientists like Werner von Braun, were even more threatening than the strategic bomber because they could strike more quickly and with little warning. By this time, it was clear that missiles would replace bombers as the preferred method of delivering nuclear weapons. Critics of Eisenhower attacked him for being weak on defense and for allowing a "missile gap" to develop between the USSR and the United States.[28] They also found fault with Eisenhower's burgeoning relationship with Soviet leader Nikita Khrushchev, as well as his attempts to engage more fully with the Soviet Union through cultural exchange programs, presidential summits, and other activities.

During the 1960 presidential election campaign between John F. Kennedy and Eisenhower's vice president, Richard Nixon, the Democrats had even more ammunition. The downing of an American U2 spy plane over the Soviet Union on May Day 1960 ended a brief thaw in the Cold War and helped the Kennedy campaign.[29] Kennedy also criticized

---

26. Thomas M. Coffey, *Iron Eagle: The Turbulent Life of General Curtis LeMay* (New York: Crown Publishers, Inc., 1986), 3.
27. Quoted in Michael Beschloss, *Mayday, The U-2 Affair: The Untold Story of the Greatest US-USSR Spy Scandal* (New York: Harper and Row, 1986), 72.
28. The missile gap, like the bomber gap before it, proved an illusion, because the United States actually had many more long-range missiles than the Soviet Union.

FIGURE 3. President John F. Kennedy and Florida Senator George Smathers (center) in 1962.

and for his arguments stressing the importance of Latin America to Florida and U.S. economic growth and trade efforts. Smathers and Senator John F. Kennedy were close friends; the two men had traveled to Cuba together in 1957. A politician who sometimes red- baited his political opponents, Smathers recognized the importance of Latin America as a battleground in the Cold War well before the crises of the early 1960s. Smathers argued that U.S. neglect of Latin America and the refusal of the nation to fund development efforts there could lead to unrest and revolution. Smathers was such an important politician in the region that Fidel Castro invited the Senator to Havana to witness personally some of the regime's trials of former Batista henchmen. After the election of Kennedy to the presidency in 1960, Smathers helped the administration decide how to "best deal with the existence of Castro's Cuba and prevent similar scenarios from developing elsewhere in Latin America." Smathers spearheaded efforts to control the U.S. sugar market and implement boycotts against Cuban products in order to deny Castro needed resources for Cuba and weaken his regime.[30]

Eisenhower for his foreign policy toward Latin America, and, more specifically, Cuba. The 1959 Cuban revolution made U.S.- Latin American relations and communist activity in the Western Hemisphere a very important issue. The rise to power of Fidel Castro and the radical character of the Cuban revolution would play a huge role in the Cold War history of the U.S. It would impact south Florida's society, culture, demographics, and history in ways unimaginable during the presidential campaign.

The Cuban revolution brought the Cold War "home" to the people of the U.S. and south Florida in the early 1960s. For a time, the region became "ground zero" in the conflict. Florida politicians were actors in the conflict in a variety of capacities. Florida Senator George Smathers became known as the "Senator from Latin America" because of his influence on U.S. Cold War policies in the region

Other politicians did not share Smathers' fear of a communist revolution in the hemisphere. Many policy makers considered Cuba and Latin America "safe" places in the Cold War. As late as 1959, policy makers believed that "there are at present no critical or strategic problems or difficulties which are major threats to the United States security or which seem likely to cause changes in the generally satisfactory status of U.S. relations with the area."[31] Cuba provided the U.S. with many important commodities such as sugar, and many large U.S. corporations had extensive holdings on the island in that field as well as in mining, telecommunications, and other important economic sectors. The

29. See Beschloss's *Mayday* for a discussion of the U2 story and its role in souring U.S.-Soviet relations.
30. Brian Lewis Crispell, *Testing the Limits: George Armistead Smathers and Cold War America* (Athens: University of Georgia Press, 1999), 151.
31. Richard Kugler, *The U.S. Army's Role in the Cuban Crisis, 1962* (Washington, D.C.: Office of the Chief of Military History, 1967), Ch. III, 2. There are numerous works on the U.S.-Cuban relationship. Some of the best include the many of works of historian Louis A Perez. See, for example, Perez's *Cuba and the United States: Ties of Singular Intimacy* (Athens: University of Georgia Press, 1990). See also Jules R. Benjamin, *The United States and the Origins of the Cuban Revolution: An Empire of Liberty in an Age of National Liberation* (Princeton: Princeton University Press, 1990); Philip W. Bonsal, *Cuba, Castro, and the United States* (Pittsburgh: University of Pittsburgh Press, 1971); and Richard E. Welch, *Response to Revolution: The United States and the Cuban Revolution, 1959-1961* (Chapel Hill: University of North Carolina Press, 1985). For a look at the relationship between Cuba and the U.S. over a longer time frame see Miguel A. Bretos, *Cuba & Florida: Exploration of an Historic Connection, 1539-1991* (Miami: Historical Association of Southern Florida, 1991). For interesting information on the pre-Revolutionary exile "scene" in south Florida see Alejandro Portes and Alex Stepick, *City on the Edge: The Transformation of Miami* (Berkeley: University of California Press, 1993).

relationship was colonial in nature despite the fact that Cuba was technically an independent nation. American organized crime operations also had interests on the island, and Florida Mafia figures such as Santos Traficante had strong ties to the Fulgencio Batista government. Indeed, authors Warren Hinckle and William W. Turner described "Pre- Revolution Havana" as "the empress city of organized crime, [a] free port for the mob where in the late 1940s "Lucky" Luciano established the Cuban Connection in the world narcotics trade."[32] Cuba was the main tourist destination in the Caribbean at this time, and people flocked to the island for its weather, beaches, and nightlife. Havana provided an even more relaxed party atmosphere than south Florida's Miami Beach, and many American tourists traveled to the island to enjoy activities less wholesome than those available in Miami. Havana offered casino gambling and infamous bordellos, in addition to the more typically available tourist attractions of the Caribbean region and south Florida.

Some U.S. officials considered the overthrow of Batista by Fidel Castro and his associated forces a good thing. In January 1959 Secretary of State John Foster Dulles reported to President Eisenhower that "The Provisional Government appears free from Communist taint and there are indications that it intends to pursue friendly relations with the United States."[33] Before the revolution, Cuba had suffered under a number of dictators, many of them ruling only because of the support of the United States. Batista was blatant in his corruption and harsh on his people. While the island did enjoy a higher standard of living than most Latin American nations, many Cubans suffered in poverty. Once Batista fled Cuba early in the morning on New Year's Day 1959, many Cuban exiles in the U.S. returned to the island.[34] Many Cuban citizens welcomed the victory of Castro's revolutionary forces, and "eagerly awaited the reimplementation of the liberal Cuban constitution of 1940, suspended under Batista, as well as new, progressive legislation that would ensure basic civil liberties."[35]

FIGURE 4. Cuban leader Fidel Castro, ca. 1960.

U.S. officials hoped Castro would bring stability to the island nation by ending the chaotic and uncertain conditions of the guerrilla war. The rebellion created concern for U.S. business interests, and any hope of achieving stability was seized upon by the concerned parties. Typically, U.S. Cold War policy makers favored stability above almost any other state of affairs. Instability was bad for business and could be exploited by subversives—i.e., communists. U.S. policy makers worried at the start about the character of the Cuban revolution. Although Fidel Castro and his Twenty- sixth of July movement (M- 26- 7) were not communist when they came to power in January 1959,[36] Castro's actions subsequent to his seizure of power raised warning flags for the U.S. government and U.S. business interests on the island. Moves to diminish the economic domination of U.S. companies by reducing rents, increasing taxation, nationalizing foreign- held assets, and demanding Cuban ownership/control were met with alarm. These nationalistic policies seemed suspiciously communist. U.S. officials responded by taking an increasingly hard line against the Cuban

32. Warren Hinckle and William W. Turner, *The Fish is Red: The Story of the Secret War Against Castro* (New York: Harper and Row, 1981), 313.
33. Gaddis, *We Now Know*, 179.
34. Portes and Stepick, *City on the Edge*, 99.
35. María Cristina García, *Havana USA: Cuban Exiles and Cuban Americans in South Florida, 1959-1994* (Berkeley: University of California Press, 1996), 14.
36. Prados, *Presidents' Secret Wars*, 172.

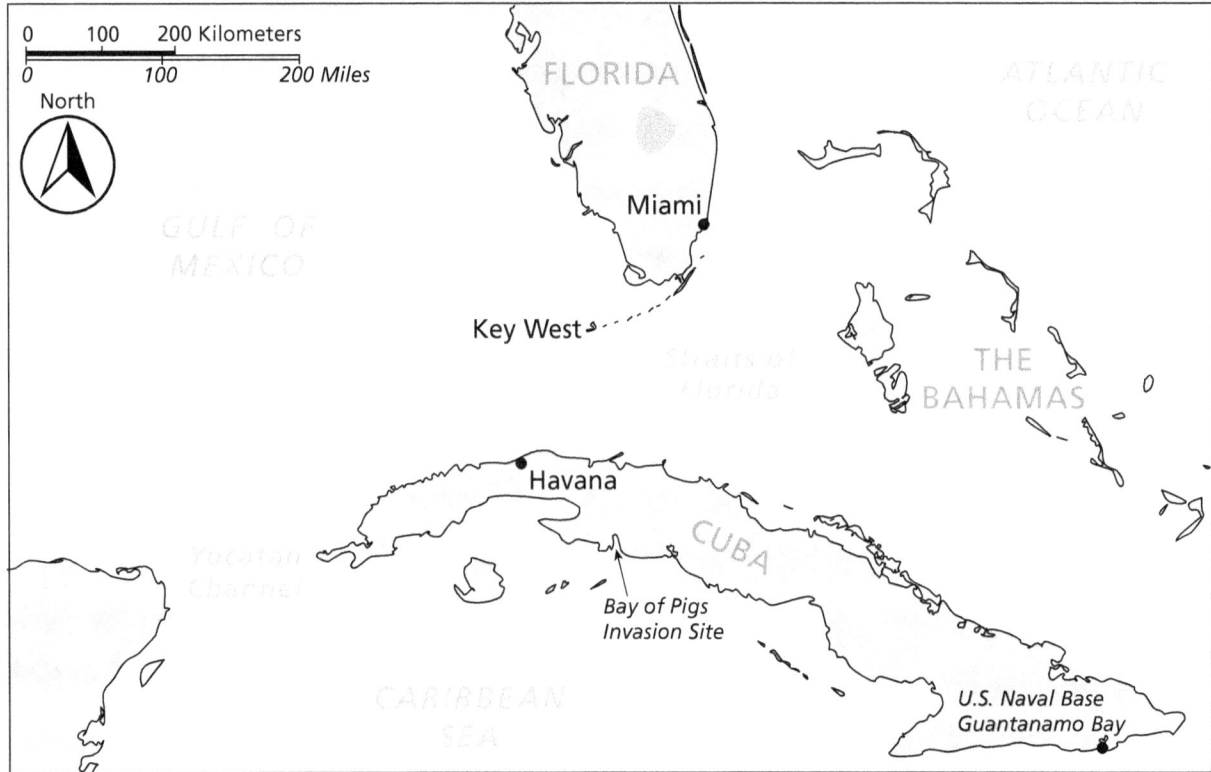

FIGURE 5. South Florida and Cuba.

government and denied the revolution needed resources. The U.S. slashed the Cuban sugar quota; seized Cuban assets; and cut off economic, military, and other aid. Castro responded in the manner expected of communists by arresting, jailing, and executing political rivals and others deemed "counter- revolutionary." Although many found the revolution to be quite limited in its reprisals and repression, U.S. cold warriors viewed any transgression by the Castro government as evidence of its communist character. U.S.- Cuban relations soured almost immediately, and Castro, needing support from somewhere to complete the revolution, looked to the Soviet Union for help.

For U.S. policy makers, Castro's overtures to the Soviet Union left little doubt that Castro was a communist and that the Cuban revolution represented yet another victory for the international communist conspiracy. The success of U.S. covert operations in Guatemala and Iran in the 1950s encouraged U.S. officials to consider similar methods when they became disenchanted with Castro's revolution.[37] As in Guatemala in 1954, the U.S. once again confronted the prospect of a

communist nation in the Western Hemisphere—this time just 90 miles from its territory. Not only did communist expansion so close to home violate the U.S. containment policy, it violated a much older claim of U.S. responsibility for the hemisphere: the Monroe Doctrine. This 1823 doctrine asserted that no foreign power should interfere in the internal affairs of nations in the Western Hemisphere.

The U.S. leadership could not allow the Cuban revolution to proceed unimpeded. In their minds, the success of Castro threatened U.S. national security and set a bad example for the other nations in the region. The radical revolution provided a living example of other paths to economic development. This threatened the U.S. goal of developing a worldwide liberal capitalist trade system. If the "dominoes" started to fall in Latin America, U.S. hegemony in Latin America would be severely damaged. The Eisenhower administration feared that Cuba might become "a symbol for the rest of Latin America—evidence, as the communists were saying, that even a small country in the shadow of the United States can defeat 'the powers of reaction and imperialism'."[38] Many Latin American

---

37. Thomas G. Paterson's *Contesting Castro* (Oxford: Oxford University Press, 1994) provides a recent synthesis of most of the important scholarship on the U.S. reaction to Castro.
38. Paterson, *Contesting Castro*, 258.

people suffered from poor medical care, high infant mortality, low literacy rates, poverty, oppressive governments, and economic domination by U.S. corporations. For years, many Latin American nations waited for the U.S. to make good on its promise of economic development and a better life for their citizens. Free trade and liberal economic principles, promoted as the only "proper" path for modernization, faltered in the case of Latin America. Instead the United States pursued a course of action designed to foster economic dependency rather than development in Latin American. As U.S. political scientist Merle Kling noted with regard to the Latin American states, "the elimination of a status of economic colonialism may diminish the diplomatic reliability of their governments."[39]

In order to fight the Cuban revolution, U.S. officials used a variety of means to isolate Cuba and deny the revolution resources. Castro responded like the communist "puppet" he was thought to be. Castro was ruthless against his opposition in Cuba, and he often used the increased U.S. pressure as an excuse to clamp down even further on Cuban dissidents. Waves of oppression followed almost every U.S. diplomatic initiative and sanction. Increasingly isolated within the international community, Castro lashed out at local political rivals. Castro's increased political oppression as well as his economic policies alienated many in Cuba's middle and upper classes. A revolution of the socialist/communist sort offered little to those who did own property and businesses. Thousands of people who did not support the revolution left Cuba and made their way to the United States. Most of them traveled only a short distance and landed in Florida. This large wave of immigration changed the face of south Florida forever and it occurred in a matter of a few years.[40] Approximately 135,000 Cubans arrived in Miami between January 1959 and April 1961.[41] By the time of the Cuban missile crisis in October 1962, there

were 248,070 Cuban exiles in the U.S.[42] Many of the Cubans who fled to Miami in the early waves of immigrants were the elites of the island. They were doctors, dentists, lawyers, engineers, and other professionals of the Cuban middle and upper classes. By 1962, even members of the working class were leaving their island behind along with members of Havana's organized crime community who "did not see the revolution as something in their interest."[43] Many of these Cuban refugees, both respectable and not, thought that Castro would only be in power for a short time. They began their exile with the belief that they would soon return to Cuba.

With exiles pouring into Miami, the communists on the move in Cuba, Southeast Asia, and elsewhere, and another round of domestic elections approaching, Eisenhower had to address the problems created by the Cuban revolution. In January 1960, CIA Director Dulles briefed Eisenhower about a series of covert actions designed to overthrow Castro's government. In March 1960, Eisenhower ordered the CIA to develop a plan of action against Castro similar to the one used against Arbenz in Guatemala.[44] The CIA believed that with similar tactics—a small army, propaganda radio stations, and covert sabotage activities—the people of Cuba could be convinced to rise up against Castro and end his communist oppression. This operation was eventually given the name "Operation Zapata."

The U.S. government quickly set its plans for Cuba in motion. Eisenhower initially authorized a budget of $13 million for the Cuban operations. The CIA poured personnel, money, and equipment into south Florida and began to train a secret army of almost 1,500 exiles for an invasion of Cuba.[45] Recruits were easy to come by with almost 40,000 Cuban exiles in Miami by the end of 1960 and another thousand to fifteen hundred arriving each week.[46] Many of these émigrés exhibited a high

39. David Green. *The Containment of Latin America: A History of the Myths and Realities of the Good Neighbor Policy* (Chicago: Quadrangle Books, 1971), 296.
40. See Juan M. Clark, "The Exodus From Revolutionary Cuba 1959-1974: A Sociological Analysis" (Ph.D. diss., University of Florida, 1975); García, *Havana USA*; Portes and Stepick, *City on the Edge*; Felix Roberto Masud-Piloto, *From Welcomed Exiles to Illegal Immigrants: Cuban Migration to the U.S., 1959-1995* (Lanham, Maryland: Rowman & Littlefield, 1996); David Rieff, *The Exile: Cuba in the Heart of Miami* (New York: Simon & Schuster, 1993); and Research Institute for Cuba and Caribbean, *The Cuban Immigration 1959-1966 and Its Impact on Miami-Dade County, Florida* (Coral Gables: Center for Advanced International Studies, University of Miami, 1967) for more on the impact of the Cuban exiles on south Florida.
41. Portes and Stepick, *City on the Edge*, 102.
42. Clark, "The Exodus," 75.
43. Hinckle and Turner, *The Fish is Red*, 313.
44. Welch, *Response to Revolution*, 48.

degree of patriotism. Those not as patriotic were often enticed by the money paid to covert personnel—$175 a month with an additional $50 if the volunteer was married and $25 for each dependent.[47] The CIA sent groups of men to Useppa Island, Florida, near Fort Myers, to learn radio operations.[48] The CIA acquired a 50- kilowatt radio transmitter from the Voice of America (VOA), installed it on Swan Island off the coast of Honduras, and began to transmit anti- Castro propaganda to Cuba.[49] At the same time, the CIA established covert facilities throughout south Florida and the Keys in order to run the covert operations, train the secret agents needed to monitor Castro's activities on the island, and attack the Cuban economy. The CIA bought its own airline, Southern Air Transport, and established operations at Miami International Airport.[50] They also bought several large troop landing craft. The CIA sent Cuban exile recruits to Opa Locka Airport and flew them to a training base in Guatemala. At famous south Florida landmarks such as the Fontainebleau Hotel in Miami Beach, the CIA negotiated with Mafia figures in an attempt to arrange the assassination of Fidel Castro.[51]

Some exile groups launched independent raids against the island, and the CIA provided many of them with military training in Florida, Panama, Guatemala, and Louisiana.[52] While covert raids proceeded, the CIA also continued to train its own army. This force, known as Brigade 2506, became something of an open secret because there was no way to keep its activities hidden in the tight- knit exile community of south Florida. "As early as November 1960, Cuban intelligence sent a report to Moscow on CIA training of the anti- Castro exiles in Guatemala; and in early April 1961, the CIA intercepted a cable from the Soviet Embassy in Mexico City accurately stating that the invasion was expected on April 17."[53] CIA officials even leaked pictures of the Guatemalan training camp to the press in an effort to increase recruitment.[54] The U.S. government and the CIA tried to manage the fractured world of Cuban exile politics and set up a unified exile government favorable to U.S. interests. This exile government would run the island once the planned invasion was successful.

Anti- Castro activities in south Florida eventually expanded to become the largest CIA operation in the world outside of the agency's headquarters in Langley, Virginia. The government devoted approximately $50 million a year to the effort to remove Castro and reverse the Cuban revolution. While covert raids tried to wreck the Cuban economy and foment dissent, Brigade 2506 continued to train in Guatemala for a large- scale invasion of the island. Eisenhower started the various covert action projects, but he never decided whether or not to invade the island. The defeat of his chosen successor Richard Nixon in the 1960 presidential race meant that John F. Kennedy would decide the fate of the proposed invasion plan.

---

45. The CIA's own declassified internal after-action report on the Bay of Pigs is an excellent resource for understanding the development of the Bay of Pigs operation; see Lyman Kirkpatrick, "The Inspector General's Survey of the Cuban Operation," in Peter Kornbluh, *Bay of Pigs Declassified: The Secret CIA Report on the Invasion of Cuba* (New York: The New Press, 1998). See also accounts of the Bay of Pigs operation such as Trumball Higgins, *The Perfect Failure: Kennedy, Eisenhower, and the CIA at the Bay of Pigs* (New York: Norton, 1987); Haynes Johnson, *The Bay of Pigs: The Leaders' Story of Brigade 2506* (New York: W.W. Norton, 1964); Peter Kornbluh and James G. Blight, *Politics of Illusion: the Bay of Pigs Invasion Reexamined* (Boulder, Colorado: Lynne Rienner Pub., 1997); and Peter Wyden, *Bay of Pigs: The Untold Story* (New York: Simon and Schuster, 1979).

46. García, *Havana, USA*, 19.

47. Ibid., 219.

48. Kirkpatrick, "The Inspector General's Survey," in Kornbluh, *Bay of Pigs Declassified*, 28.

49. David R. McLean, *Excerpts from History: Western Hemisphere Division, 1946-1965*, Historical staff CIA, 1973, NARA II Record Number 104-10301-10001, CIA Histories, JFK-MISC, ARRB files, 282. This is the same location used to transmit radio broadcasts into Guatemala during Operation PBSUCCESS.

50. This airline was involved in a number of covert activities throughout the Cold War. In the 1980s, a Southern Air Transport plane was shot down over Nicaragua and the survivor, Eugene Hasenfus, exposed the Reagan administration's illegal attempts to support the Contras, the CIA-funded forces trying to overthrow the government of Nicaragua.

51. A summary of the most infamous attempts to eliminate Castro can be found in the CIA's memo for the record, *Report on Plots to Assassinate Fidel Castro*, 23 May 1967, JFK Collection of Assassination Records, NARA II. See also Jim Kelly, "The Fidel Fixation," *Miami New Times*, 17 April 1997, available on-line at <http://www.miaminewtimes.com/issues/1997-04-17/feature.html/page1.html>.

52. While some groups were actually independent of the CIA, most sources agree that the majority of the exile military groups were, in fact, fronts for CIA-sponsored action.

53. Kornbluh, *Bay of Pigs Declassified*, 2.

54. Prados, *Presidents' Secret Wars*, 189.

Kennedy took pride in his toughness and his staunch anticommunism. A supporter of Joseph McCarthy during the worst excesses of the "red scares" during the 1950s, "Kennedy considered Latin America to be the critical Cold War arena."[55] Kennedy, a Democrat who had witnessed the repercussions of "losing" territory to the communists during the Truman administration, knew full well the political fallout that would result from failing to deal swiftly and strictly with communist Cuba. Throughout the Cold War, being painted as "soft on communism" was usually a political death sentence. When he was briefed on the covert CIA activities and plans designed to get rid of Castro, he gave the go-ahead for what would become the Bay of Pigs disaster. Kennedy, perhaps too eager to accept the CIA's promises of success for the invasion, would bear the stigma for one of the greatest fiascoes of the Cold War and one of the seminal events in the Cold War history of south Florida.[56]

With presidential approval, the CIA accelerated its plans for the invasion of Cuba and the subversion of the Cuban revolution. The invasion plan seemed straightforward and, in light of similar successful covert operations in Iran and Guatemala during the 1950s, seemed to have a high probability of success. The CIA planned to land Brigade 2506 in Cuba and announce that the revolution was being brought back to its true principles. High-ranking CIA officials and other cold warriors believed that the citizens of Cuba would rise up and join the invaders and attack their communist oppressors. This action would be supported by the same types of radio propaganda broadcasts as accompanied activities in Guatemala. Once the forces of the invasion had established a beachhead, a hand-picked group of Cuban exile politicians would be flown from Opa Locka Airport in south Florida and installed on the island as the new government of Cuba.

On April 17, 1961, the CIA-trained Cuban exile army invaded Cuba. The operation was a disaster. The CIA's "secret" training camp in Guatemala proved to be not so secret when a Guatemala City newspaper published a story about the camp.

Several major newspapers, including the New York Times and the Miami Herald soon published stories about the impending invasion.[57] Castro had ample warning and began taking measures to thwart the attack. His military forces were on full alert when Brigade 2506 hit the beach. Clandestine U.S. air strikes designed to wipe out the small Cuban Air Force were unsuccessful—and they also blew the cover on the operation when American reporters discovered and denounced attempts to portray the strike force pilots as Cuban defectors. Kennedy, now aware of his blunder and unwilling to risk overt U.S. involvement in the operation, refused to commit additional U.S. forces to the landing efforts or to provide additional air cover. The Bay of Pigs area offered the men of Brigade 2506 little protection and only one exit route into the interior of Cuba. Widespread indigenous support did not materialize, so the exile invaders received little aid from Cuban citizens. Ammunition and other supplies were lost at sea falling prey to air strikes by the Cuban Air Force. U.S. Navy ships and aircraft stood by helplessly as the Cuban exile army was cut to pieces on the beach, its men either killed or captured. While the invaders of Brigade 2506 inflicted disproportionate casualties on the much larger Cuban defense forces, they could not complete their mission without resupply and air cover. Many of them were captured and were held for ransom in Cuban jails before their eventual return to the United States. Some, however, gave their lives to rid Cuba of Castro and never returned.

Perhaps because they wanted the operation to succeed, the intelligence community and other U.S. policy makers overestimated the amount of hostility to Castro in Cuba. U.S. policy makers suffered from a form of hubris brought on by their many successful covert actions during the 1950s. They were shocked to discover that Cuba was not Guatemala or Iran and that the majority of the Cuban people were not counter-revolutionaries. Many Cubans supported Fidel Castro and his policies and they—unlike the exiles who fled Cuba for the U.S.—had less to lose from the revolution. The people on the island differed sharply in their politics and their socioeconomic status from those

---

55. Stephen G. Rabe, "John F. Kennedy and Latin America: The 'Thorough, Accurate, and Reliable Record' (Almost)," *Diplomatic History* 23 (Summer 1999): 539-552, 545.

56. Thomas G. Paterson, ed., *Kennedy's Quest for Victory: American Foreign Policy, 1961-1963* (New York: Oxford University Press, 1989) provides an excellent discussion of the JFK/Castro conflict as well as JFK's broader Cold War policies.

57. García, 31.

who fled. Exile views on Castro were not the views of the majority of the citizens of Cuba. U.S. Cuban exiles were also overwhelmingly white and thus were racially distinct from many of the Castro supporters on the island. Afro- Cubans made up almost 30 percent of the population of Cuba in the 1950s, but their numbers in the exile community in the United States were less than 3 percent of the total by 1970.[58] Afro- Cubans frequently had the most to gain from the revolution.

Castro's extremely effective political controls and his networks of secret informants meant that the island was buttoned up quite tightly. U.S. intelligence and foreign policy officials often had to rely on exile elites for their information. They therefore had no quality intelligence concerning the attitudes of the majority of the Cuban people vis- a- vis the revolution and Castro. Not surprisingly, Cuban exiles in the United States told U.S. officials what they wanted to hear in order to secure continued funding for their activities. Thus, U.S. officials possessed an extremely unrealistic picture of conditions on the island and were overly optimistic concerning the operation's chances of success.

The humiliating loss at the Bay of Pigs affected Kennedy greatly, and he vowed to do whatever he could to get Castro. The President's brother, U.S. Attorney General Robert Kennedy, constantly called on the CIA to "take immediate dynamic action" against Castro.[59] CIA efforts at covert action against the island were increased yet again. In November 1961, under the covert action plan known as Operation Mongoose, the CIA established even more extensive operations in south Florida and moved hundreds of agents and personnel to the region. The large CIA station, codenamed JMWAVE, caused a boom in Miami real estate, banking, and certain manufacturing sectors of the economy. For a while, the CIA was one of the largest employers in Miami, and Cuban exiles of lesser means used the agency as a means of support.[60] The agency bought boats and built what may have been one of the largest navies in Latin America. It hired Cuban exile agents in great numbers and trained them in commando tactics, seamanship, and espionage. Exile raids on the island, directed at its economy and designed to weaken support for Castro and thwart the progress of the revolution, occurred with increasing frequency. The CIA operation was so large that its cover was quickly blown. Almost every sector of government in south Florida became aware of the operation and participated in keeping it a secret—albeit one of the "open" variety.[61]

The U.S. military also participated in the secret war against Castro. Military advisors provided the president with numerous scenarios whereby the U.S. could stage an international incident as a pretext for invading Cuba. U.S. military leaders proposed blowing up a shipload of Cuban refugees—"real or simulated"—and blaming it on Castro. They proposed a terrorist bombing campaign in Washington, D.C., Miami, and other Florida cities which would be blamed on Cuba. They argued that if the U.S. Mercury orbital flight failed it should be blamed on Castro. They suggested staging a "Remember the Maine-incident" by sinking a large U.S. ship near the Guantanamo Naval Base. The military proposed these actions because it believed that Operation Mongoose would not promote a genuine internal revolt in Cuba. In a memo to Secretary of Defense Robert McNamara, Chairman of the Joint Chiefs of Staff Lyman Lemnitzer stated "A credible internal revolt is impossible [to] attain during the next 9- 10 months [and] will require a decision by the United States to develop a Cuba 'provocation' as justification for positive U.S. military action."[62]

58. Benignly E. Aguirre, "The Differential Migration of the Cuban Social Races," *Latin American Research Review* 11 (1976): 103-24.
59. Memo for the record by CIA Director John A. McCone of meeting with president and attorney general, 22 November 1961, *Foreign Relations of the United States 1961-1963*, 10: 684-86 cited in Rabe, "John F. Kennedy and Latin America," 547.
60. Portes and Stepick, *City on the Edge*, 126.
61. See Taylor Branch, "The Kennedy Vendetta: Our Secret War on Cuba," *Harper's Magazine*, August 1975; and Bradley Earl Ayers, *The War That Never Was: An Insider's Account of CIA Covert Operations Against Cuba* (Indianapolis: Bobbs-Merrill, 1976) for a discussion of the methods used by the CIA to ensure that local authorities did not interfere with CIA operations. Both authors indicate that law enforcement officials as well as other government agencies were well aware of CIA-sponsored activities.
62. Memorandum from Chairman of the JCS Lemnitzer to Secretary of Defense McNamara, 13 March 1962, "Justification for U.S. Military Intervention in Cuba," in Mark J. White, ed., *The Kennedys and Cuba: The Declassified Documentary History* (Chicago: Ivan R. Dee, 1999), 110-115.

FIGURE 6. Flightline, Homestead Air Force Base, Florida, November 1962.

The failed Bay of Pigs invasion, the massive CIA operation, military planning, and independent Cuban exile activities did little to weaken Castro's position and were, in fact, counterproductive because he used the foreign aggression as an excuse for more oppression. Castro rounded up thousands of "counter- revolutionaries" and jailed, tortured, and—in some cases—executed them. Kennedy came under increasing attack for failing to stop the advance of communism ninety miles from the shores of the U.S.

Fearful of another Bay of Pigs- type invasion, and with Operation Mongoose activities damaging his economy, Castro tried to defend Cuba against future U.S.- backed invasion attempts and other subversive activities. He thus established even closer relationships with the Soviet bloc. It was under the aegis of this friendship that the Soviets tried to install nuclear warhead- equipped medium- range ballistic missiles (MRBMs) and other offensive weapons in Cuba in October 1962. The discovery of nuclear missile bases and other offensive weapons by U.S. spy planes sent shock waves through the U.S. government.[63] While it was true that the U.S. had

similar weapons targeted at the Soviets in Turkey and other European nations, the establishment of Soviet missile bases in Cuba was a huge affront to U.S. national security, Cold War containment policies, and the Monroe Doctrine.[64] Kennedy acted quickly to confront this threat. Defense officials implemented portions of newly formulated military contingency plans such as Operations Plan (Oplan) 312, Oplan 314, and Oplan 316. They began a massive military alert in the United States, and all sorts of personnel, money, and military equipment flooded south Florida, blanketing Florida bases such as Homestead AFB, Key West Naval Air Station (NAS) and Naval Station, Opa Locka Airport, Port Everglades, and other facilities. The U.S. prepared to go to war over the issue of nuclear missiles in Cuba. If need be, the island would be invaded—and not by a clandestinely sponsored covert army of Cuban exiles, but with all of the might of the U.S. military.

U.S. military forces poured into south Florida in late October and early November 1962 and prepared to invade Cuba in case diplomatic efforts to resolve the crisis failed. The troops and equipment piled high at various south Florida air fields, ports, and

63. There are numerous historical studies of the Cuban missile crisis. Some of the best include Graham Allison, *Essence of Decision: Explaining the Cuban Missile Crisis* (New York: Longman, 1999); James G. Blight and David Welch, *On the Brink: Americans and Soviets Reexamine the Cuban Missile Crisis* (New York: Hill and Wang, 1989); Richard Lebow and Janet Stein, *We All Lost the Cold War* (Princeton: Princeton University Press, 1994); Aleksandr Fursenko and Timothy Naftali, *"One Hell of a Gamble": Khrushchev, Castro, and Kennedy 1958-1964* (New York: W.W. Norton, 1997); Robert F. Kennedy, *Thirteen Days: A Memoir of the Cuban Missile Crisis* (New York: W.W. Norton, 1969); and James A. Nathan, ed., *The Cuban Missile Crisis Revisited* (New York: St. Martin's Press, 1992). See also the CIA's own declassified document collection on the events of October 1962 in Mary S. McAuliffe, ed., *CIA Documents on the Cuban Missile Crisis, 1962* (Washington, D.C.: CIA, 1992).
64. Philip Nash, *The Other Missiles of October: Eisenhower, Kennedy, and the Jupiters 1957-1963* (Chapel Hill: University of North Carolina Press, 1997) discusses the Jupiter IRBM missiles in Turkey, their role in the Cuban missile crisis, and the secret agreement that resulted in the removal of these missiles after Khrushchev removed the Soviet missiles from Cuba.

FIGURE 7. HAWK missile troops prepare for an inspection by President Kennedy, Key West Florida, November 1962.

railheads made tempting targets if Castro and the Soviets decided to launch a preemptive strike. south Florida, for a variety of reasons, was bereft of the air defense missile systems protecting most major population centers in the U.S. at this time. The Soviets outflanked the extensive radar nets and air defenses that protected the majority of the nation from bomber attack by installing offensive weapons in Cuba.[65] south Florida, in the words of one defense analyst, was the U.S. air defense and warning system's "Achilles heel."[66]

Concerns about south Florida's vulnerability to air attack were apparent the first time President Kennedy convened the Executive Committee of the National Security Council (Ex- Com) to discuss the crisis. Secretary of State Dean Rusk noted that

> . . . I think there are certain military actions we might well want to take straight away. . . . [For example we] reinforce our forces in the southeastern part of the United States . . . . to take care of any MiGs or bombers that might

take a pass at Miami or at the [other parts of] the United States .[67]

Kennedy's Secretary of Defense, Robert McNamara, agreed. "We have a serious air defense problem. . . . I think we must assume that the Cuban air force is definitely capable of penetrating, in small numbers, our coastal air defense by coming in low over the water."[68]

Defense planners and intelligence analysts never really believed that a credible threat to U.S. national security could emanate from anywhere in the Western Hemisphere. The Cuban missile crisis readily exposed the fallacy of this type of thinking, and military officials scrambled to seal the breech in the U.S. air defense perimeter. To defend against the possibility of air attack on Miami and the region's strategic military staging areas, the Army deployed several air defense missile battalions to the region. Both HAWK and Nike Hercules missile battalions arrived in south Florida within days of the onset of the crisis. Missile batteries were installed

---

65. Kugler, *The U.S. Army's Role in the Cuban Crisis*, Ch. III, 42-43.
66. Jean Martin and Geraldine Rice, *ARADCOM in the Cuban Crisis, September-December 1962* (Colorado Springs: Headquarters Army Air Defense Command, 1963), ii.
67. Transcript of meeting of 16 October 1962, 11:15 a.m., Cabinet Room in Ernest R. May and Philip D. Zelikow, *The Kennedy Tapes: Inside the White House During the Cuban Missile Crisis* (Cambridge, Massachusetts: Belknap Press, 1997), 55.
68. Ibid., 60.

throughout south Florida and in Key West.[69] The deployment of these air defense missiles to the region allowed a greater degree of protection for the forces marshaling in the area. They also allowed planners to prepare for the worst if the Soviets refused to remove what the United States considered to be offensive weapons from Cuba and the Cold War turned "hot."

Meanwhile, negotiations between the Americans and the Soviets continued and the world held its breath, hoping that nuclear war could be avoided. Tensions ran high as U.S. Navy forces, ordered to enforce a quarantine on Cuba to prevent the delivery of any offensive weapons, had a series of close encounters with Soviet ships and submarines.[70] Reconnaissance flights over Cuba and Soviet ships, coordinated from Key West, brought more evidence of the Soviet buildup and offered more chances for military incidents that could lead to war.[71] Tensions escalated as Cuban and Soviet forces, using their own surface- to- air missiles (SAMs), downed a U2 reconnaissance aircraft on a mission over the island. The Strategic Air Command (SAC) was placed on Defense Condition II (DEFCON II) and dispersed its nuclear bombers—the first time this had ever happened—throughout the nation to protect them from a Soviet first strike. Thirteen percent of SAC's B- 52 bombers were placed on airborne alert. The rest of the U.S. military commands were placed on DEFCON III. In Florida, Army forces prepared for an invasion of Cuba and engaged in a series of amphibious exercises.[72]

The Cuban missile crisis was the most dangerous moment of the Cold War. Never before and never again would the Americans and Soviets come so close to initiating World War III. Both sides had their fingers on the nuclear trigger. Many hard-

FIGURE 8. Elements of 1st Armored Division practice amphibious operations in preparation for a possible invasion of Cuba, Port Everglades, Florida, November 1962.

liners in the U.S. defense bureaucracy, such as Air Force General Curtis LeMay, counseled the president to attack Cuba and the Soviet forces. Castro urged the Soviets to attack the U.S. with nuclear weapons if U.S. forces attempted to invade Cuba. These actions could have provoked a widespread escalation of hostilities and an all- out nuclear war. Fortunately, Kennedy and Khrushchev found a face- saving solution to the stand off. The Soviets would remove their missiles from Cuba while the U.S. would pledge not to invade the island or support an invasion of Cuba. The U.S. also agreed to remove its Jupiter IRBMs from Turkey in a secret side agreement. The world breathed a sigh of relief as the crisis subsided. U.S. defense officials quickly reversed the massive military buildup in south Florida following the Cuban missile crisis. Units that had deployed to the region, such as the Army's

---

69. The installation of the south Florida air defense network is discussed in some detail in Martin and Rice, *ARADCOM in the Cuban Crisis*; Jean Martin and Geraldine Rice, *History of ARADCOM January-December 1963, Book I, The Florida Units* (Colorado Springs: Headquarters Army Air Defense Command, 1963); and Timothy J. Osato and Sherryl Straup, *ARADCOM'S Florida Defenses in the Aftermath of the Cuban Missile Crisis 1963-1968* (Colorado Springs: Headquarters Army Air Defense Command, 1968). For a discussion of the role Nike Hercules missiles played in the crisis and the concerns of U.S. policy makers as to whether these missiles would be deployed to the region with nuclear warheads (they were not) see Christopher Bright, "*Still Other* Missiles of October: The Army's Nike-Hercules, Predelegation, and the Cuban Missile Crisis," paper presented at the George Washington University Graduate Student Cold War Conference, Washington, D.C., 28 April 2000.

70. Curtis A. Utz, *Cordon of Steel: The U.S. Navy and the Cuban Missile Crisis* (Washington, D.C.: Naval Historical Center, 1993), 31-39.

71. U.S. Navy, Headquarters Atlantic Command, *CINCLANT Historical Account of the Cuban Crisis-1963* (Norfolk, Virginia: Headquarters Atlantic Command, 1963), 47.

72. Utz, *Cordon of Steel*, 22-32.

First Armored Division, elements of the Navy's Atlantic Fleet, and the various Air Force interceptor squadrons, returned to their home bases. Policy makers decided, however, that Castro and the Soviets posed too big a threat to the region to once again leave it defenseless against air attack. The air defense missile battalions deployed to south Florida would remain indefinitely to protect the people of Miami and the critical south Florida staging bases. The military realized that they could not have fulfilled their mission without easy, reliable access to Homestead AFB, Key West NAS, Key West International Airport, Key West Naval Station, Opa Locka Airport, and the other airfields and port facilities in south Florida. Miami, which had been devoid of the air defense missiles prominent in other major U.S. cities, would now have a permanent, all- altitude air defense system consisting of Nike Hercules and HAWK missiles.[73]

Despite Kennedy's pledge that the U.S. would stop interfering in the internal affairs of Cuba, covert actions against the Castro regime continued. The U.S. began to cut back, however, on the scale of its anti- Castro operations. The exile raids on the island often interfered with U.S. diplomacy, and they were a constant source of complaints from Castro and the Soviets. Some exile groups were officially ordered to cease their activities against Cuba.[74] Other groups continued to receive money, training, and assistance from the CIA. The Kennedy brothers, still embarrassed by Castro and their failure at the Bay of Pigs, wanted him eliminated, and they embraced a number of covert schemes designed to rid the island of its leader.[75]

In public, the Kennedys officially denounced exile attacks on the island, but they secretly continued the CIA efforts to keep up the pressure. Propaganda efforts increased and radio programs broadcast

from Miami, Key West, and New Orleans under the name of the Cuban Freedom Committee of Miami operated as fronts for the CIA.[76] CIA personnel continued contacts with Mafia figures and plotted with members of Castro's government in the hopes of assassinating the dictator. Despite public statements to the contrary, the U.S. government continued its covert operations against the island for almost five more years. Exile groups did face increased pressure from the Border Patrol and other law enforcement agencies to stop their unsanctioned raids on the island, but at the height of the Cold War in south Florida it was difficult to distinguish officially sponsored covert operatives from their freelance counterparts.[77]

The U.S. government also continued efforts to isolate the island diplomatically and economically. In the case of commercial sugar, the U.S. government took a variety of actions designed to deny Castro the capability of increasing his regime's resources.[78] In an effort to deprive Castro of sugar revenue, the U.S. government offered assistance to exiled Cuban sugar growers displaced from the island by the revolution. In an area designed for farming by the Army Corps of Engineers south of Lake Okeechobee, post-revolution sugar operations were established in the Everglades Agricultural Area (E.A.A.). These sugar plantations proved detrimental to the fragile Everglades ecosystem; the U.S. government had not considered the environmental impact of this particular aspect of its containment strategy.

Following Kennedy's assassination in November 1963, the president's relationship with Cuba and the disenchanted CIA- backed Cuban exiles of the Bay of Pigs invasion were investigated as part of a potential assassination conspiracy. The Cuban exiles had turned against Kennedy and the Democratic party after what they viewed as their

73. Headquarters U.S. Army Air Defense Command, General Order 65, 1 April 1963.

74. García, *Havana USA*. See also relevant documents in the State Department's document collections known as the FRUS (Foreign Relations of the United States): Louis J. Smith, ed., *Foreign Relations of the United States 1961-1963, Volume X, Cuba, 1961-1962* (Washington, D.C.: Department of State, 1997); Edward C. Keefer, Charles S. Sampson, and Louis J. Smith, eds., *Foreign Relations of the United States 1961-1963: Volume XI—Cuban Missile Crisis and Aftermath* (Washington, D.C.: Department of State, 1996); and each volume's microfiche supplement.

75. See *Report on Plots to Assassinate Fidel Castro*, 23 May 1967, JFK Collection of Assassination Records, NARA II.

76. By 1965, the CIA was spending approximately $1.5 million on covert propaganda broadcasting to Cuba; McLean, *Excerpts from History*, 281.

77. Many officials were supplied with code words and other identifiers in order to discern who was "legit" and who was not. CIA-sponsored raids once identified were allowed to continue. Exile groups without official sanction could be prosecuted under the provisions of the Neutrality Act. See Branch, "The Kennedy Vendetta"; Ayers, *War that Never Was*.

78. During the MHVIPER program, CIA agents foiled a plot by Castro to overestimate the damage to the Cuban sugar crop by a hurricane in 1964 and thereby manipulate the market price of sugar. Even a one cent fluctuation in the price of a pound of sugar meant millions of dollars in hard currency for Cuba, McLean, *Excerpts from History*, 286.

"betrayal" at the Bay of Pigs. They would increasingly vote Republican, and in their extreme anticommunism they would support many right-wing causes. Some CIA- trained Cuban exiles would have long careers in CIA- sponsored activities and would go on to play important roles in covert intelligence and military operations during the Nixon and Reagan administrations.[79] The CIA's actions in south Florida and its relationship with the Cuban exile groups, Mafia leaders, and other clandestine operatives would provide fodder for JFK assassination conspiracy buffs for years to come.

Kennedy's death did not end the U.S.- sponsored covert activities against Castro, and exile groups continued their efforts to free the island from the dictator's rule. The exiles increasingly operated from a hostile environment, however, as the authorities in Miami did what they could to stop illegal raids on the island. Exile efforts to unseat Castro became increasingly ineffective because "with the Soviet Union backing Fidel and Washington preventing raids on the island, the Miami Cuban community was effectively reduced to impotence."[80]

In 1964, the administration of President Lyndon Baines Johnson recommended that the CIA focus its covert actions in Cuba away from sabotage and concentrate them in the areas of intelligence gathering and propaganda.[81] However, the new covert operations in Cuba bore little fruit. By 1965, "a chain of safe houses, training sites, and boat moorages stretched through the Florida Keys to Key West. From these [the] CIA launched maritime operations which regularly placed and retrieved agents from the Cuban coast," but information gathered in this manner "often did not justify the effort."[82] By this time, the U.S. cold warriors had more pressing problems, and Cuba and Latin America were no longer primary areas of concern in the Cold War. The attention of the U.S. government focused on the escalating conflict in Vietnam, and Asia became more of a policy concern than Latin America. The specter of falling dominoes in Southeast Asia replaced containment concerns about Cuba and Latin America as priority number one.

Local Florida politicians, however, did not believe that the United States should relent on its concern for the Cold War threat posed by its proximity to a communist state. They took a variety of steps designed to make all citizens recognize the dangers posed by communism and to protect the citizens of the state against the possibility of nuclear war. Under the leadership of Florida Governor Farris Bryant (1961- 1965), all state and local officials completed mandatory courses in survival skills and civil defense procedures during the early 1960s. The Cold War crises in the region illustrated the fact that Florida was woefully unprepared to deal with the possibility of large- scale military action and had no way of protecting its population.

Bryant and the Florida legislature also implemented programs in Florida schools designed to make citizens more aware of the threat of communism and ensure that communists were unable to infiltrate Florida schools. During the Bryant administration, teachers were required to sign loyalty oaths, and a new course was required for all Florida secondary schools. Officials designed the course, titled "Americanism vs. Communism," to promote American values and the capitalist system. Bryant presented many of his plans to the National Governor's Conference and established himself as a national leader in the areas of civil defense and "Cold War Education." Governor's aides from across the country attended workshops at the governor's conferences on the topic of the Cold War and the communist system.[83]

79. Alejandro Portes, "Morning in Miami: A New Era in Cuban-American Politics," *The American Prospect* 38 (May-June 1998) available on-line at <http://www.prospect.org/archives/38/38portes/html>. The existence of so many radical exiles with CIA-provided covert training and harsh views toward the Kennedys would provide fodder for numerous conspiracy theories after Kennedy was assassinated in 1963.
80. Portes and Stepick, *City on the Edge*, 103.
81. McLean, *Excerpts from History*, 281.
82. Ibid., 288.
83. John E. Evans, *Time for Florida: A Report On the Administration of Farris Bryant, Governor 1961-1965* (Tallahassee: n.p., 1965), 105-122.

Counterinsurgency Technology and Florida's Role as an Open Air Research Lab

While attention did move away from Florida and toward Asia as the Cold War containment needs of the U.S. shifted across the globe, the war in Vietnam did not end Cold War-related activities in south Florida. Throughout the 1960s, and as the U.S. became more embroiled in Vietnam, the U.S. military realized that it was not equipped to fight the type of conflicts demanded by the expanded containment policy of Kennedy, Johnson, and other prominent Democrats. A force structure designed to fight the Warsaw Pact armies in the Fulda Gap and on the plains of Europe was ill-suited to fighting an unconventional war in the jungles of Southeast Asia.[84] Forces designed to fight a modern, well-equipped army in the open foundered when confronted by highly motivated, agile, and stealthy guerrilla squads. Because open battles with the Soviets seemed less likely in the aftermath of the Cuban missile crisis, U.S. policy makers attempted to develop a force structure more oriented toward counterinsurgency warfare and low-intensity conflict (LIC) during the 1960s. This orientation demanded new weapons, new tactics, new training, and new technology. The U.S. military and U.S. defense contractors developed and tested some of these new technologies in south Florida's national parks.

Enemy forces in Vietnam were quite adept at operating at night and in all kinds of weather. The more heavily armed U.S. troops were often unable even to find the enemy, much less kill him or her. U.S. military and U.S. defense contractors sought technological solutions to give the edge back to U.S. forces. Companies such as Conductron and HRB Singer came to south Florida and Everglades National Park to test new visual, thermal, and acoustic sensor systems in the tropical "jungles" of the region.[85] Acoustic, thermal, and visual sensor arrays played a major role in U.S. efforts to monitor and interdict communist infiltration into South Vietnam along the Ho Chi Minh Trail. These types of sensors also eventually paid a "peace dividend" to the country's national parks and forests—HRB Singer is now one of the leading providers of advanced thermal fire detection equipment for the U.S. Forest Service. The U.S. military also frequently came to south Florida to test its equipment in conditions thought to be similar to those in Southeast Asia. The military generally found, however, that the south Florida national parks bore little resemblance to the jungles of Vietnam and generally left without achieving their goals.[86]

U.S. military and defense contractors matched new developments in counterinsurgency technology with new developments in more traditional strategic weapons. The non-existent "missile gap" that Kennedy rode to victory in 1960 and used as justification for a reinvigorated Cold War weapons-buying spree caused an arms race of huge proportions between the Soviets and the U.S. in the 1960s.[87] Strategic bombers fell out of favor, and the U.S. and the Soviets eventually deployed many new ICBMs. Defense contractors throughout the United States increased profits by providing the United States with enough weapons to meet the demands of the arms race, the reformulated containment

---

84. In a treaty lasting from May 14, 1955, to July 1, 1991, the Warsaw Pact was established as a mutual defense organization that included the USSR, Albania, Bulgaria, Czechoslovakia, East Germany, Hungary, Poland, and Romania. The organization provided for a unified military command and the maintenance of Soviet military units on territories of other participating states. The Warsaw Pact was a reaction to the 1955 admission of West Germany into the North Atlantic Treaty Organization (NATO), established in 1949 as a collective-defense agreement among Western powers in opposition to communist forces in Europe.
85. Companies such as HRB Singer tested a variety of audio and thermal sensor systems within Everglades NP. See Everglades NP *Superintendent's Monthly Narrative Reports* throughout the 1960s.
86. Military visitors to the park tried to film helicopter assault training films "against a tropical background," "test their radios under a jungle canopy," and use the soils and vegetation of the parks for "military purposes." *Superintendent's Monthly Narrative Reports* (Everglades National Park, National Park Service, Department of the Interior, April 1961); *Superintendent's Monthly Narrative Reports* (Everglades National Park, National Park Service, Department of the Interior, December 1962); *Superintendent's Monthly Narrative Reports* (Everglades National Park, National Park Service, Department of the Interior, November 1961).
87. As early as fall 1961, "new satellite reconnaissance capabilities had confirmed that even in strict numerical terms, the United States was well ahead of the Russians in operational ICBMs," proving the "missile gap" had not existed. Gaddis, *Strategies of Containment*, 206.

policies of the Kennedy and Johnson administrations, and the escalated war in Vietnam.[88] south Florida played a role here too, and community leaders did what they could to ensure that Cold War defense contractors such as the Aerojet General Corporation would locate and build weapons in south Florida. Aerojet helped the U.S. "win" the race to the moon, and it tried to win new contracts to help the U.S. close the "missile gap" and win the arms race. In the process, its operations and their aftermath also contributed to the degradation of the Everglades ecosystem.[89]

The End of the Secret War and the Legacy of Covert Activity in South Florida

With the secret war winding down in south Florida, many Cuban exiles used their covert operations training in other areas. The CIA, the U.S. military, and U.S. right-wing political operatives used Cuban exiles with covert operations experience to further a variety of agendas. Secret CIA projects in Vietnam such as the Phoenix Project of political assassination, terrorism, and clandestine action had a strong exile connection as did even more notorious events such as the Watergate break-in and the various other dirty tricks of the Nixon administration. Now-famous local historical figures such as Howard Hunt, Rolando Martinez, and others were central players in the drama that led to Richard Nixon's resignation.[90]

As the Vietnam War raged on and the U.S. suffered through the unrest of the 1960s, Cuban exiles in south Florida tried to battle Castro with little success. The exiles also fought amongst themselves in an attempt to maintain ideological purity. The more extreme exile groups, like their enemy Fidel Castro, allowed no dissent or compromise. For a time, Miami suffered a series of threats, intimidations, and terrorist bombing campaigns against Cubans deemed insufficiently hard-line against Castro and the revolution.[91] Even as Nixon was presiding over a thaw in the Cold War through détente with the Soviets and openings to China, Cuban exiles in Miami utilized their CIA connections and training to attack Cuba and, increasingly, those on American soil who disagreed with their policies.

In the 1970s and 1980s, some Miami Cuban exiles and their associates used their CIA training for a variety of illegal activities not related to ridding Cuba of Castro. Some became arms dealers while others smuggled drugs into the U.S. Former exile CIA operatives participated in the cocaine trade and related illegal activities. Two authors claim that "The rotten core of the big Miami narcotics apple— marijuana and high-grade cocaine smuggled by plane and boat from Colombia, Ecuador, and Peru—utilizes the routes, contacts, and techniques for transporting Caribbean contraband that were developed by the CIA during the secret war."[92] Some former exile CIA operatives became mercenaries, professional hit men, and money launderers. Some participated in terrorist activities including the car-bombing of foreign government officials in Washington, D.C., the bombing of Cuban government facilities in foreign countries, and the bombing of a Cuban passenger aircraft. Miami firms doing business with the island, radio hosts promoting more open relations with Castro, and others were subject to threats, intimidation, and

88. John Lewis Gaddis in *Strategies of Containment* makes much of the fact that Democrats such as Kennedy and Johnson were willing to expand containment to include many low-intensity wars. The Democrats, argues Gaddis, used a containment policy in line with their Keynesian economic policies whereby they expanded the defense budget to meet the threat of communism wherever and whenever it might occur. This stands in contrast to the policies of Eisenhower, who tried to provide containment on the cheap because of his conservative views about government spending.

89. Aerojet's use of various canals to ship completed boosters to the intercoastal waterway caused saltwater intrusion into the Everglades. Canal C-111 was a particular problem for the park. Aerojet's testing of rocket boosters also damaged local crops and polluted large tracts of land. Hach, discussions with Everglades NP Museum Director Walter Meshaka, Everglades National Park, May 1999.

90. See Felix Rodriguez and John Weisman, *Shadow Warrior: The CIA Hero of a Hundred Unknown Battles* (New York: Simon & Schuster, 1989) for discussion of the long and "colorful" career of one of Miami's most prominent Cuban exile CIA operatives, Felix Rodriguez.

91. García's *Havana USA* has an excellent chapter on exile politics that details the various bombing campaigns and assassination attempts of radical south Florida Cuban exile groups such as Omega 7. See also Historical Archivist for Miami-Dade County Gordon Winslow's web site Cuban-Exile.Com for a large number of documents from the Miami-Dade Police Department dealing with Cuban exile terrorism in south Florida and the Cold War history of the region.

92. Hinckle and Turner, *The Fish is Red*, 314.

sometimes violence. A small minority of Cuban exiles became corrupted by the darker side of their Cold War covert activities and thus damaged the good reputation of the vast majority of Cuban exiles in south Florida. While the majority of the exiles were nothing more than patriotic Cubans working to rid their island of an authoritarian leader, a small minority of them proved to be a burden to the more law- abiding members of the community and helped sour local Cuban/Anglo relations.

The effects of U.S.- sponsored Cold War activities in south Florida were not all negative. The large CIA operations in Miami did provide some benefits to the region. Besides pumping money into the local economy, the CIA operations provided a sort of temporary jobs program for many Cuban exiles. Working for the agency let a large number of exiles get on their feet and establish an economic toehold in the region. Without the CIA sponsorship of so many exile groups, many of the immigrants would have had no means of support. "The main accomplishment of the agency's massive intervention in Miami was to support a substantial number of middle class Cubans at a reasonable standard of living, allowing them time to monitor opportunities offered by the local economy and to find a suitable business niche."[93] Many exiles, supported upon arrival by the CIA's "jobs program," went on to found their own businesses and helped the region become a major center for Latin American business, banking, and international trade.

Détente and a Reduction in Cold War Tensions

During the 1970s, President Richard Nixon made overtures to the People's Republic of China and established a more open relationship with the Soviet Union. This "détente" policy allowed for a lessening of Cold War tensions. The national nightmare in Vietnam slowly came to an end by the middle of the decade and left a bitter legacy for the nation. Vietnam made many citizens wary of foreign interventions allegedly designed to stop communism. Nixon and Secretary of State Henry Kissinger, however, still kept faith with the long tradition of U.S. covert action against left- leaning regimes.

In an action reminiscent of those in Guatemala and Iran in the 1950s, the Nixon administration actively supported a coup against elected nationalist leader Salvador Allende of Chile in 1972. The regime Nixon and Kissinger helped usher in, led by General Augusto Pinochet, tortured and killed thousands of Chilean civilians in its quest to eliminate leftist influence in Chile. The regime also formed alliances with other repressive governments in Latin America and—with the help of the U.S. foreign policy establishment, certain Cuban exile covert operations veterans, and the CIA—established a reign of terror in many Latin American nations that tortured, killed, and "disappeared" many people. Despite the existence of détente, U.S. foreign policy kept up its typical Cold War posture of supporting right- wing dictators and thwarting leftist nationalist leaders.[94]

In Florida, détente did have some visible results. The Army ordered the air defense system of HAWK and Nike Hercules missiles in the region deactivated in 1979. Defense planners realized that in an era of multiple independent re- entry vehicle (MIRV) ICBMs equipped with south Florida's rather antiquated SAM systems could provide little protection to Miami and the military bases of south Florida. HAWK and Hercules missiles were designed to address the threat of bomber attack— although the Hercules units in south Florida did have some anti- missile capability. Defense officials in the late 1970s found that "there was no scenario of attack on the United States in which the [missiles of south Florida], as [they were] then deployed, could make any significant contribution to the national defense."[95] The HAWK and Hercules defenses, the last of their kind found anywhere in the country, were shipped out. Florida no longer had such a visible reminder of the Cold War in its midst.

---

93. Portes and Stepick, *City on the Edge*, 129.
94. Peter Kornbluh of the National Security Archive has been very successful in getting many classified documents on U.S. activities in Chile and Latin America released to researchers. These new documents indicate a much higher degree of U.S. complicity in the reign of terror in Latin America during the 1970s than was previously admitted by U.S. government sources. See the NSA's web site on Chile at <http://www.gwu.edu/~nsarchiv/latin_america/chile.html>.
95. Charles Edward Kirkpatrick, "The Second Battalion. 52nd Air Defense Artillery 1958-1983, [1983]" (2/52/ADA Organizational History Files, Carlisle Barracks, MHI, photocopy), 37.

The deactivated missile facilities continued to play a role in the Cold War history of south Florida, however, as they continued to have a close association with Cuban exiles in the region. The launch area of Nike Hercules site HM- 95, former home of Battery D/2/52 Air Defense Artillery (ADA), became the home of the Immigration and Naturalization Service's (INS) Krome Avenue detention center. This center would play a role in the battles over the nature of Cuban immigration to the U.S. in the 1980s and beyond. It also played an important role in various immigration crises in the region including the Mariel boat lift and the arrival of Haitian refugees in Florida after the 1991 coup against Haitian President Jean Bertrande Aristide.

Ronald Reagan, the Cold War, and the Cuban Exile- Contra Connection

Détente came to an end in the 1980s. Events in the Third World, which the superpowers could not control, brought the United States and the Soviet Union into conflict again. In 1979, a revolution in Iran deposed the Shah who came to power during the 1953 U.S.- sponsored coup against the nationalist leader Mohammed Mossadegh. The Islamic fundamentalist regime of Ayatollah Khomeini openly challenged U.S. power and damaged President Jimmy Carter's chances for re- election. That same year, the Soviets invaded Afghanistan and seemed capable of driving into Iran and threatening Middle East oil reserves. Closer to home, a coalition of rebels—some with open communist affiliations—in Nicaragua overthrew the long- time U.S.- sponsored dictatorial regime of the Somoza family.

Ronald Reagan rode this crisis- laden atmosphere to victory in the 1980 election against Carter. Reagan, a staunch anticommunist, promised an invigorated battle against the "evil empire" of the Soviet Union. His regime initiated a massive arms buildup and

fielded a variety of new strategic weapons including the B- 1 bomber and the MX missile. Reagan also initiated the anti- missile defense research program known as "Star Wars." Reagan reflected the conservative Cold War position that the U.S. should be more active and confrontational with the Soviets. Reagan's hard- line stand on communism and his conservative advisers' desire to roll back Soviet Cold War gains pushed south Florida to the forefront of Cold War activity once again.

Reagan supported a vigorous containment policy and, once again, invoked images of falling dominoes in Central America that, if left unchecked, could threaten the Panama Canal and eventually the southern border of the United States itself. Vietnam was fresh in the memory of the nation, however, and to many it did not seem prudent to become involved in another internal civil war in a less- developed nation. Congress and the American people balked at the desire of the Reagan administration to fight the Sandinistas, whose leader, Daniel Ortega Saavedra, had been elected to the presidency in 1984 in Nicaragua. Ortega and his followers were effusive in their praise of Fidel Castro, who, along with the Soviet Union, supported the Sandinistas in Nicaragua. Such clear links to communist nations seemed to confirm Reagan's fears of communism creeping across Central America. In order to get around the popular and legislative roadblocks, such as the Boland Amendments which specifically forbade direct U.S. military support for the Nicaraguan counter- revolutionaries or Contras, Reagan authorized yet another covert CIA operation.[96] Cuban exiles from south Florida participated in this effort. Training camps for Contra forces were set up in the Everglades. Cuban exiles provided money and materiel to the Contra forces battling the Sandinistas and utilized their CIA training in money laundering, smuggling, gun running, and a host of other illegal activities designed to further the hard- line, anticommunist foreign policy of the Reagan administration.[97] While many exiles were acting out of a strong sense of anticommunism, others merely acted to line their

96. See Leslie Cockburn, *Out of Control* (New York: Atlantic Monthly, 1987); Glenn Garvin, *Everybody Had His Own Gringo: The CIA & the Contras* (Riverside, N.J.: Brassey's Book Orders, 1992); Roy Gutman, *Banana Diplomacy: The Making of American Policy in Nicaragua* (New York: Simon and Schuster, 1988); Haynes Johnson, *Sleepwalking Through History: America in the Reagan Years* (New York: Doubleday, 1991); Peter Kornbluh and Malcolm Byrne, *The Iran-Contra Scandal: The Declassified History* (New York: New Press, 1993); Jonathan Marshall, *The Iran-Contra Connection: Secret Teams and Covert Operations in the Reagan Era* (Boston: South End Press, 1987); Peter Dale Scott, *Cocaine Politics: Drugs, Armies, and the CIA in Central America* (Berkeley: University of California Press, 1998); and Bob Woodward, *Veil: The Secret Wars of the CIA, 1981-1987* (New York: Simon and Schuster, 1987).

own pockets. Some Cuban exiles, sensing that something was seriously wrong with the efforts to assist the Contras, even complained publicly about the profiteering of some of the so-called patriots.[98]

A series of miscues, leaks, and other events led to the discovery of the attempts to sell American arms to the Iranians for hostages held in the Middle East and divert the profits to the Contras in Nicaragua.[99] This scandal resulted in a permanent stain on the presidency of Ronald Reagan. The administration's conduct violated U.S. law and the constitutional separation of powers. The Iran-Contra affair exposed once again the covert and often illegal orientation of Cold War U.S. foreign policy. While the nation gained some new "media stars"— such as U.S. Marine Corps Lt. Colonel Oliver North, a U.S. national security staffer whose "all-American boy" persona played exceedingly well with the scandal's large television audience and whose appearance before Congressional investigators set off a round of "Ollie-mania" in the nation—the overall result of the operation was damaging to Reagan's reputation and his legacy.

The End of the Cold War and the Legacy of the Battle

The Iran-Contra scandal damaged Reagan's ability to lead the country. Nicaragua was quickly forgotten, however, once the attention of the world and U.S. policy makers focused on newly installed Soviet leader Mikhail Gorbachev and the extraordinary events in the Soviet Union. Despite all of Reagan's anticommunist rhetoric, he developed a close working relationship with Gorbachev. Perhaps attempting to deflect criticism brought about by Iran-Contra, Reagan made a strong effort to improve relations with the Soviets.[100]

The efforts of Gorbachev, Reagan, and Reagan's successor George Bush would eventually lead to the end of the Cold War. Gorbachev's efforts to restructure the Soviet system and allow greater openness in the society—known as *Glasnost* and *Perestroika*—did not have their intended effects. The Soviet system began to crumble, and soon the whole world witnessed a series of remarkable events that had been long awaited, but often thought impossible during the darkest days of the Cold War. Reagan, however, was out of office before the truly remarkable events came to pass, and his successor, George Bush, presided over the end of the superpower conflict and some of the most memorable historical moments of the past half century.

In 1989, the walls came down all over the world, and the long and bitter Cold War, with its ever-present implied threat of nuclear holocaust and annihilation, ended with a whimper rather than a bang. By 1991 the Commonwealth of Independent States (CIS) replaced the Soviet Union, and the U.S. no longer had a superpower rival. Some praised Reagan's strategy of high defense spending and the resultant massive budget deficits because they believed it bankrupted the Soviets and forced them to cry "uncle." However, the U.S. did not escape the Cold War unscathed. Containment and its supporting ideology of anticommunism led to the debacle in Vietnam and all of its repercussions. The nation compromised its lofty principles during the Cold War by subverting the democratically elected governments of numerous states, supporting coups and terrorism, threatening liberties at home with Cold War counter-intelligence and surveillance programs, and backing dictators all over the globe in the name of stability and anticommunism. While many crowed about the U.S. "victory," others cautioned that while it was a good thing that the Cold War strategy of the U.S. prevented war between the superpowers, it should not be forgotten that it resulted in the deaths of millions of people.[101] While the superpowers never fought directly, they

97. "Inside Camp Cuba-Nicaragua," *Time* 119 (8 February 1982); "The Hothead Irregulars," *Newsweek* 99 (22 March 1982); Liz Balmaseda, "Miami's 'Little Managua,' The Contra Rebels Run Their War From South Florida," *Newsweek* 107 (26 May 1986); Ronnie Lovler, "Training For the Counterrevolution: Cuban Guerrillas in Florida," *The Nation* 233 (26 September 1981); Jose de Cordoba and Thomas E. Ricks, "Cuban Connection: Bay of Pigs Veterans Find in Nicaragua a New War to Fight," *Wall Street Journal*, 16 January 1987.
98. Cockburn, *Out of Control*, 42-45.
99. A good summary of the Iran-Contra affair can be found in Johnson's *Sleepwalking Through History*.
100. Frances Fitzgerald makes this argument in *Way Out There in the Blue: Reagan, Star Wars, and the End of the Cold War* (New York: Simon and Schuster, 2000).

did fight with surrogates in places like Korea, Nicaragua, Afghanistan, Vietnam, and Angola. Wholesale application of the containment policy resulted in local wars flaring up out of control, and it often turned local disputes into prolonged bloodbaths.

The Cold War also had a lasting impact on south Florida. Extreme applications of anticommunist fervor damaged Florida's race relations and the struggle for African-American civil rights in the 1960s. The state government spied on decent, law-abiding Floridians and ruined many reputations in an attempt to use the Cold War as an excuse to thwart reform. Wave upon wave of Cuban immigration changed the face of south Florida. Miami was transformed from a tourist resort for wealthy northerners into a center of Latin American economic power and cultural activity. The city became what some consider the "Capital of the Caribbean" thanks to the Cuban exiles and their many business ventures.[102] The region also suffered negative effects from the Cold War. Environmental damage caused by defense contractors such as Aerojet and increased sugar production necessitated by the "loss" of Cuba created many

ecological problems for the region. The "blowback" from the CIA's secret war also caused Miami and the nation untold pain. Exiles who no longer had official sanction to attack Castro attacked each other for political heresy in bombing and assassination campaigns. Some used their CIA-taught skills to smuggle cocaine into the region and launder the profits through Miami's banking system. Others made the city into a capital of covert arms deals.

Scholars and the nation as a whole are just beginning to understand the legacy of the Cold War. In south Florida, the legacy of this conflict is manifest. Despite the dissolution of the Soviet empire, the normalizing of relations with Vietnam, and all of the other remarkable changes brought on by the end of the conflict, Castro is still in power only ninety miles from Key West. For many Cuban exiles, the Cold War rages on. While the Hercules and HAWK missile sites may be abandoned and the former CIA headquarters in Richmond, Florida, has fallen into disrepair, men such as the veterans of Brigade 2506 still meet, still reminisce about their missions, and still plan for the future. In Miami, at least, the Cold War continues.

---

101. Michael R. Beschloss, *At the Highest Levels: The Inside Story of the End of the Cold War* (Boston: Little, Brown, 1993); Tom Engelhardt, *The End of Victory Culture: Cold War America and the Disillusioning of a Generation* (New York: Basic Books, 1995); Walter LaFeber, *America, Russia, and the Cold War, 1945-1992* (New York: McGraw-Hill, 1993).
102. Portes and Stepick, *City on the Edge*, 87.

Section Two: South Florida Cold War Historic Resource List

Cold War- related structures, remains of structures, landscapes, and other resources in south Florida identified in the course of this research are described in this section. This list is not exhaustive; it is likely that more resources will be identified during any follow- ups to this HRS.

Cold War Resources Located Within South Florida National Parks

Four national parks, Big Cypress, Biscayne, Dry Tortugas, and Everglades, played an important role in the Cold War history of south Florida and the United States. In many cases, park resources provided realistic training scenarios for CIA-backed Cuban exile groups as well as U.S. military personnel engaged in survival training and counter-insurgency exercises. Various military groups and defense contractors also utilized the parks as natural laboratories, seeking to develop new technologies with which to fight the Cold War. The parks provided a location for Cold War communications and intelligence- gathering facilities as well as a home for a nuclear weapon- equipped air defense missile site. Throughout the Cold War, park officials actively participated in military exercises and enjoyed a beneficial relationship with military commanders and personnel in the area. Some of the first extensive mapping of Everglades National Park (Everglades NP) took place through cooperation with U.S. Marine Corps airmen located at Opa Locka Airport. One Everglades NP superintendent was a frequent guest at Strategic Air Command functions in the region. Air Force personnel helped Everglades NP staff provide a home for alligators during the horrible droughts of the 1960s (see Sec- tion 2, Footnote 110). Air Force pilots took survival training in the waters of

Biscayne Bay and in what is now Big Cypress National Preserve (Big Cypress NP).

However, it appears that park staff may not have known how active a role the parks were playing in the Cold War. In many cases, park staff in contact with CIA and other intelligence personnel were kept in the dark by operatives who were involved in the secret war against Fidel Castro. Because of this, park records have not always provided complete information. Other sources have identified areas where the parks may have been involved in the Cold War events in south Florida but the staff may not have known it. Several seemingly innocuous items in the park records may actually be related to the various CIA covert action programs. What follows is a list of landscapes, structures, remains of structures, and other resources that played a role in the Cold War history of south Florida and the U.S.

Big Cypress National Preserve (Big Cypress NP)

Bordering the northwest boundary of Everglades NP, Big Cypress National Preserve, was the least utilized of the south Florida parks by government agencies or Cuban exile groups during the Cold War. No sources were found that positively indicated any important Cold War activities occurring within the 2400 square miles that now make up the preserve. This does not, however, rule out Cold War activities in the park. There may have been isolated training camps within what is now Big Cypress NP. Many Cold War- related activities took place in the Miami area and the Tampa area, and both communities had large Cuban populations. Big Cypress NP, by virtue of its position between Miami and Tampa, may have played some peripheral role in the Cold War in south Florida. The few possible Cold War- related Big Cypress NP resources, like the Dade Collier Training Airport,

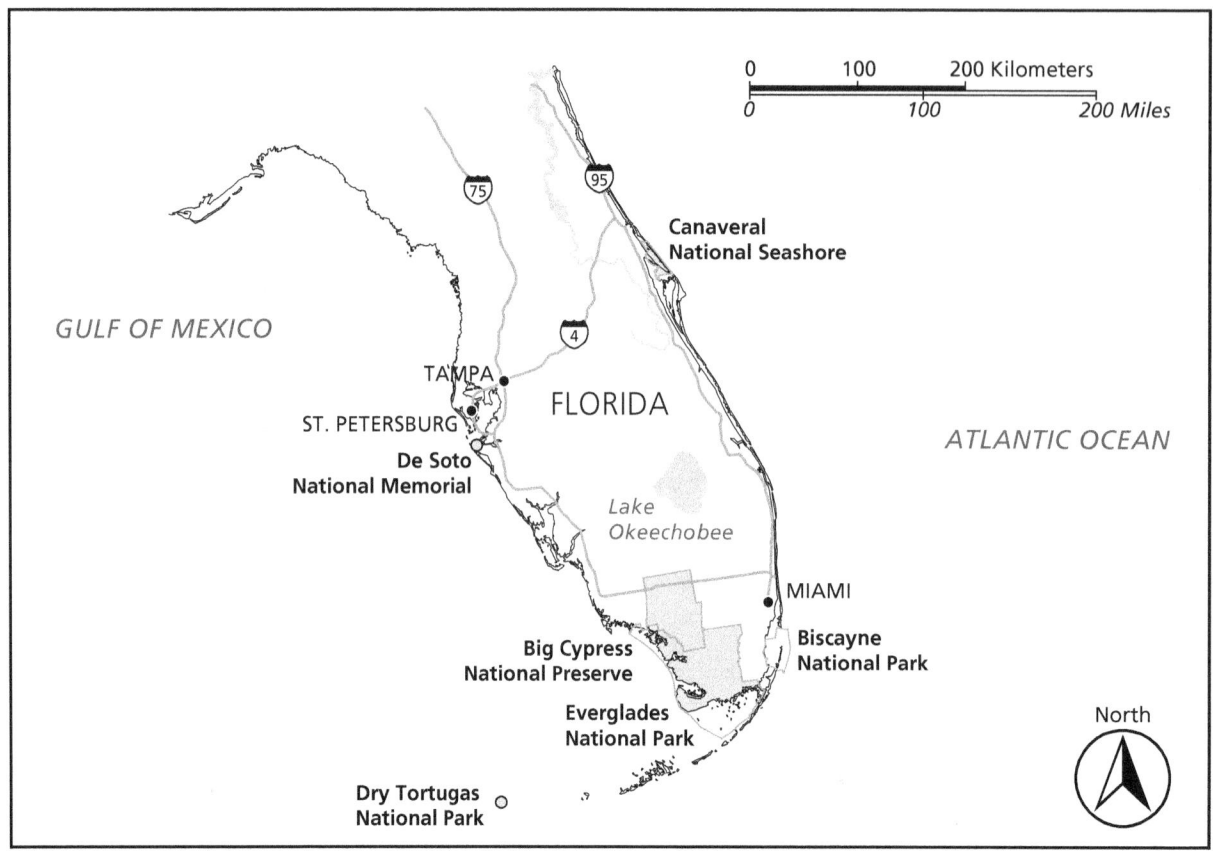

FIGURE 9. South Florida National Parks.

should be researched more fully during any follow-ups to this HRS. Also, one of the more fantastic legends promulgated among special operations warfare veterans in the U.S. intelligence community centers on activity that purportedly occurred in Big Cypress NP. This rumor, although improbable, is included below.

Dade Collier Training Airport. Throughout the Cold War era, the CIA, the U.S. military, and other government agencies used the many airports of south Florida in their operations, and Dade Collier Training Airport may have played some role in the numerous covert activities associated with the Cold War in south Florida. Everglades National Park staff report that on occasion various government agencies prevented and continue to prevent access

to the facility.[1] The training airport may serve as a support facility for clandestine Latin American operations or other classified activities. Clandestine operations often took place at lesser airports or military facilities that were supposedly closed. Opa Locka Marine Air Station, Homestead AFB, and other south Florida airports provided transport capability for the various Cold War missions and covert actions centered in and around south Florida.[2] For many Cold War activities, secret cargoes of both personnel and equipment were secured and loaded in south Florida and then flown to various locations in Latin America. In the case of the Bay of Pigs, "additional supplies [for the exile troops on the beach] were [kept] available for air landing or parachute delivery at airfields in Guatemala, Nicaragua, and Florida."[3] The Dade

---

1. Everglades National Park staff, oral interview with author. Staff report that on occasion rangers have found unusual activities at Dade Collier Training Airport. Upon investigation, park staff are met by individuals claiming membership in various "three letter government agencies." Park personnel are then instructed by the government agents to "ignore the activity at the airport." This activity reportedly continues even today.
2. Cockburn, *Out of Control*, documents the use of south Florida airports to transport weapons, money, drugs, and personnel to and from Latin America during the Contra war against the Sandinista government of Nicaragua. The use of other airports is well-documented in other histories that examine the Bay of Pigs, Operation Mongoose, Operation PBSUCCESS in Guatemala, and other Cold War events with south Florida connections. Southern Air Transport, a company which operated as a front for the CIA, is known to have utilized many south Florida airports for its operations. See also Celerino Castillo, *Powderburns: Cocaine, Contras & the Drug War* (Oakville, Ontario: Sundial, 1994).
3. Kirkpatrick, "The Inspector General's Survey," in Kornbluh, *Bay of Pigs Declassified*, 39.

Collier Training Airport, by nature of its operational status, location, and availability, could have performed a similar function for cold warriors seeking an isolated, easily secured air transport facility. The fact that the government is reported to be using this facility in a clandestine manner even today would seem to make the possibility of a Cold War connection that much more likely.

CIA Arms Cache. Among special operations personnel, a "legend" is often told about a large, secret CIA arms cache buried somewhere in the swamps of what is now Big Cypress NP. Supposedly, after the Bay of Pigs invasion, the CIA began planning another invasion of Cuba. This new effort was to be completely controlled by the CIA. In preparation for the next invasion, a large cache of arms including rifles, machine guns, bazookas, millions of rounds of ammunition, and other types of ordnance was buried somewhere within the Great Cypress Swamp:

> in the center of three large cypress hummocks or islands.. which would form a triangle. As the months then years passed with no thought of returning, the cache was slowly forgotten ... and the CIA didn't want the publicity a large scale "dig" would generate, so they destroyed the paperwork and effectively "buried" the project.[4]

Biscayne National Park (Biscayne NP)

Biscayne National Park (Biscayne NP) encompasses the waters of Biscayne Bay as well as miles of shoreline and various keys. Areas that are now within park boundaries played an important role in many Cold War events in south Florida. The park provided several training locations for official and unofficial Cuban exile paramilitary groups, maritime operations sites, support bases, and safe houses for CIA agents. Exiles and CIA agents often traveled the waters of Biscayne NP as they

completed their various tasks and missions. Scores of Cuban refugees fleeing Castro landed on the many large and small keys of Biscayne NP seeking sanctuary in the United States. Cuban exiles, CIA spies, and the various other characters who utilized its unique resources added to the colorful history of Biscayne NP that includes the park's long- time utilization as a haven for bootleggers, smugglers, and pirates.

Elliott Key. Biscayne NP's Elliott Key was a hot spot of CIA paramilitary training activity and a center for maritime infiltration operations. Throughout its history, the key served as a drug, gun, and immigrant smuggling center.[5] CIA operatives exploited the key's suitability for clandestine operations during the Bay of Pigs and Operation Mongoose era. In the early 1960s, Elliott Key had at least three facilities associated with paramilitary training, covert operations, maritime infiltration, and supply operations. One facility was the former Ledbury Lodge, the only hotel ever built on the key. Ledbury may have been a boat base or a training center or both. Carlo Abreu, a Cuban exile living in Miami, visited the Ledbury Lodge twice during his CIA- sponsored activities and loaded cargo and resupplied his vessel there.[6] The Tannehills, longtime residents of Elliott Key, reported that "Cubans were trained at this property before the Bay of Pigs incident, allegedly with CIA funding."[7] Other facilities utilized on the key by CIA operatives included a "small dock, partially concealed in the mangroves, near the center of the island and an isolated old house surrounded by palm trees and vegetation on the ocean side of the key."[8] The CIA used these facilities as a safe house and base for commandos.

Because of the isolated and primitive nature of Elliott Key, all supplies had to be transported to the site by boat, and thus CIA operatives were constantly shuttling supplies such as gas, oil, fuel for

---

4. This story was related by an Army veteran who requested to remain "anonymous" because this information was related to him when he had a Top Secret security clearance. Of course, this Top Secret conversation occurred at the officer's club. It is included here to give the reader a sense of some of the local legends surrounding this topic. For the purposes of this HRS, "resources" of this nature have been avoided and only information corroborated by secondary literature or primary documents is included in the resource listing.
5. See Nixon Smiley, "Key was a Historic Haven for Fugitives," *Miami Herald,* 14 January 1973. See also the *Herald's Tropic* magazine 29 July 1973, for more on Elliott Key and its history.
6. Carlo Abreu, oral interview with author, Brigade 2506 Museum, Miami, Florida, May 1999.
7. Oral interview with the Tannehills as quoted in T. Stell Newman, *Biscayne National Monument Historical Studies Plan— Preliminary,* Denver Service Center, Historical Preservation Team, NPS (Denver: U.S. Department of the Interior, March 1975), 45.
8. Ayers, *The War that Never Was,* 31.

stoves, and other items across Biscayne Bay. The exiles would live on the key for several weeks at a time while they underwent training in covert operations, demolitions, and maritime operations. The safe houses usually had an older exile couple or other people who cooked for the trainees and maintained the facilities. The buildings often had small shrines devoted to the memories of those who had fallen in the struggle against Castro. Trainees would build mock- ups of Cuban targets in the interior of Elliott Key and then practice locating and destroying them with simulated explosives. Occasionally, residents of Elliott Key would stumble "across squads of Cubans hiding in the interior practicing guerrilla warfare techniques."[9] Once the exiles and the CIA trainers left Elliott Key, residents found a large number of oil and gas cans left behind in the Ledbury Lodge as evidence of the various exile boating and training activities.[10] Elliott Key may have also been the home of a CIA training school for assassins hired to kill Castro.[11] The disposition of these facilities needs to be determined, but a discussion with Biscayne NP personnel indicated that the Ledbury Lodge was destroyed in a hurricane.

Despite the shut down of "official" CIA activities on the key in the 1960s, the island still occasionally played a role in exile activities. In 1988 a group of exiles selected Elliott Key as its primary target in a mock invasion of Cuba and tried to land there with their "fleet." They were arrested. The island continues to serve as a haven for smugglers of drugs, weapons, and illegal aliens, and park personnel deal with these issues on an almost daily basis.

Dry Tortugas National Park (Dry Tortugas NP)

The cluster of seven islands almost 70 miles west of Key West known as Dry Tortugas National Park (Dry Tortugas NP, known as Fort Jefferson National Monument from 1935 until 1992) was important in Cold War events related to Cuba largely because of the park's geographic location and isolation.[12] Like many of the NPS south Florida Cold War resources, Dry Tortugas NP was a frequent landing point or way station for Cuban refugees fleeing the island. In 1959, Dry Tortugas NP began to encounter boatloads of Cubans escaping the turmoil of the Cuban revolution. Park personnel worked closely with the FBI, the Border Patrol, and the U.S. Coast Guard throughout the Cold War to handle the problems associated with Cuban immigration to the U.S. National security agencies used the park during the Cuban missile crisis and for the large intelligence- gathering operations against Cuba in the early 1960s and beyond. Dry Tortugas NP was the sight of a Voice of America (VOA) transmitter in 1962.

Park officials also moderated disputes between American and Cuban fishing boat crews. These issues became much more complex once the Cold War tensions between the U.S. government and the Castro government asserted themselves.[13] Cuban and American fishermen often gathered together in the waters surrounding Dry Tortugas NP as fishermen have throughout time. Easy companionship faded as the Border Patrol implemented a strict program of inspection for all Cuban fishing vessels.[14] The practice of mixed Cuban and American crews serving on area fishing

---

9. Newman, *Biscayne National Monument*, 45.
10. Ibid.
11. Perez Jimenez, one-time dictator of Venezuela, had a house on Soldier Key. In the early 1960s his mistress, Marita Lorenz, played a role in CIA attempts to assassinate Castro. Lorenz claims to have been trained for her operation on Elliott Key. Jimenez was deposed and fled Venezuela with millions of dollars looted from the national treasury. He was extradited back to Venezuela by Attorney General Robert Kennedy. In 2000 a German film crew filmed portions of a movie about Lorenz entitled *Dear Fidel* in Biscayne NP. They are the basis for this story. Hach, e-mail conversation with Jim Adams, Biscayne NP Cultural Resources Chief.
12. Dry Tortugas National Park's isolation was readily apparent in post-World War II. Fort Jefferson National Monument superintendent reports that discuss the park receiving its current events information from Navy blimp personnel. Blimps would overfly the Fort from Key West and crewmen would drop magazines to the park staff.
13. *Superintendent's Monthly Narrative Reports* (Fort Jefferson National Monument: Department of the Interior, September 1959). The Cold War eventually affected the industry in major ways as Border Patrol officials took steps to inspect all Cuban fishing boat crews. The Border Patrol also forbade the practice of using mixed Cuban and American crews on fishing boats. *Superintendent's Monthly Narrative Reports* (Fort Jefferson National Monument: Department of the Interior, February 1960). The use of Dry Tortugas NP by Cuban fishing crews as a rest stop or as a place to gather with other fishermen declined drastically after May of 1960.
14. *Superintendent's Monthly Narrative Reports* (Fort Jefferson National Monument: Department of the Interior, February 1960).

boats was also forbidden. By May of 1960, Cold War power politics impacted the easy relations of men who made their life on the sea. The Superintendent of Dry Tortugas NP noted this fact in one of his monthly reports:

> The tense situation of the past month has created "strong feelings" of visitors toward Cuban fishing vessels using the area during storms and breakdowns. Several Cuban fishing vessels have been repaired at the Fort dock but the Cubans have "sensed" the attitude of the Americans and they have not used the harbor except in emergencies.[15]

East Key. A tower for a U.S. Coastal and Geodetic Survey (USCGS) listening station was built on East Key during 1960. This structure is no longer standing. The listening station is discussed below under Loggerhead Key resources.

In February 1964, conflicts over fishing and the protection of U.S. territorial waters at Dry Tortugas NP played a central role in an international incident between Cuba and the U.S. The U.S. Coast Guard observed four Cuban boats two miles off of East Key engaged in fishing. The boats were in U.S. territorial waters and the Coast Guard believed that the incursion "was a deliberate test or probe. It was designed to possibly survey new fishing grounds, to deliberately create an international incident, to determine limits to which the United States could be pushed, or other good reason." However, federal laws concerning such violations had no real penalties at this time. For this reason, the Coast Guard gave the state of Florida jurisdiction in the case. Florida officials were happy to assist the federal government. The fishermen and boats were taken to Key West and handed over to the Monroe County Sheriff. The Cubans were charged with violating the Florida Waters Act. Several fishermen defected once in the U.S. and they reported that they had been ordered to violate U.S. waters deliberately in order to gauge the response of the American authorities.[16]

Garden Key. U.S. Navy submarines used Garden Key as a site for infiltration exercises during May 1961 and April 1962.[17] This may be significant because the CIA reportedly used Navy submarines to infiltrate agents and supplies into Cuba at various times during the Cold War. The Navy may have used Dry Tortugas NP to practice its secret infiltration missions in a manner similar to the way in which Cuban exiles and CIA operatives used the Cape Sable area of Everglades National Park to practice their missions to Cuba.

Hospital Key. At least one tower for a U.S. Coast and Geodetic Survey listening station was built on Hospital Key.[18] No structures remain on the Key. See the discussion below for more on the USCGS listening station.

Loggerhead Key. As was the case in Everglades NP, many people visited Dry Tortugas NP in the early 1960s to undertake radio, radar, and mapping operations. Much of this activity may have been Cold War related and possibly a cover for CIA and military intelligence- gathering operations in the area. From May to October of 1960, members of the U.S. Coast and Geodetic Survey (USCGS) performed "mapping operations" at Dry Tortugas NP. However, within a month or so of the team's initial deployment, Dry Tortugas NP personnel began to refer to the mapping operation as a USCGS "listening station" in their official records. Dry Tortugas NP records indicate that this listening station, which was installed on Loggerhead Key, stayed in operation for several years. The personnel affiliated with the USCGS periodically returned to Dry Tortugas NP to maintain the listening station, and their visits coincided with key events like the Bay of Pigs invasion of April 1961.[19]

In October 1961, a Mr. Sharp and a Mr. Boyd of the U.S. Army Signal Corps visited Dry Tortugas NP and chose Loggerhead Key as the site for their own "temporary radio station."[20] This may have been yet another intelligence- gathering operation or it may have been a genuine Signal Corps team picking out a

---

15. *Superintendent's Monthly Narrative Reports* (Fort Jefferson National Monument: Department of the Interior, February 1960-June 1960) note a large drop off in Cuban vessels using the facilities of Dry Tortugas NP. The superintendent attributes this fact to the "tense international situation."
16. U.S. Department of Transportation District Office Report, "Incursion of Four Communist Cuban Fishing Vessels into U.S. Territorial Waters in the Vicinity of East Key Dry Tortugas, Florida Keys on 2 February 1964," available at <http://www.ddrs.psmedia.com>, 4.
17. *Superintendent's Monthly Narrative Reports* (Fort Jefferson National Monument: Department of the Interior, April 1962).
18. *Superintendent's Monthly Narrative Reports* (Fort Jefferson National Monument: Department of the Interior, May-June 1960).

site for a temporary VOA transmitter. As noted above, many times the CIA hid its activities under the cover of civilian technicians working for the Signal Corps, and the Army Signal Corps supported many CIA activities in south Florida.

In October 1962, at the height of the Cuban missile crisis, park officials stopped all contracted work at Dry Tortugas NP and ordered laborers to leave the park. A Navy ship docked at the park for the duration of the crisis, and Navy personnel installed a 50 kilowatt medium- wave radio station. Once operational in November, the station became part of the VOA's propaganda assets. As Donald Wilson, Acting Director of the U.S. Information Agency informed the president, "At night [the Dry Tortugas radio station] will put the most powerful signal of all [VOA stations] into Cuba." This facility remained in operation until December 1962 and was disassembled in January 1963, although the towers and ground field remained. The station, which operated on 1040 kilohertz, may have been designed for psychological warfare operations implemented by CINCLANT (Commander in Chief, Atlantic Fleet) under contingency plans Oplan 312 and Annex India to Oplans 314 and 316. The radio transmitter was originally the property of WBAL in Baltimore and was purchased by the government when WBAL bought a new one. The station even-tually moved to Sugarloaf Key where new towers were constructed for use with the transmitter.[21]

It must be noted again that VOA activities also covered for CIA operations during the Cold War. VOA personnel did visit Dry Tortugas NP during the era, but it is possible that these people were "sheep- dipped"—untraceable to the CIA or some other covert project—under VOA cover. Radio played an important role in various U.S. covert operations during the Cold War as a source of information, propaganda, and disinformation. False radio broadcasts were used to great effect during the coup against Arbenz in Guatemala in 1954, and the CIA also used them during the Bay of Pigs operation.[22] Military contingency planning regarding Castro in Cuba and—originally—Trujillo in the Dominican Republic may have called for a VOA or CIA transmitter station in Dry Tortugas NP to perform a similar function during any possible U.S. invasion.[23]

Loggerhead Key continued in its role as a communications station/listening post in April of 1963 when the U.S. Air Force (USAF) placed a mobile communications station on the island. Once again, this may have represented a legitimate military function or it may have been related to intelligence operations in the region. The USAF played a large role in the reconnaissance efforts and signal intelligence (SIGINT) monitoring efforts directed at Cuba during the Cold War. Besides USAF U2 and various military tactical reconnaissance overflights of the island, the U.S. Air Force Security Service (USAFSS) deployed a SIGINT collection component to south Florida in the early 1960s.[24] The USAFSS had one detachment on Cudjoe Key near Key West. They may have also placed some equipment in Dry Tortugas NP during this period.

Other Possible Dry Tortugas NP Resources. On nuary 6, 1960, a Navy Blue Angels aircraft crashed into the sea about one mile north of Loggerhead Key. The crash of a military aircraft is not that

---

19. Dry Tortugas NP records also call the USCGS operation a "radio substation;" *Superintendent's Monthly Narrative Reports* (Fort Jefferson National Monument: Department of the Interior, April-August 1961). The fact that both Everglades NP and Dry Tortugas NP records refer to a lot of "mapping" and other such activity on the part of individuals and agencies that may, in fact, be covers for the CIA, indicates that perhaps all of these activities should be considered as the establishment of some kind of radio net/intelligence-gathering system for the CIA and JMWAVE or the U.S. military. It may be worthwhile during any follow-ups to this HRS to consider the mapping activities at Dry Tortugas NP in conjunction with the supposed mapping and radio facilities at Everglades NP operated by the "LORAC" Corporation.
20. *Superintendent's Monthly Narrative Reports* (Fort Jefferson National Monument: Department of the Interior, October 1961).
21. Donald M. Wilson, Acting Director U.S. Information Agency, Memorandum for the President, "Brief Summary of the Strengths and Weaknesses of U.S. Broadcasting to Cuba," 2 November 1961, confidential declassified, in Jon Elliston, ed., *Psy War on Cuba: The Declassified History of U.S. Anti-Castro Propaganda* (New York: Ocean Press, 1999), 147-148; *Superintendent's Monthly Narrative Reports* (Fort Jefferson National Monument: Department of the Interior, October 1962-January 1963); U.S. Navy, Headquarters Atlantic Command, *CINCLANT Historical Account*, 46; Hach, e-mail conversation with Ron Rackley.
22. Kirkpatrick, "The Inspector General's Survey," in Kornbluh, *Bay of Pigs Declassified*, 28.
23. Some radio technicians familiar with Cold War radio operations in south Florida report that the Dry Tortugas radio transmitter may have also been designed to function as a jammer in order to block Cuban radio signals during an invasion. Hach, e-mail conversation with Ron Rackley.

significant in the overall trajectory of the Cold War. It should be noted, however, that the U.S. government used military flying demonstration teams like the U.S. Navy's Blue Angels and the USAF's Thunderbirds as recruitment tools and as a means of "showing the flag" around the world. U.S. military flight teams often performed in other nations during the Cold War as a way of displaying the technological prowess of the nation as well as its military power. It is not known if any of this wreckage remains on site at Dry Tortugas NP.

Dry Tortugas NP, like Everglades NP, sometimes served as a natural laboratory for the military and its various classified projects, but little evidence of Cold War- related weapons research was found during the course of this Historic Resource Study.[25] It should also be noted that the president most responsible for early implementation of the U.S. government's containment policy—Harry Truman—visited Dry Tortugas NP in the early Cold War period. He reportedly found Dry Tortugas NP to be very enjoyable and he liked it so much that he returned a second time to allow his wife to see the park.[26]

Everglades National Park (Everglades NP)

Encompassing much of the southern tip of Florida and Florida Bay, Everglades National Park (Everglades NP) provided a unique location for Cold War- associated activities during the Cold War. The park's vast size and its subtropical landscape made it an ideal location for a variety of covert and overt operations. At various times the park was utilized by the CIA as a paramilitary training center, by Cuban exiles as a shooting range, by the Army for an air defense site, by civil defense authorities as an evacuation center, by the State Department as a cultural resource designed to promote understanding among allies and enemies, and as a giant "real world" laboratory to develop the new technologies and weapons demanded by the Cold War's ongoing arms race and numerous proxy wars. Some of these Cold War- related activities caused damage to the park's ecosystem threatening the "River of Grass" that flows toward the sea.

Broad River. In April 1958 a military aircraft crashed in Everglades NP near the mouth of the Broad River.[27] It is undetermined whether any of the wreckage from this crash is still on site or if lives were lost. Even though U.S. forces never officially engaged in direct combat with their Soviet enemy, they had to train and be prepared for every eventuality. Highly realistic training scenarios and the simple dynamics of dangerous activities like military flight operations often led to accidents and crashes. Even in peacetime, many military members lost their lives training for Cold War operations and maintaining readiness.

Cape Sable. The Cape Sable area of Everglades NP was used by the CIA to train exile maritime operations teams and as an entry point for Cubans fleeing the island during the Cuban revolution and its aftermath. The Border Patrol was often present in the area, looking for illegal immigrant infiltration routes. Aircraft may have utilized Cape Sable as a landing zone when bringing illegal aliens into Florida from Cuba. In 1959 at least one airstrip was found to be in an operational status in Cape Sable with trimmed grass and a wind sock.[28] Clandestine trails marked with signs giving directions in Spanish were also found by the Border Patrol.[29]

---

24. Msgt. Thomas N. Thompson, *USAFSS Performance During the Cuban Crisis, Volume III, The Aftermath: Permanent Operations* (n.p.: HQ USAFSS, 1964) TOP SECRET declassified. This is a highly redacted document found in the National Security Archive at George Washington University. The report details USAFSS operations in south Florida and their activities in Cudjoe Key. The document also leaves the impression that the Cudjoe Key facility serves as a "clearinghouse" for information gathered through other means like airborne SIGINT collectors and possibly other ground stations.
25. This may be for the best; see HQ USACE Derp FUDS report # I04FL007900 Dry Tortugas chemical warfare service site, Florida, 8 September 1993. This report indicates that in 1944 Dry Tortugas NP was used by the military in a classified chemical warfare experiment. Dry Tortugas NP was signed over to the Army for three months while the Army conducted chemical warfare tests. "Testing was designed to determine the effects of tropical conditions on chemical agents and involved the use of five-gallon land mines and other methods to spread mustard-gas on the beaches of several of the keys. Decontamination methods included using flamethrowers to sweep the contaminated beaches."
26. *Superintendent's Monthly Narrative Reports* (Fort Jefferson National Monument: Department of the Interior, November 1948).
27. *Superintendent's Monthly Narrative Reports* (Everglades NP: Department of the Interior, April 1958).
28. *Superintendent's Monthly Narrative Reports* (Everglades NP: Department of the Interior, December 1959); *Ranger's Monthly Narrative Reports* (Everglades NP: Department of the Interior, December 1959).
29. *Ranger's Monthly Narrative Reports* (Everglades NP: Department of the Interior, March 1962).

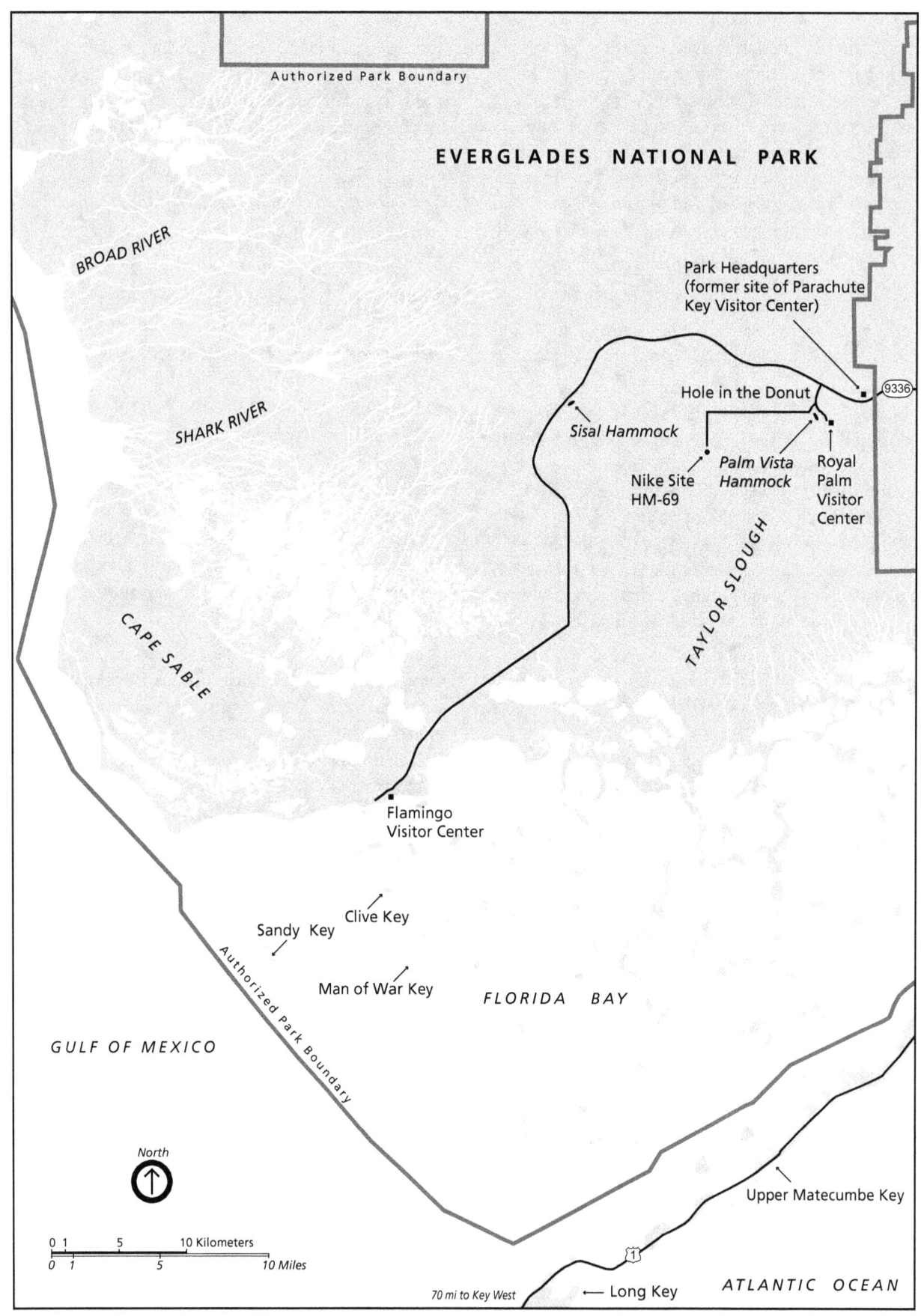

EVERGLADES NATIONAL PARK

Authorized Park Boundary

BROAD RIVER

SHARK RIVER

CAPE SABLE

Park Headquarters
(former site of Parachute
Key Visitor Center)

Hole in the Donut

Sisal Hammock

Nike Site
HM-69

Palm Vista
Hammock

Royal
Palm
Visitor
Center

TAYLOR SLOUGH

9336

Flamingo
Visitor Center

Clive Key

Sandy Key

Man of War Key

FLORIDA BAY

GULF OF MEXICO

Authorized Park Boundary

North

0 1   5   10 Kilometers
0 1   5   10 Miles

Upper Matecumbe Key

1

70 mi to Key West   Long Key

ATLANTIC OCEAN

FIGURE 10. Map of Everglades National Park.

West of Cape Sable, the CIA had a maritime operations training area. Groups of Cuban exile trainees traveled there from Flamingo in their Boston Whaler infiltration craft.[30] In 1963, exile trainees and their CIA instructors navigated the inlets and channels of Whitewater Bay as practice for their eventual operations in Cuba. The entire Cape Sable area served as a stand-in for Cuba as exiles practiced their missions by traveling to locations miles off shore and then infiltrating into the area.

The HRB Singer Corporation used Cape Sable as a "natural laboratory" for a "night sounds' recording project in 1966.[31] Given Singer's other activities in Everglades NP, this project probably represents some kind of classified military research. Throughout the 1960s the U.S. military sought technological solutions to the problems posed by counterinsurgency warfare and the increasing effectiveness of the guerrilla tactics used by "third world" insurgents. Faced with a serious guerrilla problem in Vietnam and elsewhere, the military found it necessary to develop new methods of surveillance and detection in order to maximize the U.S. military's strengths while minimizing its weaknesses. Guerrillas in Vietnam "owned the night" and were usually free to operate at will with minimal threat of detection and engagement by American air power or artillery. The Singer project may have been designed to develop audio sensors that could detect the presence of intruders in a jungle/tropical setting. Of course, the possibility also exists that the project was merely a cover for some kind of CIA, intelligence-gathering, or other covert operation.[32]

Clive Key/Man of War Key/Sandy Key. Clive Key, Man of War Key, and Sandy Key may have served as weapons cache points for exiles involved in raids on Cuba in the early 1960s. In April 1962, these keys played a role in an event known as the "Sandy Key Munitions Exposé."[33] A year later, rangers observed a vessel similar to the one involved in the "Sandy Key Munitions Exposé"—a "blue and white skiff"—launching from Flamingo and heading into Florida Bay. Rangers ordered increased surveillance of Sandy Key, Clive Key, and Man of War Key in order to determine whether the vessel was involved in any sort of illegal activity.[34] More research needs to be done on the "Sandy Key Munitions Exposé" to determine its true nature. Everglades NP records indicate that several "special incident" reports were filed on this matter, but these reports have not been found.[35]

The CIA and exile groups used Flamingo as a launch point for many Cold War operations against Castro. A typical mission might involve launching a vessel unarmed and then picking up weapons from a cache location at some uninhabited key in Florida Bay. In this manner embarrassing questions and scrutiny could be avoided because no weapons were present in the craft when it launched from U.S. facilities. After the Cuban missile crisis official sanction was removed from exile groups that launched attacks on Cuba from American soil, and authorities became much more vigilant about enforcing the Neutrality Act.

East Everglades. Near the Chekika picnic site off of 237th Avenue are the remains of a structure known to Everglades NP personnel as "the shooting gallery." This location may be the former site of an exile paramilitary training facility. Exiles utilized many facilities in and around the Everglades as training camps for their paramilitary activities. Camps would be a place to practice military drill

30. Ayers, *The War that Never Was*, 44-45.
31. *Superintendent's Monthly Narrative Reports* (Everglades NP: Department of the Interior, February 1966); the HRB Singer Corporation has a long history of involvement in the design of advanced sensor systems for the military and industry. One project of importance to NPS and the Forest Service is Singer's airborne infrared thermal imaging scanner, which is used to detect fires and hot spots in forests.
32. *Superintendent's Monthly Narrative Reports* (Everglades NP: Department of the Interior, February 1966); *Ranger's Monthly Narrative Reports* (Everglades NP: Department of the Interior, February 1966).
33. *Ranger's Monthly Narrative Reports* (Everglades NP: Department of the Interior, April 1962).
34. *Ranger's Monthly Narrative Reports* (Everglades NP: Department of the Interior, October 1963).
35. Confidential files in the Everglades NP ranger office were reviewed by Everglades NP staff for this study. While some files from the 1960s were present in the Everglades NP ranger office, reports on the "Sandy Key Munitions Exposé" and other Cold War era "special incident" reports were not present. The final disposition of "special incident" reports within the NPS is a matter that should be researched further. If these reports were filed with a higher authority within NPS or DOI then copies of these files may exist somewhere within the system. Discussions with ranger and administrative staff at Everglades NP did not reveal the typical disposition of "special incident" reports or reports which might be expected to be filed when rangers in the 1960s stumbled across the various clandestine activities occurring within the parks.

and tactics as well as marksmanship. The site near Chekika consists of the ruins and foundations of a few buildings. All over the area there are numerous expended brass shell casings. This evidence indicates that the facility may have functioned as a firing range for training paramilitary exile forces.[36]

Flamingo. Flamingo was utilized by several government agencies for various activities during the Cold War. The area's southerly location, geography, and relatively easy automobile access made it a prime candidate for Cold War- related activities such as clandestine maritime operations, intelligence gathering, and radio communications operations. It also functioned as an entry point for Cubans fleeing Castro. The Border Patrol constantly watched the Flamingo area; Everglades NP staff often assisted them as they surveyed old roads, airstrips, and other facilities utilized by illegal immigrants.[37]

In May 1958, a small Army detachment camped at Flamingo and performed a classified mission over the course of three days.[38] This mission may have involved infiltration into Cuba or the operation of sensitive communications gear. Of course, it may have also been unrelated to the Cuban situation and merely some kind of classified exercise. Four years later, an Army detachment from the Signal Corps installed an "experimental radio" in the Flamingo utility area. This activity may be significant because the Army Signal Corps worked closely with the CIA's JMWAVE operations; they may have been monitoring activities in Cuba or involved in communications with Cuban agents. Signal Corps personnel were frequent visitors to the park during the important events of the early 1960s. They may have merely been tourists or just setting up standard communications gear. The presence of so many Signal Corps visitors, often in the company of personnel from the University of Miami's

"experimental radar lab"—a known CIA cover—raises the possibility of a CIA/Cuba covert operations- connected activity.[39]

For several years beginning in early 1962, the CIA and its trainees utilized the Flamingo campground and marina for maritime infiltration training and practice.[40] Exiles slated for maritime operations would gather at an isolated, luxurious house on the edge of the Everglades several miles from Homestead for dry land exercises. At the safe house, they would learn about their Boston Whaler infiltration vessels from a former U.S. Navy instructor who now worked for the CIA. From the safe house training facility near Everglades NP, they would drive approximately 60 miles to the Flamingo marina and practice operations. From Flamingo, small groups of exiles would launch their vessels and then practice navigational techniques, emergency boat repair, and clandestine infiltration. The trainees would often travel several miles off shore and then approach the area as if they were making a landing in Cuba. They would also practice operations in the waters of both Florida Bay and Whitewater Bay. Upcoming missions were practiced by launching from Flamingo and running through every phase of the mission's "profile" while remaining in nearby waters. In this manner, valuable mission practice was obtained and problems could be corrected before the team headed to Cuba for their actual life- or- death missions. On at least one occasion, the activities of these trainees may have attracted the attention of Everglades NP staff.[41]

Florida Bay. The waters of Florida Bay within Everglades NP provided a suitable area for maritime training operations and played an important role in Cold War activities in south Florida. CIA operatives, Cuban exiles, and Cuban refugee smugglers used the numerous inlets, swamps, and

---

36. Everglades NP ranger Phil Selleck, oral interview with author, May 1999. Selleck has digital images of the ruins at the Everglades NP ranger offices.
37. *Superintendent's Monthly Narrative Reports* (Everglades NP: Department of the Interior, April 1959, November 1961, April 1966); *Ranger's Monthly Narrative Reports* (Everglades NP: Department of the Interior, December 1958, May 1960, August 1960, November 1961).
38. *Superintendent's Monthly Narrative Reports* (Everglades NP: Department of the Interior, May 1958).
39. Ayers, *The War that Never Was*, 23; Ayers notes that his cover while working for the CIA in Miami was as a "civilian technical specialist in Army Research and Development" working for "an Army support group involved in classified weapons and undersea research with the University of Miami." Throughout the 1960s, many visitors to Everglades NP and Dry Tortugas NP claimed to work for the experimental radar lab at the University of Miami while others claimed to be involved in research for the Signal Corps and its experimental research lab at Ft. Monmouth, New Jersey. All of these visitors should probably be examined as possible CIA personnel or as individuals involved in Cold War-related activities.
40. Ibid., 44-45.
41. See the Clive Key/Man of War Key/Sandy Key entry above for a discussion of the "Sandy Key Munitions Exposé."

keys of the bay and the surrounding area. CIA operatives and their trainees frequently traveled the waters of the bay as they re- supplied various safe houses and facilities and as they trained for Cuban operations. In June 1962, the Border Patrol investigated a large group of Cuban men in Florida Bay after Everglades NP rangers alerted them to their presence. Upon investigation, the Border Patrol discovered many of the men were Bay of Pigs veterans and they were practicing landing operations within Florida Bay. Because the group had no weapons, the Border Patrol let the men go. It is also possible that the men were let go because they were, in fact, CIA trainees. The Border Patrol explanation for letting the men go—they were "orderly" and "had no weapons"—seems suspect when one considers their activities may have violated the Neutrality Act and most people discovered engaging in similar activities within Everglades NP usually ended up in court.[42]

In other cases, exiles seem to have used the Florida Bay keys of as weapon cache locations. Weapons would be stored on certain keys and then recovered by groups traveling to Cuba to raid facilities. In a typical operation, exiles would travel to Flamingo or some other marina and board their vessels unarmed, avoiding the scrutiny of the authorities. Once aboard their vessels, they would head to the key where their weapons were stashed. After picking up their weapons, the exiles would travel to Cuba, complete their operation, and then return to the cache location and hide the weapons until the next operation. The U.S. government removed official sanction for most of these types of operations after the Cuban missile crisis, and exiles were forced to move their caches to locations outside of U.S. territory. Typically, the Bahamas were utilized as weapons cache locations once the U.S. government cracked down on "unofficial" exile raids against Cuba.

Ground Observer Corps Activities. Throughout the mid- 1950s, Everglades NP ranger personnel participated in the U.S. Air Force (USAF) Ground Observer Corps (GOC) program. The GOC was a system of aircraft spotters instituted to counter the threat of low- flying Soviet bombers and eliminate the threat of another Pearl Harbor- type attack. In the early Cold War period, the threat of nuclear attack came almost exclusively from bomber and long- range attack aircraft. While the U.S. and its allies eventually established extensive radar warning systems, such as the famous Distant Early Warning (DEW) Line and others, these systems took a long time to construct, and aircraft could penetrate the defenses and avoid detection by flying low.[43] The USAF utilized the GOC—first developed as a response to Pearl Harbor during World War II—as a way to spot aircraft that might penetrate the radar early warning system or come through gaps in its coverage.

Early detection of enemy aircraft was difficult due to the size of the United States, the lack of enough radars, and the short range of radars in those early years. The Ground Observer Corps was called upon to fill the gaps and supplement the radar early warning coverage. Once enemy penetrators were detected, Ground Observer Corps observers would pass information to control centers responsible for alerting fighter interceptors and the antiaircraft crews.[44]

The GOC- trained volunteers manned the observation posts, and any aircraft observed were reported by phone to the local GOC filter center. The filter center determined whether aircraft were actually intruders and then relayed this information to Air Defense Command Headquarters.

Eventually over 800,000 volunteers stood alternating shifts at 16,000 observation posts and seventy- three filter centers. The Air Force used a variety of means to recruit volunteers, including radio. One radio spot announced "it may not be a very cheerful thought but the Reds right now have about a thousand bombers that are quite capable of destroying at least 89 American cities in one raid. Won't you help protect your country, your town, your children? Call your local Civil Defense office and join the Ground Observer Corps today."[45]

---

42. *Superintendent's Monthly Narrative Reports* (Everglades NP: Department of the Interior, June 1962). The CIA worked closely with most major government agencies in south Florida throughout the Cold War period. They tried to ensure that their operatives and trainees could go about their business unmolested. Generally, "approved" groups would get code words from the CIA to give to the authorities if they were stopped. Code words could be checked out by phone with a CIA liaison officer in order to determine their legitimacy. If the code was correct, then the suspects were released immediately. Branch, *Kennedy Vendetta*, 53.
43. For more on Cold War radar defense facilities see Winkler, *Searching the Skies*.
44. Moeller, "Vigilant and Invincible."

Attempts were made to implement a nationwide 24-hour surveillance system, but the GOC never got the kind of volunteer support needed to carry out this program. Many volunteers were children and teenagers, so one often wonders whether the program could have ever provided a robust early warning system. GOC activities increasingly became anachronistic as radars improved and both the U.S. and Soviets developed missile forces with intercontinental range. By 1959, bombers were playing a less important role in the nuclear balance, and the fully operational radar warning systems made the GOC unnecessary.[46]

Everglades NP rangers were active participants in the GOC from nuary 1953 until at least February 1957.[47] The rangers would usually utilize park fire towers and other similar structures to make aircraft observations and then phone in the results to the Miami filter center for processing. The GOC held numerous alerts and exercises to test the system, and park rangers made so many observations that the GOC awarded many of them letters of commendation and GOC wings for their efforts. The wings—perhaps more coveted among the GOC's many teenage participants than among park rangers—were awarded to volunteers who made 100 aircraft observations. Park ranger staff participated in GOC alerts and exercises such as Operation Bird's Eye, Operation SKYTRAIN VI, and several SKYWATCH GOC exercises. Personnel from the 467th GOC Squadron Detachment 8, located in Miami, often met with park staff to discuss the importance of the Everglades NP observation posts and their role in protecting south Florida from aerial attack.

Hole In the Donut. The former Iori Farms location at the Hole in the Donut area was the site of Nike Hercules Missile Site HM-69.[48] Built in 1964 and operational until 1979, this Nike site became the permanent home of Battery A/2/52 ADA—the personnel originally deployed to a point just outside the main entrance to Everglades NP. Approximately 146 U.S. Army soldiers and technicians operated this missile site's three aboveground launchers and protected south Florida from Cuban air strikes. This former missile site, now the home of the Daniel Beard Research Center and an auxiliary storage area, represents the most substantial Cold War historic resource in the park.[49]

The personnel of A/2/52 deployed "under duress" as U.S. military leaders sought to protect the forces and facilities associated with the military buildup during the Cuban missile crisis. They also faced a different situation than other U.S. Nike units because they had to guard against attacks from Fidel Castro as well as the threat of Soviet bombers. As part of the overall air defense of south Florida, Nike sites like HM-69 were integrated with HAWK missile sites in order to provide an all-altitude defense capability. This occurred nowhere else within the United States.[50] The personnel of the various air defense units in south Florida received a meritorious unit commendation for their efforts from President John F. Kennedy. This award is highly significant because it represents one of the few times the award was presented for a Cold War deterrence mission.[51]

HM-69 was also significant because it used radars and missiles unlike those at any other location in the

---

45. See <http://www.bwcinet.com/acwrons/documents/GOC.html> on the internet for a good discussion of the GOC. The quotation on the web site is found in Kenneth Schaffel, *The Emerging Shield: The Air Force and the Evolution of Continental Air Defense 1945-1960* (Washington, D.C.: Office of Air Force History, 1991), 158-159.
46. <http://www.spacecom.af.mil/norad/maschron.html> contains an official NORAD chronology of radar defense and surveillance.
47. *Superintendent's Monthly Narrative Reports* (Everglades NP: Department of the Interior, nuary 1953, July 1953, March 1955, July 1955, August 1955, October 1955, nuary 1956, February 1956, February 1957); *Ranger's Monthly Narrative Reports* (Everglades NP: Department of the Interior, nuary 1953, July 1953, March 1955, July 1955, August 1955, October 1955, nuary 1956, February 1956, February 1957).
48. Everglades NP archives contains the special use permits and title deed transfers related to the Iori property and its transfer to the Army. See Everglades NP Superintendent files, box 8 folder d5015 acc# 406. Everglades NP also has HQ USACE documents related to the hazmat survey and cleanup of the site after deactivation in Everglades NP Superintendent files, box 9.
49. For more on the unique nature and history of HM-69, see Appendix A.
50. The deployment, construction, and history of the south Florida Nike sites is best summarized in Kirkpatrick, "The Second Battalion." Osato and Straup, *ARADCOM'S Florida Defenses*; Martin and Rice, *ARADCOM in the Cuban Crisis*; Martin and Rice, *History of ARADCOM*; and the 2/52 unit history by James R. Hinds, "History of the 2d Missile Battalion [1965]" (2/52/ADA Organizational History Files, Carlisle Barracks, MHI, photocopy). See also contemporary local newspaper accounts as well as accounts in the *Argus*, ARADCOM's monthly command newspaper found at MHI, Carlisle Barracks, Pennsylvania. A good general discussion of Cold War missile programs may be found in Lonnquest, *To Defend and Deter*.

continental United States (CONUS).[52] HM- 69 had a mobile high- power acquisition radar (HIPAR) in order to fulfill its mission as a fully mobile air defense system. Mobile HIPARs were rare among Nike sites operating in fixed locations. The site also had the Nike version of the Army's anti- tactical ballistic missile (ATBM). This was one of the earliest weapons systems designed to shoot down incoming missiles. This implies that one of the missions of HM- 69 was to provide a defense against missiles launched from Cuba against south Florida. The ATBM was an important early step in the quest to defend the nation against a ballistic missile attack.

In addition to its highly significant role in the Cold War history of south Florida, Nike site HM- 69— along with the other Nike sites in south Florida—is important because it represents the last group of active Nike sites to operate within the CONUS. The Nike sites of south Florida were still in operation a full five years after all other similar installations were shut down. The former integrated fire control (IFC) area was converted into the Daniel Beard Research Center in the early 1980s, but the former IFC's main structure is still intact. Florida's water table precluded the construction of underground magazines like those found at other CONUS missile sites, so aboveground missile storage buildings were constructed. These storage buildings, along with several other launch area structures, such as earthen berms and the missile assembly building are still intact.

Long Pine Key. The Long Pine Key fire tower was the scene of some Cold War- related research and development in 1968 and 1969.[53] At that time, scientists from the Massachusetts Institute of Technology (MIT) working for the Department of Defense secured a special use permit to utilize the fire tower in an effort to develop an anti- infiltration radar system designed to expose "live man infiltration attempts." This project, most likely related to the ongoing war in Vietnam, illustrates the fact that the south Florida national parks were used as giant natural laboratories by the military throughout the Cold War. The war in Vietnam was

often a guerrilla fight, and guerrillas could use their ability to move at night and in bad weather in ways that overcame the strengths of U.S. military forces. The U.S. government, involved in counterinsurgency conflicts throughout the Cold War, tried to bring new technologies on line in order to combat the typical enemy mode of operation in Vietnam and elsewhere. The MIT project at Pine Island fire tower, directed by Paul Cusick, demonstrates again the role the park had in helping to develop and test advanced Cold War military technologies.

Palma Vista Hammock. During 1965, the HRB Singer Corporation conducted tests of new military technology within the Palma Vista Hammock area of Everglades NP. Contemporary park ranger and superintendent records indicate that Singer was designing and testing some type of infrared (IR) ground surveillance sensor system. Singer was eventually joined in their Everglades NP project by personnel from the Conductron Corporation. Conductron, a research and development consortium from the University of Michigan, used DC- 7 and DC- 3 aircraft to overfly the Palma Vista Hammock and East End of Long Pine Key to test the experimental IR sensor system.[54]

Because the Cold War nuclear weapons balance precluded a direct U.S. confrontation with the Soviets—and vice versa—proxy wars functioned as substitutes for direct conflict all over the globe as each side tried to maximize its respective sphere of influence. The military searched for technologies that would allow them to successfully combat the new type of enemy faced in the many struggles for national liberation and independence—such as the Vietcong forces in Vietnam. In many cases, these conflicts pitted the relatively slow and cumbersome U.S. military apparatus against highly agile enemies that could move about undetected and then attack U.S. forces on their own terms. Faced increasingly with an enemy it often could not see or otherwise detect, the U.S. military tried to develop weapons and surveillance systems that would eliminate the advantages held by guerrilla forces. U.S. combat

51. Bob Wright, chief of records, CMH, Washington, D.C., pointed out the significance of this award to the researcher. He believes that it may be one of the only times an award of this type was made to units that had not engaged in actual combat operations—it may be the only time that a deterrence mission was so rewarded.
52. Colonel Bud Halsey, e-mail to author, July 1999.
53. Everglades NP archives, superintendent files, box 15 308019, Folder L30#1-160-35, acc#327. The records include pictures of the operation as well as copies of documentation related to it.
54. The CIA is known to have used surplus DC-7 aircraft in its operations.

forces in Vietnam deployed many new sensor systems and other intelligence- gathering equipment designed to eliminate the advantages of the Vietcong and North Vietnamese forces. IR sensor arrays, like those tested by Singer at Palma Vista, would eventually give the U.S. military a greater capability to detect and engage enemy guerrillas and conventional forces operating under cover of darkness. IR, audio, and other types of new sensor systems were used extensively in Vietnam in such activities as the interdiction of the Ho Chi Minh Trail.[55] Eventually, the Persian Gulf War would demonstrate the stunning effectiveness of advanced U.S. military sensor systems.

Parachute Key Visitor Center. Parachute Key Visitor Center served as an auxiliary civil defense and military hospital location.[56] As the Cold War developed into a hardened stalemate and some began to think of a nuclear exchange as a survivable event, the U.S. government and military planners began to pay more than lip service to the idea of civil defense and emergency preparations for the aftermath of nuclear combat. In the early 1960s, Florida Governor Farris Bryant took a leading role in the implementation of a number of state- level civil defense and "survival" projects. Under his leadership, local and state officials received civil defense training. For a time, Florida also led the nation in the number of fallout shelter spaces identified and stocked for its citizens. Bryant took his program of civil defense to the National Governors' Conference, and state officials from across the U.S. participated in Bryant's special Cold War educational seminars.[57]

Government officials designated several areas in Everglades NP as fallout shelters and emergency facilities. Following the Cuban missile crisis, the military formulated a variety of contingency plans to deal with Cuba and the Soviet troops stationed there. They needed to ensure that facilities were available to handle casualties if hostilities commenced. Military and civil defense officials designated Parachute Key Visitor Center as a

location where the wounded could receive treatment if casualties overwhelmed the various military and civilian medical facilities in the area in the event of a "major catastrophe."[58] The visitor center was destroyed by Hurricane Andrew in 1992. Four years later, a new facility, the Ernest F. Coe Visitor Center, opened in the same location.

Pine Island. In March 1958, a B- 47 SAC bomber from Homestead AFB crashed into the glades of Everglades NP just east of the Pine Island area.[59] The B- 47 was SAC's first nuclear- capable jet bomber, and it served as the backbone of the U.S. strategic bomber force until the B- 52 entered into service. The B- 47 had an intermediate range, and many of them served with SAC all over the world. The crash served as a reminder that even though the Cold War never went "hot," many military personnel lost their lives ensuring that the concept of deterrence was not hollow. SAC's motto, "Peace is our Profession," meant extraordinary sacrifices had to be made in providing a combat- ready nuclear force capable of responding to a Soviet attack in a credible and effective manner. Military planners believed that the U.S. could deter Soviet aggression only by possessing a credible threat.

The significance of this crash depends, in part, on the status of the aircraft at the time of the incident. SAC, under the direction of General Curtis LeMay, developed much of the USAF's strategic bombing theory and many hallmarks of nuclear deterrence strategy. One of LeMay's innovations was the practice of airborne alert. With airborne alert, SAC kept fully loaded nuclear bombers airborne and ready to attack targets in the Soviet Union if given the order. During SAC exercises and crisis periods, the entire bomber fleet could be placed on airborne alert.[60] On several occasions, airborne alert aircraft crashed while carrying nuclear bombs. If the aircraft that crashed in Everglades NP was on airborne alert then it may have been carrying nuclear weapons. It is unclear from park documents whether this was a concern at the time of the crash, but it is worth

---

55. See James William Gibson's *The Perfect War: Technowar in Vietnam* (Boston: Atlantic Monthly Press, 1986) for a discussion of technology and the U.S. reliance on it in Vietnam.
56. *Superintendent's Monthly Narrative Reports* (Everglades NP: Department of the Interior, March 1963).
57. Evans, *Time for Florida*, 107-109.
58. "Major catastrophe" refers to the possibility of a large scale conventional battle for the island or a nuclear exchange.
59. *Superintendent's Monthly Narrative Reports* (Everglades NP: Department of the Interior, March 1958, November 1959); *Ranger's Monthly Narrative Reports* (Everglades NP: Department of the Interior, March 1958, November 1959).
60. During the Cuban missile crisis CINCSAC General Thomas S. Power placed 1/8 of the SAC B-52 fleet on airborne alert. Utz, *Cordon of Steel*, 32.

exploring further. It is also uncertain at this time whether any debris from the crash remains on site at the park today.

The Air Force designated several areas in Everglades NP as temporary hospital and evacuation sites. Pine Island served as a location for a mobile base hospital from Homestead AFB.[61] During the 1960s, military planners implemented various measures designed to ensure survivability in the nuclear war fighting scenarios of the Cold War. These measures often involved the construction of off- base fallout shelters and contingency facilities that would not be damaged in the event of a nuclear strike. In the aftermath of the Cuban missile crisis, the U.S. military took steps to provide for emergency facilities throughout the region. During exercises at military bases in south Florida, the facilities at Everglades NP would be activated to test the procedures involved in setting up military operations off base.

Pine Island Utility Area. The Pine Island Utility Area served as an emergency equipment storage area for the various missile forces deployed to south Florida during the Cuban missile crisis. The construction of permanent installations took over a year, and missile troops were forced to serve in temporary locations during the crisis. Until they had more substantial facilities, troops were often at the mercy of south Florida's tropical climate and the more violent tropical storms and hurricanes. The weapons systems used state- of- the- art equipment consisting of several primitive computers and a digital network at each missile emplacement. This equipment was notoriously difficult to maintain in south Florida's climate, and the troops quickly learned that any rain or excessive moisture could cause all kinds of glitches in the system.[62] When needed, missile troops would store more sensitive equipment at Everglades NP facilities like the Pine Island Utility Area until the bad weather had passed. In October 1963, soldiers from Battery B/2/52 ADA used the utility area to keep mobile equipment out of the weather, and personnel moved into the ranger office to guard the sensitive equipment.[63]

Royal Palm Visitor Center. During the Cuban missile crisis, "hundreds of military personnel" in search of rest and recreation (R&R) utilized the various interpretive programs at Everglades NP's Royal Palm visitor center.[64] So many troops visited Everglades NP that overall attendance figures did not decline that much from previous years despite the ongoing crisis. Any reduction in tourism was almost completely made up by the numerous troops in the area who visited the park. Troops deployed to Florida faced problems of morale and boredom once the initial adrenaline of the rapid deployment wore off and they realized that they would not be facing combat. Troops found themselves with little money and even less to do. Pay rates in the draft military of the 1960s were quite low. In a tourist area like Florida, service members were unable to afford more expensive entertainment and thus made good use of any free or inexpensive recreational activities.

The HRB Singer Corporation utilized the area around Royal Palm Visitor Center as another location for its experimental "night sounds" recording project in the spring of 1966.[65] As noted previously, this project—if not merely a cover for some other CIA/intelligence activity—may have been designed to develop some sort of sensor system or other surveillance device in order to combat the difficulties faced by the U.S. military as they increasingly fought counterinsurgency/guerrilla- type wars throughout the 1960s. The expansion of the containment doctrine to include battles in various Third World nations meant fighting battles where U.S. military advantages could not easily be brought to bear. Advanced sensor systems were one way of negating the advantages of those enemies who utilized guerrilla tactics—such as stealthy nighttime attacks.

Seven Mile Road. Throughout the history of Everglades NP, park personnel have always faced the problem of armed hunters and others engaged in poaching or other illegal activities traveling through the park. The events in Cuba at the end of the 1950s and early 1960s meant that park staff had to deal with a new type of armed visitor—the Cuban exiles. As numerous exile paramilitary groups

---

61. *Superintendent's Monthly Narrative Reports* (Everglades NP: Department of the Interior, April 1965). The Everglades NP headquarters and main visitor center was designated as an evacuation area for base personnel in the event of an attack.
62. Kirkpatrick, "The Second Battalion," 12.
63. *Superintendent's Monthly Narrative Reports* (Everglades NP: Department of the Interior, October 1963).
64. *Superintendent's Monthly Narrative Reports* (Everglades NP: Department of the Interior, October-December 1962).
65. *Superintendent's Monthly Narrative Reports* (Everglades NP: Department of the Interior, February-March 1966).

prepared to overthrow Castro, they increasingly used the Everglades for training purposes. Throughout the Cold War, especially during the time of the Cuban revolution, exiles of many different political persuasions used the isolation of the glades to practice their marksmanship and other military skills. As early as 1958, park staff discovered heavily armed Cubans in the park looking for places to practice their marksmanship.[66] Ironically, the first exiles caught in the park with weapons were on the side of the Cuban rebels led by Castro. Three men found with weapons on Seven Mile Road in March 1958 identified themselves as "anti-Batistianos" when confronted by park rangers. The three men had their weapons seized and received thirty- day suspended sentences for their violation of park rules.

Seven Mile Tower. On Seven Mile Road, north of Seven Mile Tower, Homer W. Hiser, Paul Norman, and Douglas Hirth—"radar technicians" for the University of Miami—and Mr. Carter of the U.S. Army Signal Corps Research and Development Lab, Fort Monmouth, New Jersey, participated in a project studying "night radar operations and light distance studies."[67] The project at Seven Mile Tower may have been a clandestine intelligence-monitoring effort, classified military research, or a classified project related to CIA or military covert activities in south Florida. The CIA used a Cold War- era cover for its employees in south Florida where agents claimed to be civilian technicians working on classified projects for the Army.[68] CIA JMWAVE operatives also used the University of Miami and other local colleges as a cover for many of their activities.[69] The CIA worked closely with the Army Signal Corps for its communications needs, so any visitors who claimed to work for the Signal Corps, the University of Miami, or U.S. Army Research and Development within the park should

raise some suspicion of Cold War- related covert activities.

Sisal Hammock. In February of 1960, Everglades NP rangers discovered a large bomb in an old U.S. practice bomb case in the Sisal Hammock area. Rangers believed that the bomb had been built by a group of Batista supporters seeking to foment a counterrevolution against Castro. As noted previously, Cuban exiles may have used areas of Everglades NP as weapons cache points. They stored weapons and munitions within various areas of the park and then picked them up on the outbound legs of their missions to Cuba. The early date of this bomb discovery indicates that this was probably not an action connected to officially sanctioned U.S. government activities against Cuba.[70]

U.S. Department of State Activities. Everglades NP served an important role in U.S. State Department initiatives designed to promote cultural exchange and understanding with both Cold War allies and enemies. Visitor programs run by the State Department brought high- ranking government officials, college students, and business officials from many other nations to the park throughout the Cold War. The State Department's park guest lists provide a window on shifting U.S. Cold War concerns throughout the period. At first, visitors to Everglades NP with the State Department program reflected the almost exclusively Western European focus of containment and U.S. diplomacy. Visitors in the 1950s tended to come from Western European nations and from countries behind the Iron Curtain.[71] In the 1960s, however, visitors from many Asian nations began to show up in the park. As the containment policy of the United States spread beyond the Kennan- conceived focus on Europe, the U.S. increasingly became involved in Southeast Asia and other areas of the world. By the 1960s, the threat of communism was thought to be

66. *Superintendent's Monthly Narrative Reports* (Everglades NP: Department of the Interior, March 1958).
67. *Superintendent's Monthly Narrative Reports* (Everglades NP: Department of the Interior, February 1964).
68. Ayers, *The War that Never Was*, 23. Ayers writes that his cover while working for the CIA in Miami was as a "civilian technical specialist in Army Research and Development" working for "an Army support group involved in classified weapons and undersea research with the University of Miami." Throughout the 1960s, many visitors to Everglades NP and Dry Tortugas NP claimed to work for the experimental radar lab at the University of Miami while others claimed to be involved in research for the Signal Corps and its experimental research lab at Ft. Monmouth, New Jersey.
69. Kirkpatrick, "The Inspector General's Survey," in Kornbluh, *Bay of Pigs Declassified*, 28, mentions the fact that JMWAVE facilities were leased from the University of Miami, while Hinckle and Turner, *The Fish is Red*, note that the CIA used university cover for its mother ship, the *Explorer II*.
70. *Ranger's Monthly Narrative Reports* (Everglades NP: Department of the Interior, March 1960).
71. The term "Iron Curtain" refers to the political, military, and ideological barrier established by the Soviet Union around itself and its allies after World War II. Former British prime minister Winston Churchill used the term to refer to this situation in a speech made in the United States on March 5, 1946.

focused on the "emerging" nations of Asia. Park visitor rosters of official State Department tours reflect this fact and document that in the 1960s the park was visited by government officials from Laos, Indonesia, South Vietnam, and other Asian nations.[72]

Other possible Everglades NP resources.
Everglades NP's monthly narrative reports document the existence of a special use permit issued to the LORAC Corporation. According to park records, this project involved extensive radio communications gear and mapping facilities. The LORAC Corporation was supposedly an oil company engaged in oil exploration activities in the Gulf of Mexico and the Caribbean. LORAC said that it was coordinating its project within the park with the activities of its oil exploration ships in the waters surrounding Florida. Research revealed, however, that the CIA used decoy ships for its infiltration operations into Cuba and that these decoy vessels were "U.S. registered and officially operated by a phony Delaware CIA petroleum corporation [which] was supposed to be doing offshore [oil] research and mapping."[73] This discovery demonstrates the need for a more thorough examination of the LORAC Corporation and its activities in Everglades NP to determine whether LORAC was in fact a front for the CIA. It is possible that the CIA used the legitimate operations of the LORAC Corporation to cover its own clandestine activities.

Cold War Resources Located Near South Florida National Parks

Numerous Cold War- related historical sites and resources are located throughout south Florida near the various south Florida National Parks. This is not surprising given that during the early 1960s the area was literally ground zero in the Cold War. Events in Cuba during the late 1950s and early 1960s resulted in massive changes to the south Florida region as a large Cuban exile community sprang up almost overnight.[74] Miami, long a tourist destination, soon became a center of international intrigue and espionage. At one point, the largest CIA detachment outside of the agency's Langley, Virginia, headquarters was located in the Miami area. With a budget of approximately $50 million a year, the CIA Cuban operations and its Miami headquarters—code named JMWAVE—provided a substantial boost to the local economy.[75] The CIA established an extensive network of safe houses and training facilities in the region. For a brief time, duty in Miami was a hot career choice among CIA operatives.[76]

> The CIA's influence over the transformation of Greater Miami into a center of international finance and business can probably never be determined, but it's clear that the Company and its subsidiaries had a finger in almost every pie in the Magic City: real estate, banking, shipping, air transport, you name it.[77]

Only the growing conflict in Southeast Asia would eventually relegate Miami to a lesser status among "up and coming" CIA agents.[78]

More obvious Cold War sites can be found all over the region as well because the Cuban missile crisis resulted in a massive deployment of U.S. military forces to south Florida. While mostly temporary in nature, this deployment did result in the permanent establishment of an all- altitude, anti- aircraft missile defense system designed to counter the threat of both Soviet and Cuban air attacks. The Cold War arms and space race led to some defense industry work occurring in Miami; infrastructure connected to this work resulted in salt water intrusion into the Everglades and other negative impacts on the environmental health of the region. Furthermore, strategic Cold War economic policies, designed to

---

72. Everglades NP *Superintendent's Monthly Narrative Reports* throughout the 1950s and 1960s contain lists of visitors to the park from State Department programs.
73. Ayers, *The War that Never Was*, 57.
74. The history of the Cuban exiles and their role in the development of Miami is well explored in Clark, *The Exodus*; García, *Havana USA*; Portes and Stepick, *City on the Edge*; Rieff, *The Exile*; and Research Institute for Cuba and Caribbean, *The Cuban Immigration*.
75. David Corn, *Blond Ghost: Ted Shackley and the CIA's Crusades* (New York: Simon and Schuster, 1994), 75.
76. Kirkpatrick, "The Inspector General's Survey," in Kornbluh, *Bay of Pigs Declassified*, 28.
77. Kelly, "The Fidel Fixation," 1. See also Hinckle and Turner, *The Fish is Red*, especially the last chapter, "A Murderous Legacy."
78. Corn, *Blond Ghost*, 119.

deny Castro benefit from the fruits of the Cuban economy, also harmed the environment of south Florida in an unforeseen manner.

If one takes a broad view, there are probably hundreds of Cold War- related resources located in and around Miami. This list has identified the most notable of these resources where possible. Additional resources probably exist, and any follow- up HRS research will most likely identify many more of these resources in the region.

Other Cold War-Related Resources in South Florida

Aerojet General Solid Rocket Booster Facility.

Aerojet General, a division of the General Tire Corporation of Akron, Ohio, had a solid rocket booster (SRB) and rocket engine facility in south Dade County near Everglades NP. The factory was designed to take advantage of the massive arms race between the Soviet Union and the U.S. and to support U.S. competition with the Soviets in the space race. A key issue in the 1960 election between Nixon and Kennedy was the so- called missile gap. Like the "bomber gap" before it, this was largely a case where an incumbent President was accused of allowing the military to fall behind the Soviets, putting the nation at risk. The typical solution to the various Cold War "gaps" was generally an increased arms building program that benefited defense contractors, such as Aerojet General, and the military- industrial complex. In this case, the "missile gap" proved a red herring. During the 1960 election cycle, Eisenhower and Nixon could not challenge eventual presidential candidate Kennedy and the Democrats on the issue directly because such a challenge would have revealed the existence of certain U.S. intelligence assets like the U2 spy plane. Ironically, the use of the U2 by Eisenhower to assess the purported "missile gap" resulted in the infamous U2 incident. Combined with other contemporary Cold War events, such as the launch of Sputnik and Soviet repression in East Berlin, the

U2 incident led to increasing superpower tensions just prior to the Bay of Pigs and the Cuban missile crisis, and further spurred the arms race.[79] Kennedy also supported National Aeronautics and Space Administration (NASA) efforts to put an American on the moon by the end of the 1960s. This Cold War- related policy goal created even more work for the aerospace and defense industries.

Kennedy and his successor, Lyndon Johnson, continued to build new missiles, escalating the arms race. New missile programs involved a switch from primitive, liquid- fueled booster engines like those of the Titan, to more stable systems that relied on solid fuel boosters, like the Minuteman.

> Aerojet [employees] soon began working around the clock to help close the Missile Gap declared by President Eisenhower [sic]. Propulsion systems for Titan, Minuteman, and Polaris [missile systems] became the backbone of Aerojet's propulsion business. Even after the gap had been eliminated, work continued on the three programs, providing long- lasting business for Aerojet.[80]

Aerojet built a factory in south Dade that made rocket engines for the Apollo program; they also tried to obtain the NASA space shuttle SRB contract. Florida politicians gave the company tax breaks and a lease with an option to buy on a large quantity of south Dade county land. It was hoped that the Aerojet facility would eventually provide many jobs for the region and help secure Florida's position as a leader in the emerging high tech aerospace industry.

Aerojet established operations and commenced production of solid fuel boosters and other NASA rocket engines at the plant. On September 19, 1964, Aerojet tested a 120" SRB, and in October 1965, the company tested a 26" SRB. During one test, the chemical fallout from the rocket exhaust killed much of the citrus crop in south Dade County.[81] The south Dade Aerojet factory never achieved the scale promised by the corporation although the company did do a large amount of work for NASA

---

79. See Beschloss, *Mayday,* for a discussion of this crisis.
80. "Official" Gencorp Aerojet history web site, <www.aerojet.com/About_Aerojet/history/1950>. It is interesting to note that the official web site still discusses the missile gap as if it actually existed. "Unofficial" history can be found at <www.csz.com/history/>. See "Aerojet General Corporation 1964," a film held by the Florida Department of State Library and Information Services Division for coverage of the Aerojet facility in Dade County.
81. Everglades NP archives, superintendent files, box 20, has a large clipping file related to the Aerojet property and the Aerojet land deal.

and the space program. This work, however, caused environmental problems because Aerojet dug and utilized various south Dade canals for its operations. Aerojet shipped completed boosters down the canals and up the intercoastal waterway for delivery to Cape Canaveral. Some of these canals—such as Canal C-III—posed a major threat to the environment of the region and Everglades NP because they permitted saltwater intrusion into the delicate Everglades ecosystem and interrupted the flow of freshwater across the "River of Grass."[82] Park officials fought hard to close Canal C-III and prevent a major ecological disaster. The history of Aerojet and Canal C-III in south Florida demonstrates how the Cold War impacted the environment of the region in an unforeseen manner.

To add economic insult to environmental injury, once land values skyrocketed in south Dade in the late 1960s, Aerojet attempted to exercise its option on the thousands of acres set aside for the SRB factory. Despite having never fulfilled its part of the bargain with local and state authorities who arranged the corporate incentive package, the company now wanted the land for a massive real estate development and in the then-booming south Dade market.[83] The state was forced to sell the land to the company at a deeply discounted price following a court battle, and Aerojet reinvented itself as a land development company.

Big Pine Key. Big Pine Key was the site of at least one Cuban exile paramilitary training camp or maritime operations facility. It is unclear whether this camp was CIA operated or an exile-run operation. Both the CIA and Cuban exiles had

camps in numerous locations and deciphering the lineage of all of them is rather difficult. Big Pine Key had a facility known as the Susan Ann base where PT (patrol torpedo) boat raids would be launched.[84] It is now a University of Miami research facility. Follow-up research should attempt to determine the provenance of lesser-known training camps and maritime facilities like the one reported to have existed on Big Pine Key.

Boca Chica Key. Boca Chica Key near Key West was the home of HAWK Missile Site KW-10. Battery D/6/65 occupied this site from the Cuban missile crisis in 1962 until September 1972. At that time, battery D/1/65 replaced D/6/65 and served at the site from September 1972 until the deactivation of the Key West missile defense in 1979.[85] The HAWK sites located in the keys helped to protect the various military facilities in the area from Soviet and Cuban attack during the Cuban missile crisis and served as a deterrent against attacks from Fidel Castro throughout the Cold War. The batteries of the keys are unique in that they represent the first time HAWK missiles were deployed in defense of the CONUS by the Army Air Defense Command (ARADCOM). The HAWKs provided much-needed protection for the Key West area during the Cuban missile crisis because this critical staging area was essentially wide open to aerial attack. These batteries were often in the news during the Cold War as politicians, generals, and other VIPs demonstrated a strong propensity for visiting them at certain times of the year.[86]

Boca Chica is also the home of Key West Naval Air Station (NAS), a facility that played a huge role in

82. Everglades NP archives, superintendent files, box 23, contains information concerning problems caused by Aerojet's Canal C-111 and the park's efforts to keep the canal closed. Hach, oral discussions with Everglades NP museum curator Walter Meshaka, Everglades NP, May 1999. Meshaka discussed the problems caused by Canal C-111.
83. Everglades NP archives, superintendent files, box 20, have a great deal of information on the Aerojet factory and the famous land case. The files include extensive newspaper clippings from the era and they provide insight into the political dynamics of big-time Florida real estate development deals. Aerojet's option was to buy 25,000 acres of county land at approximately $50 an acre. By the time they attempted to exercise the option the land in question was valued at approximately $2000 an acre.
84. Hach, e-mail from Gordon Winslow, Dade County Historical Archivist.
85. HAWK missile information is best presented in Morgan, *Nike Quick Look III*; Osato and Straup, *ARADCOM'S Florida Defenses*; Martin and Rice, *ARADCOM in the Cuban Crisis*; and Martin and Rice, *History of ARADCOM*. There are also numerous articles on south Florida HAWK sites in contemporary issues of the ARADCOM *Argus* newspaper, as well as the locally produced *Defender* newspaper of the south Florida missile units. JFK reviewed some of the HAWK sites in Key West during his trip to south Florida during the Cuban missile crisis. NARA II Army Signal Corps photo archives contain photos of this visit.
86. Of course, these "official" visits most often coincided with tourist season. Many VIPs demonstrated a preference for reviewing the troops at times when the weather in their own home towns may not have been as pleasant as that of the keys in winter. This analysis is bolstered by the fact that Nike Hercules and HAWK sites in remote locations—such as HM-69 in the Everglades NP—most often received "flyover" inspections while HAWK sites in Key West received direct personal inspections lasting several days. Osato and Straup note this VIP "problem" in *ARADCOM'S Florida Defenses*.

the Cuban missile crisis. Key West NAS was a fighter base as well as an important staging area for activities during the military buildup of the missile crisis. Its vulnerability necessitated the permanent deployment of HAWK missiles to the Key West defense area. Navy aircraft were instrumental in ensuring the safety of U.S. forces in the region as well as providing important low-altitude reconnaissance photographs of Cuban missile installations. The naval aircraft also played a key role in detecting and tracking the Soviet submarines in the waters surrounding Cuba during the crisis period.

Key West NAS was the home of HAWK missile facilities KW-18 and KW-19. These sites were the locations of the associated missile control computers and other facilities for the management of the Key West air defense missile sites. Control facilities at NAS Key West included a Missile Master computer as well as a TSQ-51 Missile Mentor. The Headquarters and Headquarters Battery (HHB)/6/65 ADA manned KW-189 and KW-19 until 1971 when they were replaced by HHB/1/65 ADA.[87]

Card Sound Area. CIA trainees used various facilities in south Florida as practice targets for their missions. Some utilized the Bell South (formerly Southern Bell) microwave facility on Old Card Sound Road near Homestead/Florida City as an example of the type of facility they might have to infiltrate in Cuba.[88] To "graduate" from training, exiles would have to infiltrate the microwave facility and simulate destroying it with explosives and then make a clean getaway. The facility had electric fences and its own security guards, so trainees were assured of as realistic an exercise as possible. Exile trainees also used the numerous swamps, rivers, and inlets of the Old Card Sound Road area as a huge natural training ground for their activities. Trainees would leave the various safe house/training facilities throughout the keys and then practice navigation, infiltration, and other seamanship skills in the areas between Upper Key Largo and Card Sound.[89]

Of course, not all CIA-connected activities in the region were necessarily life and death matters. CIA personnel frequently needed to unwind after spending days on end in the swamps and glades of south Florida. Unfortunately, they could not usually mix freely with the general population while out seeking R&R. Thus, CIA personnel typically patronized a few select establishments when looking for a little fun. One location popular with CIA personnel stationed at facilities in the keys was "Alabama Jack's," a bar on Card Sound Road with a reputation for "raffish clientele."[90]

Coconut Grove. The CIA made use of countless facilities throughout the Miami area, several of them located within Coconut Grove. In his memoirs, Captain Bradley Ayers mentions one safe house for Cuban exile trainees in Coconut Grove, and it is probable that many CIA employees lived in the Grove during their assignment to Miami's JMWAVE operation.[91]

Perhaps the most famous of the CIA Cold War-related facilities in Coconut Grove was the safe house of noted Watergate figure E. Howard Hunt. Hunt worked for the CIA during operation PBSUCCESS in Guatemala during 1954 and played an important role in the Bay of Pigs. At his Coconut Grove safe house, located on Poinciana Drive and now demolished, Hunt performed many of his CIA-related duties. Among the more important activities of Hunt at this location were his attempts to instill unity among the many disparate Cuban exile political factions. The exile voice in the early 1960s consisted of many diverse elements including former Fidelistas, Batistianos, and other opposing political groups all vying for control and favor within the exile movement. Hunt and other CIA officials often faced great difficulty when seeking consensus among them. Many times these groups vehemently opposed the inclusion of other factions with whom they disagreed. Hunt often met with exile leaders such as Manuel Artime and Antonio de Varona at his safe house in Coconut Grove to formulate the Cuban exile political structure that would take control of the island after the then-expected success of the Bay of Pigs invasion.[92]

---

87. Berhow and Morgan, *Rings of Supersonic Steel*, 85-86.
88. Ayers, *The War that Never Was*, 83.
89. Ayers, *The War that Never Was*, 89.
90. Kelly, "The Fidel Fixation," 1.
91. Ayers, *The War that Never Was*, 56.
92. Kelly, "The Fidel Fixation," 1.

Coral Gables. Several facilities in Coral Gables played a large role in the JMWAVE CIA operations during the Cold War in south Florida. The first headquarters for CIA operations against Castro was located in Coral Gables and opened in May 1960. Like many CIA facilities in the area, the first headquarters was "backstopped"—rendered untraceable directly back to the CIA—under a cover story. In the case of the Coral Gables headquarters facility, the cover was that of "a New York career development and placement firm, backstopped by a Department of Defense contract" and known as "Clarence A. Depew and Sons." This facility was later replaced by the much larger and more extensive JMWAVE operation—backstopped as "Zenith Technical Enterprises"—at the former Richmond Naval Air Station property leased from the University of Miami.[93]

Coral Gables was also the location of several CIA safe houses and operational facilities with one of the most significant being a house located at 6312 Riviera Drive. This house—and its attached boat house on the Coral Gables Waterway—served as both a CIA boat base and safe house. Famous Cuban exile figures involved in numerous CIA-sponsored missions to Cuba such as Rolando "Muscolito" Martinez frequently operated from this location. The covered boat house right on the canal offered a location where infiltration vessels could be hidden from plain view, thus shielding their extensive modifications and true nature from prying eyes.[94]

CIA agents often used very public and seemingly innocuous locations as part of their work in south Florida during the Cold War. Some agents would meet potential paramilitary recruits in public locations in order to determine their suitability for CIA- sponsored activity. In one case, an agent used the Sears Store in Coral Gables to meet with and interview potential recruits.[95]

Cudjoe Key. Located near Key West, Cudjoe Key was utilized as a radio facility and SIGINT collection station by the USAFSS and other agencies during the Cold War.[96] This site was responsible for collecting SIGINT from Cuba and coordinating its activities with airborne SIGINT collection activities over Cuba and other intelligence operations in the region. The disposition of these facilities is unknown.

Cudjoe Key also serves as the site for TV Marti, which began broadcasting in 1990. This program, along with Radio Marti, which began broadcasting from Marathon Key in 1985, was instituted by the U.S. government as part of its renewed emphasis on fighting communism in nearby Cuba. President Reagan had strong Cuban exile support and was a friend of powerful Cuban exiles such as Jorge Mas Canosa, co- founder of the Cuban American National Foundation (CANF). Thanks to CANF's efforts, Cuban exiles significantly increased their political power in Washington, D.C. during the 1980s.

TV Marti was controversial when President George Bush gave the order to commence broadcasting. National Security Adviser Richard Allen noted that "the only reason there is a TV Marti is because Jorge Mas twisted every political arm he could reach."[97] Radio and TV Marti were designed to provide a source of uncensored news and programming to the people of Cuba, but prominent Cuban exiles used their political influence to promote their own views on the stations. The influence of Jorge Mas and CANF on the broadcast content was a continuing source of controversy. Former Radio Marti director Ernesto Betancourt argued that

> An influential lobby has been able to use its congressional clout to pressure USIA management to give them control, for their own political purposes, of a broadcasting station financed by the American taxpayer.... [Radio Marti is] being converted into a vehicle of propaganda for Mr. Mas.... Mas has misled the

---

93. Kirkpatrick, "The Inspector General's Survey," in Kornbluh, *Bay of Pigs Declassified*, 28; "backstopped" refers to the CIA practice of providing plausible covers for all CIA facilities so that they could not easily be traced back to the CIA.
94. Corn, *Blond Ghost*, 74; see also Branch, "The Kennedy Vendetta," 49-63. The disposition of this site is unknown, but Cuban exile CIA operative Rolando Martinez suggests that to get a true picture of its suitability for clandestine activity it should be viewed from a location across the waterway rather than from the from the street in front of the address.
95. Ayers, *The War that Never Was*, notes numerous sites throughout the area that were utilized by CIA operatives.
96. Thompson, *USAFSS Performance During the Cuban Crisis*, 1-16.
97. Alvin A. Snyder, *Warriors of Disinformation: American Propaganda, Soviet Lies, and the Winning of the Cold War* (New York: Arcade Publishing, 1995), 241.

Cuban- American community about the feasibility of TV Marti in a deliberate effort to build up public expectations to force the [Bush] administration into a confrontation with Castro.[98]

Florida City. Two temporary Nike Hercules missile sites were based in Florida City during the Cold War. Upon deployment during the Cuban missile crisis in 1962, the troops of Battery A/2/52 ADA established operations at site HM- 65 near the main entrance to Everglades NP. This site was problematic because the commander ignored the advice of local farmers and located the battery in an area prone to flooding. The soldiers improved their living standards considerably when they moved to their permanent home at HM- 69 within the Hole in the Donut area of Everglades NP. HM- 66, home of battery B/2/52 ADA, was also located near Everglades NP in Florida City. This site was moved to a permanent location on Route 905 in Key Largo once ARADCOM secured funding and built the facilities. The Florida City Campground and RV Park, located on Krome Avenue, 1/4 mile north of Palm Drive on the west side, currently has a static display of HAWK missiles.[99]

Flo-Sun Sugar Corporation/Fanjul Family/Cuban Exile Sugar Growing Operations. Once the Cuban revolution took on its overtly Marxist character, the U.S. government imposed economic sanctions to limit the sale of Cuban goods and to deny Castro needed economic resources. These sanctions included a ban on the importation of Cuban sugar into the United States. The sugar industry was very important to Cuba, and the U.S. provided one of its most important markets. In addition to the overt steps designed to lower the price of sugar on the world market and thus deprive the Castro government of much- needed foreign exchange, the U.S. government—with the CIA's Operation

Mongoose and Cuban exile groups like Alpha 66— frequently targeted the Cuban sugar industry.[100] CIA and Cuban exile activities against the Cuban sugar industry included burning sugar cane fields with aerial Napalm attacks, destroying Cuban sugar processing facilities, and attempting to damage refined Cuban sugar through the application of various chemical substances designed to ruin the crop's palatability.

Perhaps more important when considering the impact of the Cold War on south Florida are the efforts of the U.S. government and state politicians to boost local sugar production. Extensive efforts were made to ensure that displaced Cuban sugar growers, such as the Arab- Cuban Fanjul family, would find a welcome environment in which to continue their agricultural operations. Certainly, the U.S. wanted to provide U.S. companies and consumers with access to inexpensive sugar. At the same time, they could not abide doing business with Castro to get this resource. If Cuban sugar growers moved their operations to Florida, U.S. access to inexpensive sugar could be secured and Castro would be denied much- needed foreign exchange. If the United States provided Cuban exile sugar operations with a friendly operating environment, the world supply of sugar would stay high, resulting in a lower commodity price and less money for Castro's government. With the aid of federal, state, and local governments, Cuban sugar growers like the Fanjuls swiftly transferred their operations to the U.S. and the Florida sugar industry increased operations.

Florida Senator George Smathers was at the forefront of economic efforts to hurt the Castro regime through manipulation of the sugar market, and he advised President Kennedy and other policy makers accordingly. At first, Smathers believed that

---

98. John Spicer Nichols, "Broadcast Wars," *NACLA Report on the Americas*, November 1990, quoted in Elliston, *Psy War on Cuba*, 279.

99. Photographs of these missiles can be found in the *Miami Herald*, "Cold War Relic is Hot: Missile Site May Become Attraction," 3 October 1999. The reporter, Peter Whoriskey, has copies of the photos.

100. See State Department FRUS Cuba volumes X, XI, and the microfiche supplements for documents detailing NSC and cabinet discussions on the topic of how the U.S. could manipulate world sugar prices and thus damage the Cuban economy. Operation Mongoose often targeted Cuban sugar operations. Branch, "The Kennedy Vendetta," argues that these raids did not do that much damage to Cuba's sugar industry and that they may have served more to fulfill the CIA's demands for revenge against Castro and the loss at the Bay of Pigs. See also Thomas J. Heston, *Sweet Subsidy: The Economic and Diplomatic Effects of the U.S. Sugar Acts, 1934-1974* (New York: Garland Pub., 1987). Everglades NP archives contain numerous files and reports detailing the severe drought conditions and lack of water flowing into the park during the 1960s and beyond. Phosphorous fertilizer runoff from Florida sugar operations has been a serious problem for the region. The linkages of the Cold War economic policies of the U.S. government and the environmental degradation of the Everglades ecosystem by the south Florida sugar industry should be further explored in any follow- ups to this HRS.

economic sanctions would provide a better means of eliminating the communist menace in Cuba than would overt military action. While most projects designed to impact directly the price of sugar on the world market were never implemented, economic warfare against the Castro regime did occur. Once the U.S. took action at the Bay of Pigs, however, Smathers counseled President Kennedy to launch air strikes and increasingly advocated a hard-line policy against the Castro regime. Smathers's criticism of the administration's Cuba policies led to increased tension between the President and his long-time friend. However, Smathers still made sure that increased sugar production in the U.S. paid direct benefits to Florida sugar manufacturers.[101]

Sugar growers like the Fanjuls found south Florida perfect for their needs. Big sugar producers in the region and many of the environmental issues related to their operations have a direct link to the history of the Cold War in the region. Florida's sugar industry grew remarkably in the aftermath of the Cuban revolution. The industry doubled the amount of land devoted to sugar as a direct result of economic sanctions imposed against Cuban sugar.[102] Any follow-ups to this HRS should research the role of the U.S. government in the "soft-landing" achieved by Cuban exile sugar concerns as they transferred their operations to south Florida and the increase in sugar production following the Cold War conflict with Cuba.

Goulds. HAWK Missile Site HM-05, which was manned by battery A/8/15 ADA upon deployment in 1962 during the Cuban missile crisis, was temporarily based in Goulds, Florida.[103] As mentioned previously, HAWK missiles were integral to military efforts to protect forces associated with the military buildup in the region during the crisis and to provide protection for the people of south Florida from attacks by Fidel Castro. HAWK missiles in and around the Homestead-Miami area provided protection for Opa Locka Airport and

Homestead AFB—important staging facilities for U.S. forces during the Cuban missile crisis. HAWK missiles served in tandem with Nike Hercules missiles in the Homestead-Miami defense—the only time HAWK and Nike missiles served together in the same missile defense in the history of ARADCOM. Battery A/8/15 eventually moved to a permanent location in Miami once it was decided that the HAWKs would stay in south Florida and ARADCOM secured the funds required to build the facilities.

Homestead Air Force Base (Homestead AFB).

Homestead AFB was a SAC facility and a Tactical Air Command (TAC) facility for many years, supporting B-47s and B-52 nuclear bombers as well as fighter interceptor/attack aircraft. It was home to air defense fighters and provided strip alert aircraft to defend against Cuban attacks as part of the overall air defense package for south Florida. The base served as one of the critical staging points for the military buildup associated with the Cuban missile crisis and provided support facilities for many of the air defense missile units deployed to the region during the Cold War. John F. Kennedy toured Homestead AFB during the missile crisis and reviewed some missile troops deployed there.[104] Homestead AFB served as the headquarters for the U.S. Army forces associated with the Cuban missile crisis—known as the U.S. Army Forces Atlantic (USARLANT)—and provided command and control capability for the more than 100,000 Army personnel assigned to Cuban missile crisis operations.[105] Homestead AFB also provided facilities and support to the massive numbers of fighter aircraft deployed to the region during the Cuban missile crisis.[106]

Homestead AFB was the location of the HHB units for the 2/52 ADA and the headquarters location for all of the missile forces deployed to south Florida during the Cuban missile crisis—the 13th Artillery Group, the 47th Artillery Brigade, and the 31st ADA

---

101. Crispell, *Testing the Limits*, 168-175.
102. Ibid., 175.
103. See Morgan and Berhow, *Rings of Supersonic Steel*, 79-83; Osato and Straup, *ARADCOM'S Florida Defenses*; and the still classified ARADCOM reports on the Air Defenses of south Florida by Jean Martin and Geraldine Rice. There are also numerous articles on south Florida HAWK sites in contemporary issues of the ARADCOM *Argus* newspaper, as well as the locally published *Defender* newspaper of the south Florida missile units.
104. NARA II Signal Corps photo archives has pictures of JFK reviewing the troops at Homestead AFB.
105. U.S. DOD press release *Actions of Military Services in Cuban Crisis Outlined*, 29 November 1962, 1; Jean R. Moenk, *USCONARC Participation in the Cuban Crisis 1962* (Ft. Monroe: Headquarters U.S. Continental Army Command, 1964), 1-10.
106. McMullen, *The Fighter Interceptor Force*, 8-16.

Brigade.[107] The base provided the lion's share of support facilities and recreational opportunities for the many Army missile troops deployed to the region. Homestead AFB also played a role in some of the more controversial Cold War activities of the Reagan Administration during the Contra war against the Nicaraguan Sandinistas.[108] Homestead AFB suffered severe damage from Hurricane Andrew in 1992 and has largely ceased operations. It now functions as a reserve USAF base. Recent proposals to replace the facility with a large commercial airport are extremely controversial due to the facility's location in the environmentally sensitive region between Everglades NP and Biscayne NP.

Throughout the Cold War, Everglades NP staff interacted with the personnel and leadership of Homestead AFB on numerous occasions.[109] High-ranking SAC officials were frequent visitors to the park in the early 1960s. Homestead AFB escape and evasion (E&E) staff utilized the park as a survival training location. As mentioned previously, Homestead AFB staff located a base auxiliary hospital within the park in case an attack destroyed facilities at the AFB itself. Close cooperation with SAC personnel at Homestead helped Everglades NP in countless ways. Cooperation could be as simple as AFB personnel providing charts for ranger pilots, assisting in the digging of alligator survival holes or involving the superintendent in important Cold War milestones achieved by the base.[110] For example, park staff were present when the Boeing Corporation delivered the first B-52H model strategic bomber to Homestead AFB. The B-52H was a mainstay of the Cold War nuclear deterrence triad and they still serve with the USAF today. B-52H models played a key role in the Persian Gulf war and in the Kosovo crisis. Everglades NP staff

flew to SAC headquarters at Offutt AFB, Nebraska, for a tour of the nation's Cold War nuclear command post at the height of Cold War tensions in 1962.

Homestead Area. A house at 26145 SW 195th Avenue served as one of the many exile training locations scattered throughout south Florida during the Cold War.[111] This guerrilla training location demonstrates that paramilitary training in south Florida was a rather open secret. In August 1960, some young children in the area were playing in the neighborhood and threw firecrackers in the driveway of the home. The Cuban exiles inside, perhaps taking their training a bit too seriously, opened fire on the children with automatic weapons. At least one of the neighborhood youths was wounded. Of course, the CIA took many steps to ensure that its involvement was not revealed and to minimize the scrutiny of potentially embarrassing events.[112]

A blue stucco house located off Quail Roost Drive in the Homestead area served as a CIA safe house/training center for teaching intelligence trade craft to Cuban exiles. Run by agents with the pseudonyms of Greg and Otto, this location provided Cuban exiles instruction in the various tricks of the trade.[113] An isolated, luxurious house on the edge of the Everglades several miles from Homestead was the base of operations for Flamingo maritime training. At this location, Cuban exiles received training on their Boston Whaler infiltration vessels and in basic seamanship. Once the trainees demonstrated competence in maintaining the boat engines and other equipment, they drove sixty-miles every day to Everglades NP's Flamingo marina to practice their missions.[114]

---

107. Morgan and Berhow, *Rings of Supersonic Steel*, 79-83.
108. Cockburn, *Out of Control*, details the use of Homestead AFB by the CIA, the Contras, and other clandestine operators involved in what would come to be known as the Iran-Contra scandal. One of the more serious allegations is that covert operatives associated with Reagan's efforts to continue Contra support after the Congress ordered it stopped with the Boland Amendment smuggled drugs into the U.S. using their CIA-supplied immunity from custom's scrutiny. The CIA denies that this type of activity ever occurred.
109. Contemporary Everglades NP superintendent and ranger monthly narrative reports document numerous instances where AFB staff and Everglades NP staff coordinated activities.
110. Base explosives personnel would help provide survival holes for alligators threatened by the severe water shortages the park suffered in the late 1960s. Explosives were used to "dig" holes which would then fill with water/mud. Alligators would enter these holes in an attempt to survive the severe drought.
111. Kelly, "The Fidel Fixation," 1; contemporary newspapers also discussed this incident.
112. Branch, "The Kennedy Vendetta," 53, discusses the enormous liaison effort the CIA instituted with local authorities to cover its Cold War activities in the region.
113. Ayers, *The War that Never Was*, 39.
114. Ibid., 44-45.

The Homestead marina, like many of the marinas in south Florida during the Cold War, served as a base for some of the CIA's V-20 infiltration boats. These vessels were specially modified by the CIA and local Miami boat shops to provide extra protection for the crews and they were equipped with hard points for mounting automatic weapons. Many Cuban exiles crewed these boats on missions to Cuba throughout the secret war era.

Hutchinson Island.   During the military activities associated with the Cuban missile crisis, Hutchinson Island was used by the military as a site for practicing the proposed invasion of Cuba.[115]

Key Biscayne.   Many CIA safe houses were located on Key Biscayne. The area provided living quarters for many CIA personnel attached to JMWAVE and CIA Cold War operations in south Florida.[116]

Key Largo.   In April 1958, an airborne Everglades NP ranger patrol spotted a ship loading cargo at a strange location on Key Largo.[117] The unusual activities prompted Everglades NP rangers to contact the Border Patrol. Upon further investigation, the Border Patrol discovered that the ship's cargo consisted of ammunition destined for Cuba and the fight against the dictator Batista. This incident demonstrates that the connection between Florida and Cuba during the Cold War predated Castro's assumption of power. The region supported efforts to rid the island of Batista, and thus helped the forces arrayed against him. Ironically, these forces included Fidel Castro, who would soon assume power in Cuba and become the impetus for so many more clandestine activities on the part of the CIA and Cuban exiles.

The Key Largo region, like so many of the isolated rural areas of south Florida, was well suited for smuggling activities including the transport of illegal Cuban immigrants. While many exiles arrived in the U.S. by boat, some arranged to be smuggled to the U.S. through the air. In January 1959, a plane carrying illegal Cuban immigrants went down off of North Key Largo. Everglades NP rangers assisted the Border Patrol in an attempt to apprehend the two illegal Cuban passengers of the plane, but only the American pilots were caught.[118]

Southwest of the Carrysfort Reef light, toward a finger of land called Point Mary on Key Largo, there was yet another CIA safe house/training area complex. Accessible by a good road from Key Largo and 200 yards from a small subdevelopment of vacation homes were two old wooden buildings controlled by CIA operatives known as Julio and Bob.[119] This may be the same facility visited by Miami Cuban exile Carlo Abreu, who identified Key Largo as the site of a maritime operations base during his employment by the CIA. Abreu attempted to visit this location a few years ago and found that it was now some kind of marine park or sea lion show.[120] Key Largo provided an excellent area for exile maritime training and practice. The Dynamite Pier area of the key was used by CIA paramilitary trainer Bradley Ayers to provide survival training for Cuban exile paramilitary trainees.[121]

Key Largo was also the home of Nike Hercules Missile Site HM-40. Battery B/2/52 ADA was located on Route 905 adjacent to the Crocodile Lake National Wildlife Refuge. This site was the permanent location of the battery once ARADCOM secured the funds to build permanent missile facilities in the region. The battery's integrated fire control (IFC) area and launch area (LA) are extant.

Key West.   The military facilities on Key West played an important role in the Cuban missile crisis, the Bay of Pigs, and many other activities connected with the Cold War. It was also an important port of entry for Cubans fleeing Castro. Dry Tortugas NP personnel would often refuel and resupply Cuban exiles fleeing the island and then either direct them to Key West or contact authorities there to have the refugees picked up. The island was also the site of the Key West conference that established the mission responsibilities of the post-World War II

---

115. Joe Crankshaw, "Mock Invasion Warned Castro of U.S. Determination," *Miami Herald*, 26 October 1992, sec. B, p. 1.
116. Ayers, *The War that Never Was*, 25.
117. *Superintendent's Monthly Narrative Reports* (Everglades NP: Department of the Interior, April 1958); *Ranger's Monthly Narrative Reports* (Everglades NP: Department of the Interior, April 1958).
118. *Ranger's Monthly Narrative Reports* (Everglades NP: Department of the Interior, January 1959).
119. Ayers, *The War that Never Was*, 36.
120. Abreu, oral interview with author.
121. Ayers, *The War that Never Was*, 88.

U.S. military services. The Key West conference was supposed to eliminate duplication of missions among the various branches of the service and allow for the creation of a streamlined and more "rational" defense bureaucracy. Despite President Truman's best efforts, the services to this day still fight over which branch should perform which mission. The Key West conference is important for later Cold War- related events in south Florida because it was here that the president delegated to the respective services their responsibilities for missiles, missile defense, and other missions. The delegation of responsibilities at Key West is important background to later Army/Air Force conflicts over weapon systems like the Nike Hercules missile.[122]

Key West Naval Air Station was an important base and staging area for the military buildup during the Cuban missile crisis. In addition to aircraft already on site, a Navy F- 4D squadron was sent to Key West NAS. The island also served as the home of the Air Reconnaissance Center. This center played a key role in the Cuban missile crisis because it provided "coordination of all air reconnaissance operations in the Cuban peripheral area."[123] It was also home to the radar control facilities of the HAWK air defense missile installations—sites KW- 18H and KW- 19H— installed throughout the area. Units manning these locations were the HHB/6/65 from 1962 to September 1972 and the HHB/1/65 from September 1972 to 1979.[124] The Naval Air Station also served as the "Winter White House" for President Truman who would spend several weeks each year in the former home of the base commandant.[125]

A CIA detachment at Key West monitored Cuban operations and the CIA beamed propaganda into Cuba from Key West on local commercial radio station WKWF. Commercial transmissions into Cuba from WKWF were ostensibly supported by the Cuban Freedom Committee (CFC), a supposedly independent organization of American citizens who were upset by the communist direction of Castro's government and provided private support for radio broadcasting to Cuba. In reality, the CFC was a front for the CIA created prior to the Bay of Pigs to support agency anti- Castro propaganda efforts. The CIA used two ships, the *Barbara J* and the *Blagar*, based at Key West, to supply weapons, explosives, and supplies to teams in Cuba. The *Barbara J* sank at the Bay of Pigs. The CIA used a warehouse at the Key West- Havana ferry terminal for storage.[126]

Lignum Vitae Key. Cuban exiles sometimes built and operated their own radio transmitters, using them to broadcast news, music, and propaganda to Cuba. In many cases, these unlicensed operations were vigorously pursued by the FCC and shut down. In other cases, however, the operations were actually fronts for the CIA. As early as March of 1960, the agency was already supporting opposition broadcasts from Miami.[127] Agency radio activities included both shore- based and marine- based transmitters.[128] The CIA fed several local radio stations information and programming. Of course, the agency had a tough time controlling all of the information broadcast by exiles. In the early phases of the CIA- sponsored plan of action against Castro even "the Democratic Revolutionary Front (FRD) coordinator had his own radio boat, which made unauthorized broadcasts until halted by the Federal Communications Commission and the Federal Bureau of Investigation."[129] In April 1963, another unsanctioned transmitter was discovered on a boat in a canal on Lignum Vitae Key. The operators, Cuban exiles Emiliano de Cardenas and Aurillo Lugez, were arrested, and the FCC seized their equipment.[130]

Linderman Key. Linderman Key was the site of a CIA safe house complex and maritime operations training area known as the "Pirate's Lair." The CIA

---

122. The Army and Air Force fought bitterly for control of the nation's air defense missile systems. Nike air defense missiles competed with the Air Force's longer-range BOMARC system.
123. U.S. Navy, Headquarters Atlantic Command, *CINCLANT Historical Account of the Cuban Crisis*, 46-47.
124. Morgan and Berhow, *Rings of Supersonic Steel*, 85-86.
125. "President Truman's Travel Logs," available at <http://www.trumanlibrary.org/calendar/travel_log/>.
126. Kirkpatrick, "The Inspector General's Survey," in Kornbluh, *Bay of Pigs Declassified*, 87; Donald Wilson, USIA Deputy Director, "Radio Propaganda Plan," 20 October 1962, in Elliston, *Psy War on Cuba*, 132-134; Elliston, *Psy War on Cuba*, 175; Hinckle and Turner, *The Fish is Red*, 61.
127. Kirkpatrick, "The Inspector General's Survey," in Kornbluh, *Bay of Pigs Declassified*, 26.
128. Ibid., 27.
129. Ibid., 33.
130. *Miami Herald*, 7 April 1963.

leased this facility from the University of Miami. The safe house complex consisted of "four houses which were dispersed about the heavily wooded three- acre island in such a manner that only one [building] could be seen from the single deep- water canal that strung its way through the mangroves."[131] The former hideaway had been built by a Florida millionaire many years before. This complex was used to teach Cuban exiles V- 20 boating techniques. In addition to Boston Whaler- type vessels and rubber rafts with silenced motors, the CIA and Cuban exiles used the small, fast, and agile V- 20 boats on many of their Cold War missions.[132] These craft were specially rebuilt to CIA specifications by local south Florida boat yards and their modifications included reinforced hulls, armor plating in key areas, modified engines, electronic gear, and hard points for mounting heavy automatic weapons.

Marathon Key. Marathon Key was the site of a CIA- operated maritime operations safe house and base. Miami Cuban exile Carlo Abreu operated out of this base on occasion. He indicated that on his last recent visit to the facility it was still there but it had been fenced and marked with "no trespassing" signs.[133] CIA files on John F. Kennedy referenced Marathon Key and operations known as "Starlight Cruises." It is not known if this is a reference to the activities Carlo Abreu mentioned on Marathon Key or if this refers to another program or base on the key.

Marathon Key was the site of a VOA radio station installed during the Cuban missile crisis and, since 1985, has been the site of the Radio Marti transmitter. As was the case with the VOA station at Dry Tortugas NP, the USIA quickly constructed the VOA facility in order to support propaganda broadcasts during the crisis. This station was a fifty kilowatt medium wave transmitter and its signal violated international broadcast regulations. This transmitter, unlike the Dry Tortugas facility, stayed on the air after the missile crisis along with a similar transmitter operated by the Navy on Sugarloaf Key.

These stations were controversial because their signals interfered with the frequencies assigned to commercial radio stations in New York and Iowa. The broadcasts did reach their intended audience, however, and the Cuban government responded to them by jamming their signals.[134] The Marathon Key station continued to operate long after other propaganda efforts in the region were shut down, focusing on general Latin American programming when the U.S. government scaled back anti- Castro efforts in the 1970s.

In 1985 Radio Marti began broadcasting its 1180 kHz signal from Marathon Key. The radio broadcasting effort, along with TV Marti, were pet projects of various Cuban exile groups and powerful conservative patrons such as Joseph Coors and Richard Mellon Scaife. These new facilities created more tension between Cuba and the U.S. with both sides threatening to jam the other's broadcasts. At one point, U.S. officials proposed military action against any Cuban stations jamming Radio Marti. The program worsened U.S.- Cuban relations. The station even played a role in U.S. Cold War operations in Angola—where U.S.- backed forces battled against Cuban and Soviet- supported troops. These stations sometimes violated international broadcasting agreements and provoked the ire of radio station owners as far away as Iowa when Radio Marti broadcasts interfered with already assigned frequencies.

Miami Area. The city of Miami is the site of countless Cold War- related resources. The city provided a good environment for covert activities for many reasons. Miami provided easy access to Cuba. Florida's lenient gun laws made almost any type of firearm readily available. The Miami area and its tourist destinations were the playgrounds of mobsters, movie stars, and members of the jet set in the 1950s and 1960s, and activities which surely would have drawn attention in almost any other major city in the country often went largely unnoticed—or at least unreported. It was full of newly arrived Cuban exiles eager to help liberate their country from Castro. It possessed cooperative

131. Ayers, *The War that Never Was*, 134.
132. Carlo Abreu was a crewman on a V-20 boat and visited Elliott Key and at least two other safe house/training complexes in the Upper Keys. It is unclear whether he ever visited the "Pirate's Lair" complex. Abreu, oral interview with author.
133. Ibid.
134. Donald M. Wilson, "Brief Summary of the Strengths and Weaknesses of U.S. Broadcasting to Cuba," in Elliston, *Psy War on Cuba*, 147-148; Donald M. Wilson, Acting Director USIA, "Memorandum for Mr. Ralph A. Dungan, Special Assistant to the President," 14 October 1963, in Elliston, *Psy War on Cuba*, 156-157; Office of the Engineering Manager, USIA Frequency Division, "Reception of Broadcasts in the Cuban Area," March 1971, in Elliston, *Psy War on Cuba*, 183-187.

local and state institutions ready to assist the U.S. government in its fight against communism.[135]

CIA money poured into Miami in the early 1960s as the agency hired agents, rented houses, bought boats, chartered aircraft, and installed the huge infrastructure necessary to conduct its not- so- secret war against Cuban Communism.

> There were, besides the phantom "Zenith Technological Services" that was JMWAVE headquarters itself, fifty- four other front businesses, providing employment and cover and various services required by JMWAVE operations. There were CIA boat shops. There were CIA gun shops. There were CIA travel agencies and there were CIA real- estate agencies and there were CIA detective agencies. Anyone who spent any time at all on the street in Miami during the early 1960s, then, was likely to have had dealings with the CIA.[136]

Cold War- related resources in Miami are numerous. The old Holiday Inn at 2500 Brickell Avenue in Miami had a lounge called "the Stuff Shirt." This bar was a favored rest and recreation location for CIA agents and employees serving in the Miami area. Also on Brickell were the law offices of Paul Helliwell at 600 Brickell Avenue. Helliwell, a veteran of the Office of Strategic Services (OSS), the CIA's World War II predecessor, used his offices as the contact point for "Red Sunset Enterprises"—a CIA front company set up to recruit frogmen and demolitions experts for Operation Mongoose. At Southwest 27th Avenue and Bird Road was Big Daddy's bar, another hangout popular with the CIA operatives. Called "27 Birds" by CIA agents because of its address, it is now Flanigan's Loggerhead Seafood Bar and Grill.[137]

Miami was the site of many events connected with the Cold War as people working for the CIA and those that wished they were frequently carried out

their "missions" within the city limits. On February 5, 1961, near the then- under- construction Julia Tuttle Causeway, five American mercenaries hijacked the tugboat *Gil Rocke* and set off for Cuba's Escambray Province for an invasion. They never made it and wrecked the boat off Bay Point. On the MacArthur Causeway, in September 1968, Cuban exile Orlando Bosch—former leader of the CIA-supported Movement for Revolutionary Recovery (MRR)—fired a homemade rocket launcher at the Polish freighter *Polanica*. An apartment building at 1925 SW Fourth Street served as a sort of flophouse for the various characters who associated themselves with the entire Cuban exile/CIA scene in the early 1960s. Known as "Nelli Hamilton's paramilitary boardinghouse," the Fourth Street location was a hangout for "the freelance fringe, the amateur adventurers and mercenaries who lurked around the edges of the early Sixties secret war, hoping to be let in on the action." People who stayed at Nelli's included Gerry Patrick Hemming, leader of the Intercontinental Penetration Force (Interpen), Little Joe Garman, and Howard K. Davis. These men "used Nelli's as their bunkhouse, packing parachutes on the sidewalk, cleaning weapons in the backyard and occasionally practicing close- order drill with their mascot, a midget known only as Pete." The Interpen group was just one of the many non- governmental organizations that sprang up in Miami and tried to make money from the Cuban exile desire to fight Castro. Interpen operated training camps in Miami at 955 West Flagler Street and in the keys at a camp on No Name Key. Cuban exiles paid the Interpen people in order to learn the skills needed for carrying on the war against Castro.[138]

The CIA utilized several Miami boat shops to purchase and modify vessels for missions to Cuba during the secret war. Several large ships were refurbished in order to act as motherships for

---

135. There are several general histories of Miami and the Cuban exiles that emphasize the history of the city from the time of the Cuban Revolution until the present. While not specifically focused on the Cold War in south Florida, they discuss a great many issues of relevance to this HRS. These include T.D. Allman, *Miami: City of the Future* (New York: Atlantic Monthly, 1987); Sheila L. Croucher, *Imagining Miami: Ethnic Politics in a Postmodern World* (Charlottesville, Virginia: University Press of Virginia, 1997); Joan Didion, *Miami* (New York: Simon and Schuster, 1987); García, *Havana USA*; Rieff, *The Exile*; and David Rieff, *Going to Miami: Exiles, Tourists, and Refugees in the New America* (Boston: Little, Brown, and Company, 1987). For information on Miami's role in the Cold War and clandestine operations see William R. Amlong, "How the CIA Operated in Dade," *Miami Herald,* 9 March 1975; and Hinckle and Turner's, *The Fish is Red*, especially the last chapter, "A Murderous Legacy."

136. Didion, *Miami*, 91.

137. Kelly, "The Fidel Fixation," 1; Miami CIA investigator Marty Casey is reported to have entered these "law offices" stating that he was an ex-Navy underwater demolitions expert looking for work. The secretary then handed him a job application without batting an eye.

smaller craft. The CIA motherships would tow the smaller, more agile boats—like the V-20s—to an area off Cuba where they would be dropped off to complete their missions. The CIA had its own boat shop at SW 117th Avenue in Miami, and it also was a frequent user of the services provided by Miami Ship, Tommy's Boatyard, and Merrill Steven Jones Boatyard.[139]

The CIA and the USIA used commercial radio stations in Miami to broadcast propaganda to Cuba in the early 1960s. Stations WGBS and WMIE beamed Spanish language programming to Cuba for several hours each day. The stations transmitted official government programs and those secretly funded by the CIA and broadcast under ostensibly independent front groups such as the CFC. These stations complemented the VOA network and other regional commercial stations broadcasting to Cuba in Key West, Atlanta, and New Orleans.[140]

Miami International Airport (MIA) was used throughout the Cold War by the CIA for a variety of covert activities. The CIA owned its own airline, Southern Air Transport (SAT), that operated out of MIA. The airline was involved in a variety of Cold War activities including supply efforts for the Contras in Nicaragua. The CIA recruited pilots for its various covert activities at the nearby Double-Chek Corporation on Curtiss Parkway.

The MIA Howard Johnson's was the scene of much intrigue during the Reagan administration's efforts to oust the Nicaraguan Sandinistas from power. It re-portedly offered "guerrilla discounts" to freedom fighters. According to some sources, personnel affil-iated with the Contra war met at the cocktail lounge of the Howard Johnson's to plot the assassination of the American ambassador to Costa Rica. They planned to blame the assassination on the Sandinistas. It was hoped that this action would provide the pre-text for a U.S. invasion of Nicaragua.[141]

Many of the most important Cuban exile groups—such as Alpha 66, Commandos L, the infamous Omega 7—established their headquarters in Miami and played an important role in the official and unofficial efforts to remove Castro's communist government from the island. The exile groups often provided cover for the CIA when Cuban security officials discovered clandestine CIA operations. Whenever Castro accused the U.S. government of meddling in Cuban affairs, the U.S. government could assign blame to one of the many Miami-based Cuban exile groups. Of course, these groups were frequently established, trained, and paid by the CIA. Many of these groups are still in existence today, and their exploits are well known in the exile community. However, the history of these groups is controversial. When the CIA removed official sanction for these groups, they showed a disturbing tendency to attack each other. Disagreement within the exile community about the proper course of action to take against Castro resulted in bombings, murders, and terror campaigns. The exiles, having learned many dirty tricks from the CIA, often practiced their newfound skills on those whose politics did not mesh exactly with their own ideology.[142] While the majority of exiles were law-abiding citizens, some hard-line right wing elements of the exile community resorted to violence in order to settle disputes. These elements were often connected to the Batista regime and its associated corruption and violence.

Miami was the location of numerous air defense missile sites. Miami-area missile sites included the following: HAWK site HM-12 on Old Cutler Road, manned by personnel from A/8/15 ADA until 1971 and then A/3/68 ADA until 1979; HAWK site HM-39 on North Canal Drive, staffed by B/8/15 ADA until 1971 and then A/3/68 until 1979; HAWK site HM-59, manned by D/8/15 ADA until 1971 and D/3/68 ADA until deactivation in 1979; temporary HAWK site HM-60, manned by D/8/15 ADA from

138. See Gordon Winslow's web site Cuban-Exile.com for documents relating to Cuban exile terrorism and associated activities in south Florida; García's chapter on exile politics in *Havana U.S.A.*; and Kelly, "The Fidel Fixation," 1. Heavily redacted CIA documents at NARA II mention No Name Key but they do not make clear whether or not the CIA was actually running operations there. Many people tried to get in on the action in Miami in the early 1960s. These included crooks, Mafia arms dealers, and all other kinds of unsavory characters. On at least one occasion, con men also got involved in the Cold War frenzy. Some Cuban exiles were tricked into giving money to a person claiming to have CIA affiliations. The con man was only using exile patriots to line his own pockets, *Miami Herald*, 13 March 1960.
139. Ayers, *The War that Never Was*, 136; Kelly, "The Fidel Fixation," 1; and Hach, e-mail conversation with Gordon Winslow.
140. Wilson, "Radio Propaganda Plan," in Elliston, *Psy War on Cuba*, 132-134.
141. Didion, *Miami*, 199-202.
142. Gordon Winslow's web site, Cuban-Exile.com, has a variety of documents on-line related to exile terrorism from the files of the Dade County and Miami police as well as the FBI.

1962 until a permanent site was built at HM- 59; temporary HAWK site HM- 80, moved to HM- 84 and run by the members of C/8/15 ADA until 1971 and then C/3/68 ADA until 1979; and site HM- 85, the temporary site of the headquarters of the 13th Artillery Group and the HHB/2/52 ADA upon deployment in 1962 until permanent facilities were installed at Homestead AFB.[143]

Of perhaps more significance than the above-mentioned missile facilities was Nike Hercules missile site HM- 95 in southwest Miami. This location, home of Battery D/2/52 ADA, was a typical south Florida Nike site with three aboveground missile launchers and a nearby IFC site. Upon deactivation, however, this site became the INS's Krome Avenue processing center and detention facility. In this capacity it became a place where Cuban exiles coming into the United States could be debriefed and detained if they were found to be of questionable background. Krome's history addresses the changing nature of Cuban and Caribbean immigration to south Florida. When Castro released citizens for immigration to the U.S. in 1980, he also emptied his jails and mental hospitals. Of the 124,776 new immigrants who came to the U.S. during the Mariel boat lift, four percent were found to be felons.[144] These criminals attempted to hide themselves among the other immigrants. The U.S. government and local authorities were swamped with refugees and had to try and screen out the former inmates and patients from the more typical Cuban exiles. As María Cristina García has noted, "the Mariel Cubans became one of the most stigmatized immigrant groups in American history."[145] The government refurbished facilities like the abandoned HM- 95 Nike Missile site to hold and process the many immigrants trying to enter the United States from Cuba and later, other Caribbean nations like Haiti. Since the Cold War's end, Cuban immigrants to the United States lack the priority they were once afforded for their status as "living" propaganda. Cuban immigrants to the U.S. were, in effect, "voting with their feet." They provided good propaganda by helping the U.S. demonstrate the failures of communism. Now, when Cubans try to enter the United States they are no longer provided the same easy reception given to political refugees, and they are sometimes detained at the Krome Avenue detention center.[146]

The Miami Orange Bowl also has a strong association with the history of the Cold War in south Florida. On December 29, 1962, President and Mrs. Kennedy met with 1,113 veterans of Brigade 2506 at the Orange Bowl. These men were held prisoner by Castro in Cuban jails until the U.S. government paid a ransom for their return. First Lady Jacqueline Kennedy told the men in Spanish that she hoped her son grew up to be "a man at least half as brave as the members of Brigade 2506." The returned prisoners presented JFK with the Brigade 2506 combat flag. Kennedy promised the men that "this flag will be returned to this brigade in a free Havana." The failure of the president to live up to the promise gave rise to feelings of betrayal on the part of the Cuban exiles and it is one of the reasons they eventually turned against the Democratic party. Among Cuban exiles, JFK is often referred to behind Castro as the "number two most hated man in Miami." The Orange Bowl also served as a temporary refugee facility during the Mariel Boatlift.[147]

Miami Beach. Miami Beach was the region's best-known tourist attraction, and even the Soviets could not resist its appeal—they included it on the official itinerary for one of their cultural exchange visits in February 1960. Miami Beach was also the site of numerous Cold War activities. Famous landmarks like the Fontainebleu Hotel—considered one of the premier resort hotels in the world during its heyday in the 1960s—provided the favored lodgings of famous entertainers such as Frank Sinatra and the other members of the "rat pack." CIA operatives used Miami Beach locations as meeting places and often patronized them when they were in the area. The Fontainebleu Hotel was the site of some of the most controversial activities of the entire secret war against Castro.

143. Morgan and Berhow, *Rings of Supersonic Steel*, 79-83.
144. García, *Havana USA*, 6.
145. Ibid.
146. It should be noted that there are many others in "exile" in Miami besides the readily apparent Cubans. Miami is often the preferred haven for the many dictators and their families who fled Latin America, Central America, and the Caribbean upon being overthrown.
147. Didion, *Miami*, 85-90.

Meetings to arrange the assassination of Castro first took place during the Eisenhower administration. Later, when John F. Kennedy and Robert Kennedy were humiliated by their failure to deal successfully with Castro at the Bay of Pigs, they approved a highly secret program of covert actions designed to rid Cuba of its charismatic and popular leader. Some of these actions included trying to assassinate Castro under a plan known as ZR/Rifle and other code names. While attempting to arrange the assassination of Castro, CIA operatives met with members of the Mafia.

CIA personnel met with Mafia figures Sam Giancana, Santos Trafficante, and Johnny Rosselli—who had all run Mafia operations in Cuba prior to the revolution—in August of 1960. Many of these mobsters were important players in organized crime in Florida cities such as Tampa and Miami. Congressional witnesses later testified that the first meeting led to another rendezvous at the Fontainebleu, where poison was given to a Cuban exile to put into one of Castro's meals. Famous meetings were also held at other Miami Beach landmark restaurants like Joe's Stone Crab. In April 1961, just prior to the Bay of Pigs, Howard Hunt held meetings with exile leaders like Antonio de Varona at Joe's to discuss exile group politics and the problems associated with unifying the numerous groups.[148]

The CIA used the Miami Beach marina as a base of operations for maritime infiltration operations. Docked at the marina in the early 1960s was the ship *Explorer II*. This vessel, supposedly a research ship for Florida Atlantic University in Boca Raton, was actually a CIA mother ship that would support the smaller V-20 and Boston Whaler boats on their missions to Cuba. Typically, the mother ship would tow the smaller vessels to Cuba after a rendezvous somewhere off the coast of south Florida. The *Explorer II* was one of several CIA motherships—others included the *Rex* and the *Leda*.[149]

Florida Governor Farris Bryant presented some of his Cold War education and civil defense plans to national conventions of U.S. governors in Miami Beach. He held a "Conference on Cold War Education" in July 1962 attended by more than 1,000 people. His aim was to provide "good" Cold War information and to counter Soviet propaganda. Conventions on Cold War education were also held in Tampa, and a report on the topic was presented to the National Governor's Conference in Miami Beach in July 1963. Bryant's efforts led to the establishment of a two-week Cold War education course for governor's aides. The first class of this type was held in Florida in December 1964, run by Bryant aide John A. Evans.[150]

Naranja. Naranja was the site of the headquarters for the HAWK missile troops of the Homestead-Miami defense area. The Headquarters and Headquarters Battery (HHB)/8/15 ADA deployed to Naranja in 1962 during the Cuban missile crisis. This unit supplied support functions to the HAWK batteries serving in the region. It eventually moved to facilities at Homestead AFB where it was replaced in 1971 by elements of the HHB/3/68.[151]

No Name Key. No Name Key was the site of the Interpen group's training base for Cuban exiles. Interpen was an association of mercenaries who formed a training camp and then charged exiles a fee to receive military training. Run by Gerry Patrick Hemming, this camp is illustrative of the fact that the Cold War in south Florida was a lucrative business. People tried to take advantage of the situation and profit from the desires of the Cuban exiles to help their country. A colorful cast of characters happily provided the training, adventure, and risk associated with the secret war to all those who, for one reason or another, could not participate in CIA programs.[152]

Opa Locka. The Opa Locka Airport served as a base of Cold War operations for the CIA in south Florida. The CIA ran elements of Operation PBSUCCESS, the operation to overthrow the

148. Hinckle and Turner, *The Fish is Red*, 36-37. There were many assassination plots against Castro; see U.S. Senate, "Alleged Assassination Plots Involving Foreign Leaders," Interim Report of the Select Committee to Study Government with Respect to Intelligence Activities, 20 November 1975. See also files in the House Select Committee on Assassination (HSCA) collection, the Assassination Records Review Board (ARRB) Files, and *Report on Plots to Assassinate Fidel Castro*, 23 May 1967, JFK Collection of Assassination Records, NARA II.
149. Hinckle and Turner, *The Fish is Red*, 144-148.
150. Evans, *Time for Florida*, 105-122.
151. Morgan and Berhow, *Rings of Supersonic Steel*, 79-83.
152. Hinckle and Turner, *The Fish is Red*, 158-159.

Arbenz government in Guatemala in 1954, from Opa Locka Airport. The CIA also used the same two-story barracks building as a headquarters during the training of Brigade 2506 for the Bay of Pigs invasion. Many 2506 recruits were flown from Opa Locka to the main military training camp in Guatemala. Opa Locka also served as a marshaling point for members of the Cuban Revolutionary Council (CRC)—the exiles selected by the U.S. government to lead Cuba following the invasion—during the operation in April 1961. Members of the CRC were ordered to Opa Locka so that they could be quickly transported to Cuba and set up as a revolutionary government under arms once the Brigade 2506 members established a beachhead at the Bay of Pigs. Detaining the CRC at Opa Locka also ensured control of the members by the U.S. government. The operation's leadership did not want CRC members to blow its cover or affect the outcome through ill-timed statements or actions. Opa Locka Airport also served as a Cuban refugee reception center. Several weeks prior to the discovery of Soviet weapons by U.S. U2 overflights, two refugees processed through Opa Locka told debriefers that the Soviet Union was installing offensive missiles in Cuba.[153]

The Army utilized Opa Locka Airport as the headquarters for 2nd Logistical Command activities during the Cuban missile crisis. The massive military buildup in the region required huge amounts of medical, logistical, and administrative support. More than 10,000 troops in medical, engineering, ordnance, transportation boat, and transportation service units were based at Opa Locka as part of the Peninsula Base Command.[154]

Opa Locka was also the location of several air defense sites. Nike Hercules Missile Site HM-01 Battery C/2/52 ADA operated at a temporary site in Opa Locka when it deployed to the region during the Cuban missile crisis. This battery moved to a permanent location at HM-03 Opa Locka/Carol City once funds were secured to build permanent

installations in the region. HM-03 defended south Florida until 1979. The former launch area of this site is now a National Guard reservation. The IFC area is gone and is now covered by a subdivision. [155]

Palm Beach/Peanut Island. President Kennedy often visited his family's Palm Beach estate during his time in office. The Palm Beach Maritime Museum has a bunker/fallout shelter reportedly built for the use of JFK. The museum recently restored the bunker and opened it for public display. During the Cold War, the bunker's existence was kept secret, and cover stories described it as a munitions storage area.[156]

During the late 1950s and early 1960s, the nation went on a fallout shelter building spree as events like the Cuban missile crisis made the likelihood of nuclear war more possible in the minds of many policy makers and common citizens. "Preparing for war to keep the peace" was a commonly heard justification for the shelters. Local civil defense authorities took a much more aggressive stance toward fallout shelter building and installed fallout shelters at most government facilities. Many civilians followed suit and installed protection in their own homes. However, the typical homeowner's shelter was more of a psychological crutch than a plausible means of surviving a nuclear attack. While the Kennedy bunker on Peanut Island was certainly more survivable than most, the typical homeowner's shelter would have provided little protection from an H-bomb explosion in the megaton range. Everglades NP and Dry Tortugas NP also installed fallout shelters and received fallout shelter supplies from civil defense authorities at this time.[157]

Port Everglades. Port Everglades was the site of some of the activities associated with the Cuban missile crisis military buildup. Army and Navy personnel used Port Everglades to load tons of equipment and practice for an invasion of Cuba. Troops from the Army's 1st Armored Division

---

153. John Prados, *President's Secret Wars*, 99; Kelly, "The Fidel Fixation," 1; Kirkpatrick, "The Inspector General's Survey," in Kornbluh, *Bay of Pigs Declassified*, 58; official CIA documents as quoted in Corn, *Blond Ghost*, 91.
154. U.S. Army, *Congressional Fact Paper—Cuba Threat and Army Plans* (Washington, D.C.: Deputy Chief of Staff for Operations, Headquarters U.S. Army, 11 November 1962), Ch. 5, 3.
155. Morgan and Berhow, *Rings of Supersonic Steel*, 79-83.
156. This story was forwarded by e-mail to the author by Jim Adams, Biscayne NP cultural resources manager. It comes from a recent AP wire report and can be found at <http://www.usatoday.com/life/travel/leisure/1999/t0628ap4.htm>.
157. *Superintendent's Monthly Narrative Reports* (Everglades NP: Department of the Interior, November 1962, April 1964); *Superintendent's Monthly Narrative Reports* (Fort Jefferson National Monument: Department of the Interior, May 1963, August 1963).

embarked at Port Everglades, traveled up the coast of Florida, and made a practice landing at Ft. Pierce. This activity was part of the ongoing practice implementation of various contingency plans concerning Cuba—such as Oplan 312, Oplan 314, and Oplan 316.[158]

Richmond. The University of Miami South Campus, situated at the former home of Richmond Naval Air Station, was the site of the CIAs JMWAVE operations for most of the covert war against Cuba. The CIA used this 1,571- acre property between Coral Reef and Eureka Drives as a site for communications operated under Army cover after leasing it from the University of Miami. Eventually, the CIA directed its entire operation in south Florida from this site, and they set up a phony corporation known as "Zenith Technical Enterprises" to hide the nature of the activities there. At the height of the Cold War, JMWAVE was the largest CIA field station in the world.[159]

The Richmond facility also served as the Army Air Defense Command Post (AADCP) location for south Florida air defenses until 1979. HM- 01 was the site's designation. This location was the home of the air defense missile control computers like the Missile Master and the Birdie system, as well as master radar systems like the TSQ- 51 Missile Mentor and the ARSR- 1. HM- 01 contained the missile command infrastructure components for the entire south Florida air defense system. HM- 01 was run by the 13th Artillery group from deployment in 1962 until November 1968. At that time, control passed to the 47th Artillery Brigade Detachment until June 1971. HM- 01 and the south Florida defenses were then controlled by the 31st Artillery Brigade Detachment until the Army dismantled the defenses in 1979.[160]

The Richmond facilities are still in use by a number of government agencies, including the CIA's Foreign Broadcast Information Service (FBIS), which monitors Cuba and other places. The Air Force has a facility there and the Army also uses the site. Some of the original JMWAVE buildings are still standing.[161]

Sugarloaf Key. Sugarloaf Key was the home of HAWK Missile Site KW- 15, which was manned by battery C/6/65 ADA. This facility provided protection to important assets in the keys, including the Key West Naval Air Station, the Key West Naval Station, and the Key West Airport. The military buildup of the Cuban missile crisis illustrated the importance of these facilities, so U.S. military planners left the HAWK missiles in place until 1979. Like the other HAWK batteries in the Key West defense area, this battery is significant because it is the only place within ARADCOM and the U.S. where HAWK missile batteries served solely within their own defense.[162]

Sugarloaf Key was also the home of a Navy radio transmitter that was part of the VOA network. This transmitter ran VOA programming, but it may have been originally intended to support some type of psychological warfare operations connected to the Cuban missile crisis and contingency plans to invade Cuba.[163]

Useppa Island. Used by the CIA to train Cuban exile radio operators for the Bay of Pigs invasion, Useppa Island was one of the first south Florida resources utilized by the CIA in its efforts to depose Castro. Useppa Island was reportedly "acquired as a site for assessment and holding of Cuban paramilitary trainees and for training radio operators."[164] Approximately twenty Cuban exiles were taken to Useppa Island to receive training. Eventually, many larger training facilities for the Bay of Pigs operation would be established in Louisiana, Guatemala, and Panama.

158. U.S. DOD, *Actions of Military Services*, 2.
159. Kirkpatrick, "The Inspector General's Survey," in Kornbluh, *Bay of Pigs Declassified*, 28.
160. Morgan and Berhow, *Rings of Supersonic Steel*, 79-83.
161. Hach, e-mail conversation with Gordon Winslow; see Winslow's Cuban-Exile.com for pictures and maps of the Richmond NAS site.
162. Morgan and Berhow, *Rings of Supersonic Steel*, 85-86.
163. Hach, e-mail conversation with Ron Rackley.
164. Kirkpatrick, "The Inspector General's Survey," in Kornbluh, *Bay of Pigs Declassified*, 28.

Section Three: Notes on Sources and Suggestions for Further Research

This section describes the various libraries and archives consulted for this study. Time constraints did not always allow for an exhaustive review, so suggestions for further research during any follow-ups to this HRS are also included.

Archives and Research Facilities Visited for this Report

Everglades NP Museum Archives. Everglades NP holds the records of Dry Tortugas NP, Biscayne NP, and Big Cypress NP as well as its own records within its museum library and archive. At this facility, a thorough search was performed which included reviewing both Superintendent and Chief Ranger monthly narrative reports from 1945 until the termination of these reports in the late 1960s. These narrative reports were a key resource for this study. Unfortunately, the NPS discontinued them because of time concerns in the late 1960s. All other files from the respective parks' superintendent file collections were also reviewed. Cultural resource managers, ranger personnel, and public affairs staff at Everglades NP and Biscayne NP were queried as to any knowledge they might have about possible Cold War resources within the parks. All of the park personnel consulted for this study were exceedingly professional and extremely helpful.

Some of the relevant Everglades NP records appear to have been destroyed or misplaced. Monthly narrative reports often refer to "special incident reports" written at various times during the early 1960s. These reports were written in response to unusual activities taking place within the boundaries of the parks. In particular, records refer to something called the "Sandy Key Munitions Exposé" and the reports filed in response to this incident in April 1962. A search of the law enforcement division's confidential files did not turn up any of these reports. If these files could be located, they may shed additional light on the sensitive activities undertaken by various agencies within the park during the Cold War.

Nike Hercules Missile Site HM- 69 was also visited at Everglades NP. With the additional documentation and information on the significance of the site provided by this report, any follow- ups should allow for the development of relevant historical contexts and a National Register of Historic Places nomination. Blueprints were located for site HM- 03 in Carol City, Florida, and HM- 69 construction is similar enough that these primary documents should prove quite helpful. Hand- drawn site diagrams for the launch area of HM- 69 were found that provide documentation on all of the buildings in the launch area. Everglades NP museum curator Nancy Russell is in possession of one blueprint related to Nike Hercules Missile Site HM- 69, but this document is merely a real estate map designating the site of the complex. She also has the names of several individuals who served at the site and should be contacted for this information during any follow- up studies. The park has aerial photography that covers the site, but it is from a high altitude and of low resolution and it did not prove to be very useful. When combined with site layouts and diagrams discovered during subsequent research for this report and the survey of other local Nike sites performed for this HRS, the photos may become more useful.

National Archives and Records Administration (NARA) I-Suitland, Maryland. Research at NARA I in Suitland, Maryland, focused on reviewing the Army Forces Command (FORSCOM) records concerning the 2/52 ADA Nike Hercules Battalion and the Army Corps of Engineer files related to the construction of the south Florida air defense sites. Three boxes of material were examined. This information was generally of little value to the HRS. Six additional boxes of the materials listed in the HQ USACE finding aid on Nike missiles was either missing or checked- out of NARA I- the materials checked out had been out for about five years. The missing/checked- out files are supposed to contain information on Nike construction and the aboveground Nike site building project. It is possible that they contain blueprints or other primary documents relating to Nike in south Florida. It may be difficult to locate these boxes, however, and NARA I personnel did not seem to be able to immediately determine which government agency had the files.

National Archives and Records Administration (NARA) II-College Park, Maryland. Research at NARA II in College Park, Maryland, focused on corroboration of CIA utilization of south Florida National Park resources during the Cold War, locating photos of Cold War military activities in south Florida, including air defense missile installations, and verifying the use of Dry Tortugas NP as a VOA broadcast site during the Cuban missile crisis.

Approximately forty boxes of CIA, Kennedy, and Cuba- related materials were reviewed. These files were mostly contained in the declassified records in the various Kennedy assassination collections. These include the House Select Committee on Assassination (HSCA) files and the Assassination Records Review Board (ARRB) files. While no "smoking guns" were found, evidence was discovered that corroborates the Ayers and Abreu information as well as the other less official sources that purport to detail CIA operations in south Florida during the Cold War. One document gave a nice synopsis of a typical CIA infiltration mission. Known as a "TYPIC- operational progress report," this document gave a summary of a specific mission to Cuba, and it included a deck log of the infiltration mother ship. Any and all reports of this type that can be secured from the CIA should be reviewed during any follow- ups to this HRS. A top secret redacted report on the Bay of Pigs indicates that the CIA holds approximately 322 reports on the operations of JMWAVE from 1962 to 1968. Recently, the CIA has been releasing some information to the public dealing with the Bay of Pigs and the Kennedy

matter. More information may be declassified during future HRS studies.

Any FOIA requests should attempt to request as specifically as possible items related to Elliott Key bases and Flamingo activities. Latin American Division work files seem to contain the most information of use to the HRS, especially those that provide detail about training operations. These are the files that the CIA is the most reluctant to release. Operations are given code names beginning with the prefix "AM." Look for files and documents with words like AMTRACK, AMARK, AMTHUMB, AMTRUNK, AMFAUNA, AMLASH, etc. These words represent code names of agents and operations run by the CIA Miami station JMWAVE. If the NPS can access documents that discuss the details of these coded operations, documentation on HRS resources may be obtained. A contact in the CIA historian's office- Mike Warner- suggested that the public affairs office of the CIA be contacted for official CIA information relating to this HRS.

The NARA II imagery archive was searched with some success in order to locate photos of Cold War military activities in south Florida. NARA II's U.S. Army Signal Corps photo archive does contain many photos documenting the military buildup associated with the Cuban missile crisis. There are, however, only a few pictures of air defense activities. One photo was located that depicted the A/2/52 ADA at their temporary field site outside Everglades NP in 1962, but this photo was missing from the collection at NARA II and the collection at the Army Center for Military History. It may be lost or it may still be classified- the description of the photo was marked "confidential."

A brief search of State Department and USIA files related to VOA activities did not uncover much information on the Dry Tortugas NP VOA site. Further research should be pursued in this area in order to determine the true nature of the activities at Dry Tortugas NP. Archivists at NARA II suggested contacting individual agencies directly in order to determine the disposition of records related to possible USIA, VOA, and State Department broadcast programs.

National Security Archive-George Washington University, Washington, D.C. The National Security Archive contains numerous declassified documents on the Cold War and important Cold

War events such as the Cuban missile crisis. Their Cuban missile crisis collection, intelligence collection, and Iran- Contra collection were reviewed for the HRS. Many of the documents held by the archive have not yet been declassified in the various military branch repositories. Thus, one can be told by a military historian/archivist/librarian that a certain record is still classified and unavailable to those without clearance, but often a copy may be reviewed if it is in the National Security Archive. Documents in the National Security Archive detail relevant HRS topics like the deployment of military forces to south Florida, the activities of the U.S. Air Force Security Service- which was involved in Cudjoe Key SIGINT activities and perhaps similar ones at Dry Tortugas NP, CINCLANT activities, and the various CIA operations connected to the Bay of Pigs, Operation Mongoose, and the Cuban missile crisis. HRS researchers should note that many research libraries have copies of the National Security Archive's collections on microfilm. Also, the indexes to the various collections themselves are a very useful source because they contain in- depth bibliographies, summaries of each document in the collection, and exhaustive chronologies of events. The archive also has a very useful web site.

Naval Historical Center-Washington Navy Yard, Washington, D.C. The Naval Historical Center has a large collection relating to naval operations. Their records were searched for information relating to the military buildup during the Cuban missile crisis, the activities of the Navy at Dry Tortugas NP during the crisis, and any other materials of relevance to the HRS. Many of the Navy's records relating to the mil- itary buildup are still classified- although some are available at the National Security Archive. Deck logs of the intelligence- gathering ship U.S.S. Oxford were consulted to determine whether this ship happened to be the vessel docked at Dry Tortugas NP during the crisis, but large portions of the log are still classified.

Another review of the Everglades NP archive's Dry Tortugas NP records might prove useful if the name of the ship that docked at Dry Tortugas NP during the crisis can be discovered. This would allow a check of the ship's deck log at the Naval Historical Center. An archivist at the Naval Historical Center suggested that the oral histories collected from various naval leaders concerning events like the Bay of Pigs and the Cuban missile crisis might be of use to the HRS, but this researcher doubts they will

contain the level of operational detail necessary to shed light on the various activities that utilized park resources.

Richter Library-University of Miami, Coral Gables, Florida. Richter Library holds an extensive collection of primary documents related to Cuban exile political activities during the Cold War in its archives. Most of these documents are in Spanish. The library also holds a collection of the Miami Herald newspaper on microfilm that proved quite useful for this study. The impact of the arrival of the exiles and the numerous Cold War confrontations with Cuba in south Florida is easily discerned by reading the contemporary accounts provided in the Miami Herald. Follow- ups to this HRS should include inquiries at the University of Miami to determine what the university knew about its CIA tenant at the south campus. ARRB files indicate that there may be some information on JMWAVE at the University of Miami. Suggested contacts include Ms. Esperanza de Varona and Mr. William Brown of the University of Miami rare books collection and library.

U.S. Army Center for Military History (CMH)-Fort Myer, Washington, D.C. The CMH holds many Army publications and documents which hold some Nike information of a general nature and may be of relevance to the HRS. They have a large collection of after- action reports detailing Army activities associated with the Cuban missile crisis. They also hold several official studies that detail the history of ARADCOM units in south Florida. Unfortunately, several of these studies- the ones detailing the deployment and initial installation of the air defenses in south Florida- are still classified "SECRET." They may provide useful information on the early history of the air defenses in south Florida if the NPS can gain access to them. Also, the CMH has yearly summaries of ARADCOM historical information that, for the most part, remain classified. These documents include the relevant years of 1962 to 1974 and may merit FOIA action. All declassified records held by the CMH on Nike missiles, the Cuban missile crisis, and other known Cold War events in south Florida were reviewed for this report. Declassified records reviewed at CMH provided good background on Army activities during the Cuban missile crisis but were not very useful as far as park- related resources go. The staff at the CMH were very helpful, however, in suggesting further areas of inquiry that ultimately proved to be quite useful to the HRS.

U.S. Army Corps of Engineers Headquarters (HQ USACE) Historical Archives. At the HQ USACE historical department library and archive, three boxes of materials were reviewed relating to air defense construction in south Florida and the Nike Hercules missile project. Most records were rather general in focus and provided little additional information. HQ USACE does, however, have finding aids that document holdings related to Nike design, construction, and deployment contained at NARA I, Suitland, Maryland. They also have a folder that contains copies of the original leases and deeds for the Nike and HAWK sites in south Florida. The archivist indicated that these were the only copies known to exist of these records. These deeds concerned the original locations of the various ARADCOM facilities and did not fully document all of the sites in their eventual permanent locations. HQ USACE does not have deeds and titles related to HM-69 within Everglades NP. Because HM-69 was located on USDA land by virtue of the bankruptcy of the Iori farms business, this site was secured by interagency government transfer. These documents are located at the Everglades NP museum library and archives in the superintendent files collection.

U.S. Army Military History Institute (MHI)-Carlisle Barracks, Pennsylvania. MHI proved to be the single best resource consulted for this study. MHI has a large library and archive as well as a huge collection of military newspapers. They are also the repository for the organizational history files of deactivated units. They have the 2/52 ADA history files as well as a complete run of the ARADCOM newspaper Argus. These records provide a lot of detail about air defense operations in south Florida and life at the missile sites. In the unit history files, two unpublished manuscripts were discovered that document the history of the 2/52 in south Florida. Also, a hand-drawn layout of the launch area of HM-69 was found among the records. This is the only known documentation of the HM-69 site layout; official records and photographs have not yet been discovered. It may be worthwhile to take another trip to Carlisle during any follow-ups to this HRS because the MHI may have more important sources related to air defense in south Florida as well as Cold War activities in the region.

For this study, only the organizational history files of 2/52 ADA, the photographic archives, and the Argus from 1962 to 1974 were reviewed. MHI does not hold copies of the 13th Artillery Group newspaper, The Defender. Efforts should be made to determine whether an archival collection of this publication is maintained at any facility in south Florida. This newspaper was published throughout the era when missile forces were deployed in south Florida. It may provide a level of detail about the air defense forces in south Florida beyond that of the more broadly focused Argus.

Suggestions for Further Research

All researchers pursuing topics dealing with the CIA, Cuban exiles, and covert operations in south Florida should be aware that much of the information available is perhaps untrue or at least not completely reliable. The material of concern to this HRS often overlaps the same ground mined by Kennedy assassination researchers. For this reason, some sources may contain a lot of conspiracy theory fantasy mingled with a few nuggets of true information of relevance to this HRS. Many of the individuals named in this HRS have a long history of covert operations. For reasons of security, they may not be completely forthright when talking to researchers. On the other hand, some of the people named in this HRS study have made a career out of telling researchers exactly what they want to hear. Many hoaxes have been perpetrated where the CIA, Cubans, and Kennedy are involved. This fact merits particular attention where internet resources are concerned. While the internet is a valuable resource for any historical research these days, there are a lot of web sites with bad information.

Researchers should also be aware of the tendency for some Cuban exiles to exaggerate the amount of their involvement in the secret wars. While most of the exiles mentioned in this report are major, documented players in the Cold War in south Florida, some are not. No doubt many exiles- like veterans everywhere- may have a tendency on occasion to tell tall tales. Researchers should be cautious when relying on oral interviews as a means to confirm the CIA utilization of resources mentioned in this report.

While oral histories certainly have problems of reliability and accuracy, the nature of this project makes it likely that oral history will have to provide the lion's share of information during possible follow-ups to this HRS. The CIA is notoriously slow in releasing documents concerning the Cold War in south Florida, and they seem particularly loath to release the types of operational reports and work files that might shed light on park resources. If individuals can be located who trained at the facilities within the parks, the HRS will be able to circumvent the refusals of the CIA to provide a full accounting of its activities in south Florida during the Cold War. This may be difficult, however, because many agents trained by the CIA and then infiltrated into Cuba were captured or killed. It is suggested that NPS consider creating a historical survey/questionnaire and then distributing it through the various exile associations in Miami. In this way, a large number of Cuban exiles could be contacted and surveyed about their activities during the Cold War. Likely candidates for interviews could be identified from this project at a relatively low cost. A similar effort could be undertaken for missile troops by posting a survey to the various Nike and HAWK-related web sites on the internet. It is important to note, as with all interviews, that information on south Florida missile operations obtained from Nike veterans reflects the personal recollections of the interviewees and should be weighed against all other sources of available evidence.

Similar efforts should be made with former CIA officers such as Grayston Lynch and Howard Hunt. Many of the CIA staff involved in Cold War operations in Florida are now at least eighty years old. Elderly subjects raise issues of memory and coherence of delivery and cannot be expected to live long. For this reason, it would be prudent to place special emphasis on talking to surviving CIA personnel as soon as possible.

This report has turned up additional information relating to the significance of Nike site HM-69 in Everglades NP which indicates that the south Florida missile sites were highly significant in the Cold War history of the region. The south Florida missile sites had a different history, construction, mission, and complement of equipment than any of the other missile sites in the CONUS. For this reason, listing HM-69 on the National Register of

Historic Places should prove to be an achievable goal. No other air defense missile sites in the CONUS deployed "under duress." No other Hercules sites served in a defense with HAWK missiles. No other Hercules troops received the Army's Meritorious Unit Commendation for a Cold War deterrence mission. No other Hercules sites had to defend against "mad man" attacks on the part of a communist dictator in addition to defending against Soviet bombers. No other CONUS Hercules sites were equipped with one of the Army's earliest anti-missile systems.

Some primary source documents have been located for the south Florida missile sites in the course of this research. Researchers should continue the search for blueprints and other official documents related to site construction at HM-69 in follow-ups to this HRS. Possible sources for HM-69 primary source materials not searched in the course of preparing this report include regional National Archives sites and the regional U.S. Army Corps of Engineers office in Jacksonville, Florida. A search should be performed in the Miami region to see whether any local library or military facility has a collection of The Defender, which was the local paper for the missile troops in the region. FOIA and declassification requests should also be filed for the various early studies on the history of the missile units deployed to the region. The studies by Jean Martin and Geraldine Rice document the deployment and history of the Florida missile units at the height of Cold War tensions. The Historical Museum of south Florida in Miami is home to the archives, library and documentary collections of the Historical Association of Southern Florida. The collection includes an extensive collection of photographs, newspapers, maps, and manuscripts related to south Florida.

NPS may want to explore the possibility of a land swap or annexation in order to protect Nike Hercules site HM-40 on Key Largo. This site is by far the most intact of any of the south Florida Nike sites. At a minimum, NPS cultural resources personnel in the region should visit HM-40 to get a clearer picture of Nike operations in Florida.

Follow-ups to this HRS should make an effort to explore radio operations in the region, especially those at Dry Tortugas NP. Researchers should examine USIA records in Washington, D.C., as well as State Department and VOA records related to Cold War broadcasting projects. These types of sources were not examined for this HRS. At a minimum, it should be possible to get transcripts or actual tape recordings of the propaganda and other programming beamed to Cuba from radio facilities in south Florida. Ron Rackley of DLR Inc. may be a good contact for this type of information.

It is also important to note that the Cold War occurred at the same time that the south Florida region underwent a boom in real estate and development, and the links between these two transformational events should be explored. The CIA pumped massive amounts of money into the local economy, while at the same time a huge influx of Cuban exiles arrived on U.S. shores. It is probable that the Cold War in south Florida led to a measurable increase in economic development. Thus, the Cold War may have broadly impacted the history of the region.

Florida politicians used their offices and their roles in the Cold War to gain national prominence. Governor Farris Bryant was a leader in the area of civil defense, while he also helped implement school curricula to indoctrinate Florida students into the mind-set of the Cold War superpower competition. Bryant's Cold War activities also had a relationship with civil rights issues in the state. During the Cold War, "civil rights agitator" was often interchangeable with "communist" in the minds of many politicians-especially southern ones. The HUAC-like Florida Legislative Investigation Committee (FLIC), often demonstrated a propensity to harass blacks, gays, and other "subversives" rather than the communists it was ostensibly designed to investigate. Links between anticommunist activities and the civil rights struggles in Florida that occurred concurrently with the most important Cold War events in the region should be explored in follow-ups to this HRS.

Florida Senator George Smathers was known as the "Senator from Latin America" because of his advocacy of greater U.S. involvement in Latin American economic and political development years before the crisis mentality erupted during the Cuban revolution. His career and relationship with President Kennedy should also be explored.

Time and money constraints did not allow for a thorough examination of records at the state level for this HRS; however, follow-up research should not neglect state-level sources found in archives in Tallahassee. At a minimum, the papers of people such as George Smathers and Farris Bryant should be examined as well as those of the Florida Legislative Investigation Committee (FLIC).

It may also be worthwhile to examine some Cold War-related activity in the region under the aegis of the region's long-standing status as a tourist mecca. Many high-ranking government officials-such as John F. Kennedy, Florida Senator George Smathers, and others-used Miami Beach and Havana as their personal playgrounds. An investigation of the loss of Havana as a venue for activities too shady even for wide-open Miami could be fascinating. Furthermore, sources consulted for this study are filled with information about VIPs and their propensity to show up for inspection tours in the region just when the weather got cold in the northern U.S. Missile troops reported difficulties in completing their duties because of the continual parade of VIPs. Contexts created for the Cold War HRS could include the uses and misuses of south Florida and Havana as a VIP tourist destination. It should also consider the role played by Florida mobsters in the Cold War history of the region. The link between Florida gangsters, the Batista regime, crime, and violence in the region and the Cold War efforts of the U.S. government to eliminate Castro is a fascinating topic. Of course, one must be very cautious to avoid the numerous conspiracy theories and hoaxes that permeate this subject matter.

Some Cold War-related events in south Florida have gone unstudied because few people have realized that many issues of contemporary importance in the region are Cold War-connected. The role of Aerojet and Canal C-111 in the Cold War history of south Florida and the region's environmental problems should be explored further. Aerojet, as a company with both Cold War missile contracts and a role in the space race, is a product of the Cold War era. The fact that its activities may have led to a major environmental disaster like salt water intrusion into the Everglades must be further explored and the Cold War impact on the environment in south Florida documented. Additionally, Aerojet's involvement in real estate development in the region provides a fascinating example of how Cold War concerns interacted with the powerful real estate/developer lobby in the state and how the attempts to land Cold War- related jobs in the region led to further sprawl and runaway land development.

Similarly, the U.S. government's efforts to affect the world sugar market in the aftermath of the Cuban Revolution and the effects of the transfer of major sugar growing operations from Cuba to south Florida should also be explored in the HRS. Sugar production in south Florida damaged the environment of the Everglades. Activities undertaken by the government and Florida Senator George Smathers to ensure that large- scale Cuban exile sugar growers like the Fanjuls were able to easily relocate to Florida's Everglades Agricultural Area warrant further study.

If the above suggestions are followed, then research may demonstrate that the history of the Cold War in south Florida, thought by some NPS personnel consulted for this study to be irrelevant in light of the more pressing concerns facing the parks, is actually quite important when considering several of the parks' major environmental challenges. The Cold War may be directly responsible for some of them.

Contexts developed for this HRS could probably be divided into three main subject areas. One could focus on the entire history of the Cuban exiles in south Florida, discussing the arrival of the exiles as a result of the Cold War struggle with communism in Cuba, the Cuban exile war against Castro, and the impact of the exiles on south Florida. Another context might deal strictly with military Cold War issues in south Florida. These would include overt military actions like the Cuban missile crisis buildup, the secret development of new military technologies as necessitated by shifting tactics in the battle for containment, and the establishment and history of the south Florida air defense missile system. A third context could analyze the most fascinating issue in the Cold War history of south Florida, the CIA JMWAVE activities and the various covert actions run from Miami such as the operation against Guatemala, the Cuban secret wars, and activities in Nicaragua. Of course, all of these contexts have significant overlap, and it may be best to discuss the park resources in one overall context concerning the Cold War in south Florida.

Stories of Cuban exiles in Miami have been told since their arrival in the region. CIA agents have published accounts of their activities in south Florida. Many accounts of the Bay of Pigs and the Cuban missile crisis have been written. Some histories document the construction of Nike missile sites in the nation- but most of them are vague about missile activities in Florida. Certainly, the Cold War has prompted the writing of numerous histories both good and bad. Studies are rare, however, that examine the impact of the Cold War on a single community or region. The Cold War in south Florida HRS could produce a very interesting historical context that examines the impact of the Cold War on south Florida in all of its many facets. This context could also make an important contribution to Cold War historiography more generally. The stories of the Cuban exiles, the covert CIA war against Castro, the environmental degradation of the local ecosystem, the military buildup during the Cuban missile crisis and the construction of the air defense system, and the drug, weapons, and money- laundering industries of south Florida could all be discussed as part of a broad overview of Cold War- related activities in the region.

Such a context could not only establish the importance of park resources in the history of the Cold War, but could be used as the basis for an interpretive exhibit or tour of the Cold War history of south Florida. A tour or exhibit could help the south Florida parks boost their visitation by some members of the local community who as of now spend little time in the parks and may not feel that the parks are relevant to their history or their lives. A tour that focused on Cold War sites within the parks could use the Nike site HM- 69 as a very overt display of the real threats faced during the Cold War and it could use the various sites utilized by the CIA and the Cubans during the secret wars as an example of the covert nature of much of the prosecution of the Cold War. A tour focused on the intrigue of the secret war against Castro in Florida would highlight important issues in the politics of the region by focusing on the history of the south Florida Cuban exiles. Many of them made their way into the country through the parks and then they used those same parks to fight- with the CIA and U.S. government's help of course- for the liberation of their nation.

The history of the parks in the Cold War is an important topic. Placing the various south Florida national park resources identified within this report into their proper Cold War context will provide a fascinating history of the region. It will also illuminate the fact that the parks were utilized by the military, the CIA, and the Cuban exiles in order to battle communism across the globe. Properly executed, this HRS can provide a means of better understanding the Cold War's impact on American society as well as the history of south Florida. Researchers should try, wherever possible, to take a broad view of the Cold War history of south Florida. Doing so will ensure that the HRS achieves its maximum utility.

Appendices

Appendix One: A Brief History of Air Defense in South Florida

FIGURE 11. Nike Hercules Missile Test, Santa Rosa, Florida, 1959.

Air defense units in Florida faced numerous difficulties during their initial deployment to the region during the Cuban missile crisis.[1] Battery B, 1st Automatic Weapons Battalion, 59th Artillery arrived in Florida on October 25, 1962. This unit had no missiles; rather it was equipped with World War II-vintage self- propelled 40mm "Dusters." These weapons were of little threat to the supersonic Soviet aircraft then in Cuba and they provided psychological support more than defense. The 40mm weapons battalion remained in Florida until December 15, 1962. Air defense missile units and their support groups began arriving in Florida at the

end of October 1962. Nike Hercules troops left Fort Bliss, Texas, on October 28, 1962, and arrived at Homestead AFB on October 31. The unit's missiles—with only conventional warheads rather than the nuclear W- 31 warheads—arrived in the region on November 1. Nike Hercules troops had their batteries ready to fire by November 14, 1962. HAWK troops of the 8/15 ADA came to Florida on November 1, 1962, and set up defenses at Patrick AFB, MacDill AFB, and Homestead AFB within 24 hours. HAWK units from the 6th Battalion 65th Artillery arrived in Key West on October 26. The HAWK units' missiles in Key West were ready to fire on October 29, 1962.[2] Despite the necessity of almost overnight deployment and the challenges of the field environment, the soldiers of the Nike and HAWK units rapidly achieved operational readiness.

The missile troops deployed during the Cuban missile crisis faced the challenge of setting up an operational air defense under field conditions with

FIGURE 12. HAWK Missile Launcher, Key West, Florida, November 1962.

little outside support. Their experience was unique within ARADCOM. South Florida missile troops deployed to the region with minimal warning. Commanders as far away as Ft. Lewis, Washington, held emergency evening formations, canceled all passes, ordered their troops to settle their personal affairs, and commenced the move to Florida. Troops arrived via rail with minimal equipment, usually in the middle of the night. They then set up working air defenses under the most primitive conditions. Planners typically located U.S. air defense sites in major cities and their suburbs. In south Florida, the first duty stations were located in the middle of the Everglades or in the midst of south Dade County bean and tomato fields. At these primitive south Florida field locations, constantly running tactical generators provided electricity. Soldiers lived in tents at the sites—at first, their squad tents did not even have walls or floors—and constantly battled mosquitoes and snakes. Rats were yet another problem, and the soldiers usually slept in shifts with one person staying awake at all times to fight the rodents. The number of rats grew at the sites, and personnel resorted to shooting them with small arms.

Because showers were not available at the temporary sites, soldiers dove into canals or used their helmets for bathing.[3] The Army scheduled regular showers only once a week for those able to travel to Homestead AFB, and the temporary shower facilities there attracted numerous gawkers. The Army tried to improve the conditions for the troops at the temporary sites as quickly as possible by installing wooden floors for the tents and wood walkways to permit dry travel between battery facilities. Showers were soon built in order to provide proper hygiene and boost morale; however, "little could be done to ameliorate the heat, humidity, and effects of the insects. Altogether, it was a rather rustic existence."[4]

Nike Hercules troops from Battery A/2/52 deployed to an area near the main entrance to Everglades National Park (Everglades NP), Battery C/2/52 deployed near Carol City, Battery D/2/52 went to a site near the Broward County line, and the Headquarters and Headquarters Battery (HHB)/2/52 based its operations at Princeton. Battery B/2/52 was not in the CONUS at the time of the crisis. They were in the Pacific participating in a series of nuclear tests. They joined Battery A near Everglades NP upon their return.

Tactical considerations and the requirements of each particular weapons system determined the site locations. These considerations often meant locating the sites in areas prone to flooding. Commanders did not always listen to the warnings of local residents about the hazards associated with the temporary sites. When A/2/52 set up operations near the entrance to Everglades NP, local farmers told the commander that a better location should be found because any rain would flood the area. Ignoring the local knowledge, the commander deployed his troops anyway. Frequent rains subjected the unlucky soldiers to constant flooding. Soldiers had to truck in numerous loads of fill dirt just to stay above water.[5] Flooding was not the only problem at the temporary sites. Richard Krenek, of

1. This essay is meant to provide some insight into the unique history of the south Florida air defense missile installations. It is not meant to provide a general history of Cold War air defense weapons systems or general day-to-day Nike and HAWK operations. For a more general discussion of the history of Cold War air defense programs and the day-to-day operations of Nike and HAWK missile installations see the various sources listed in the bibliography of this report. Nike history and daily operations are covered particularly well in John A. Martini and Stephen Haller, *What We Have We Shall Defend: An Interim History and Preservation Plan for Nike Site SF-88L, Fort Barry, California* (San Francisco: National Park Service, 1998). This appendix draws heavily on the following sources: Charles Edward Kirkpatrick, "The Second Battalion. 52nd Air Defense Artillery 1958-1983, [1983]" (2/52/ADA Organizational History Files, Carlisle Barracks, MHI, photocopy); James R. Hinds, "History of the 2d Missile Battalion [1965]," (2/52/ADA Organizational History Files, Carlisle Barracks, MHI, photocopy); U.S. Army, "Battery D, Second Battalion, 52nd Air Defense Artillery Welcome Guide and Fact Booklet (1970?)" (2/52/ADA Organizational History Files, Carlisle Barracks, MHI, photocopy); Richard Krenek, e-mail to author, October 1999; Richard H. McCormick, Col., U.S. Army (ret.), telephone interview with author, October 1999; and numerous articles found in the ARADCOM *Argus*, the official newspaper of the Army Air Defense Command.
2. Osato and Straup, *ARADCOM'S Florida Defenses*, 4.
3. The troops of Battery C were allowed to utilize the showers of Carol City High School thanks to the generosity of the principal who had witnessed the soldiers bathing in a canal; Kirkpatrick, "The Second Battalion," 11. Kirkpatrick cites an interview with the C/2/52 XO (executive officer) Thomas W. Kirkpatrick, 22 December 1977, as the source for this information.
4. Ibid., 9.
5. Ibid., 10; see also contemporary local news coverage of the deployment such as "Missile Sites Up to Ankles," *Cutler Ridge-Perrine Post*, December 1963; and "Mud and Missiles," *Cutler Ridge-Perrine Post*, 26 September 1963.

Battery D/2/52, remembers his first Thanksgiving dinner at his missile site.

> We were served sliced turkey breast. While going through the serving line I thought, wow, this looks pretty good for G.I. food. When I got to my table and put my tray down, I noticed a lot of black specks on the white turkey breast and I thought somebody had put some pepper on it. I kept looking and noticed the specks were moving. They were actually gnats. The tomato fields were rotting and were full of bugs and gnats. Everybody just scraped them off and ate the turkey anyway.[6]

The ongoing crisis of Soviet missiles in Cuba led the people of south Florida to welcome the missile troops with open arms. To ensure continued good relations, local commanders participated in civilian outreach and education programs. An accident with a Hercules or HAWK could seriously damage the initial goodwill that greeted the troops. Battery commanders carefully briefed their new neighbors on the operations of the missile sites for both safety and public- relations reasons. Local farmers and their workers made a habit of ignoring warnings to evacuate missile exhaust backblast areas during launch alerts. Anyone in the backblast zone would be severely injured if troops launched a missile.

Sites had to be improved in a variety of ways to ensure that the defenders could perform their mission. The heavy Hercules missiles often sank into the earth, while the typical Florida weather wreaked havoc on sensitive military equipment. Primitive electronics and other related equipment did not do well in the humid atmosphere of south Dade. Sites had to be drained and flooding controlled. This was usually achieved by plowing, scraping, and packing enough rough coral soil to provide a level and dry operations area. Security had to be enhanced by replacing primitive barbed-wire fences with the more secure concertina wire-topped fences.

The typical south Florida vegetation presented other hazards, including the risk of fire. Soldiers deployed to Florida had a bare minimum of supplies and no grass cutting- equipment. High grass in the launch area was matted down to provide a flat surface, becoming a serious fire hazard in the dry season. In December 1962, Battery C/2/52 narrowly avoided a disaster when a spark from one of their tactical field generators ignited the dry underbrush in the launch area. As the fire quickly advanced on the battery's supply of Hercules missiles, the troopers fought it with their blankets, their shirts, and the few pieces of fire fighting equipment at the site. The blaze injured several of the fire fighting soldiers. Until the batteries received mowers and other maintenance equipment, they tried to eliminate the fire hazard by scraping the ground in the launch area down to bare earth.[7]

Once the individual sites were operational, they had to be tied together into a fully integrated air defense network. The air defense systems of the Cold War era represent some of the first fully integrated and networked computer systems in history. Tying together all of the radar, missile, communications, and computer gear of the Hercules and HAWK sites presented a challenge for the Army and the Southern Bell telephone company. Signal Corps personnel worked with the phone company to provide all of the connections necessary to allow full integration of the 2/52 and 8/15 missile sites with the 13th Artillery Group Headquarters in the Homestead- Miami defense area. This was an important milestone for the Army because it represented "the first time that Field Army air defense units had been used in an active air defense role within the CONUS, and it was the first successful integration of Nike Hercules and HAWK in the same defense in a static CONUS situation."[8]

Despite these milestones, being a part of history began to take on less significance for the soldiers of the south Florida air defenses. Morale suffered at the sites because of the temporary and primitive nature of their living arrangements. As the initial crisis over Soviet missiles in Cuba faded, the troops lost the adrenaline "boost" provided by the sudden nature of their deployment and the necessity of getting their respective batteries operational under threat of enemy attack. For a considerable time, the soldiers suffered in the limbo of being deployed on a temporary duty (TDY) status in a permanent location with no prospect of returning to their home posts. Soldiers missed their families, their homes, and their belongings. They deployed so quickly that

6. Krenek, e-mail to author.
7. Kirkpatrick, "The Second Battalion," 13.
8. Ibid.

they had no time to secure their personal effects. Some left their cars at the railroad sidings where they boarded trains for Florida. In the draft Army of that era, the soldiers knew full well that most of the items they left behind in the barracks would be stolen. The field locations offered limited recreational opportunities with soldiers having access to only a pool or Ping- Pong table. Field location post exchanges (PXs) typically stocked only essential hygiene items, soda, and beer. The soldiers constantly asked their superiors when they might return home. In a well- remembered incident, when the soldiers of a HAWK battery asked a visiting officer when they would leave south Florida he replied that they should "begin planting corn." Luckily, for morale and sanity's sake, the missile troops soon received a less cryptic answer to their questions.

In the aftermath of the Cuban missile crisis, military planners realized that they had erred by not including south Florida in the air defense network of the United States. While they had planned on defending most large population centers in the U.S., budget constraints necessitated the construction of air defenses according to strategic considerations. The military believed that Soviet bombers would attack the U.S. from over the North Pole, and they prioritized their efforts accordingly. The discovery of Soviet missiles and jet bombers in Cuba, ninety miles from American shores, provided the necessary impetus for a rethinking of the strategic importance of Florida and Key West. As U.S. forces poured into south Florida, they quickly exceeded the capacity of the defense installations in the area to hold them. Planners realized the importance of these facilities to their contingency plans and shuddered to think of the consequences if Cuban or Soviet air strikes destroyed them. As a result, the temporary missile sites of south Florida became a permanent feature of the air defense network of the U.S. Not only would these defenses serve to deter and protect against future Soviet moves in the area but, more importantly, they would protect south Florida against any sort of "madman" attacks from Cuba. "[Castro's Air Force] could [have] launch[ed] an 'irrational' attack upon the southern United States with 'little or no warning.'"[9]

With HAWK missiles in Key West and Nike and HAWK missiles in the Homestead- Miami defense, military planners could provide protection to crucial military facilities as well as the civilian population of the region. The U.S. military commanders, "outflanked" by Soviet and Cuban scheming during the crisis with their staging areas vulnerable to air attack, thus ensured that they would never be so vulnerable again. The HAWK missile battalions could protect Florida from low-level attack while the Nike Hercules batteries could guard the medium and higher altitudes. Florida would finally get its own air defenses, and they would be unique within the CONUS. The Homestead- Miami area would be the only place within ARADCOM that Nike and HAWK batteries were integrated into a local missile defense.

In August 1963, the Army officially announced that the missile sites of south Florida would become a permanent feature of the U.S. air defense network. The Army assigned the troops under the control of the 13th Artillery Group to the 53rd Artillery Brigade and the 2nd Region of ARADCOM at the beginning of the 1963 fiscal year. The soldiers could now go off TDY status and bring their families, cars, and personal effects to south Florida. They could also move into more permanent living facilities and get access to amenities available at permanent CONUS duty locations.

The happiness resulting from this announcement was short- lived. Hurricanes pummeled the soldiers of south Florida's Cold War air defenses on an all-too- frequent basis during the 1960s. In October 1963, Hurricane Flora ravaged the temporary south Florida HAWK and Nike positions. The hurricane's storm surge and flooding overwhelmed the troops serving with HAWK units in the Keys. These storms would be an ongoing challenge for the soldiers of the region's missile defenses.[10] During hurricanes, shelter was sought wherever it could be found. Soldiers sometimes stored missiles and equipment within Everglades NP. The damage caused by Flora further illustrated the necessity of building permanent missile installations as soon as possible.

The massive construction plan would ultimately cost approximately $17 million. In the short term,

---

9. Osato and Straup, *ARADCOM'S Florida Defenses*, 13.
10. In 1965 Hurricane Betsy knocked out almost all of the communication circuits in the Homestead-Miami defense area and caused over $500,000 in damage just to the communications facilities. Osato and Straup, *ARADCOM's Florida Defenses*, 82.

FIGURE 13. HM-40 Integrated Fire Control Area under construction, Key Largo, Florida, 1964.

the Army tried to address the immediate needs of the soldiers with a quick construction plan focused on improving morale. As a stop- gap measure, ARADCOM invested approximately $600,000 for improved mess- hall facilities, water purification, tent lighting, and drainage systems. The Army implemented this construction program to improve the living conditions at the sites until permanent facilities could be designed, funded, and constructed. The Army Corps of Engineers completed the program with the help and participation of local contractors.[11] Some lucky soldiers, like those of the HHB/8/15, moved into leased living quarters in Naranja, Florida in August 1963, while the soldiers of HHB/2/52 moved into barracks at Homestead AFB. These barracks improved morale because they were closer to local recreation facilities, possessed air conditioning and hot showers, and—perhaps most importantly— provided relief from the vicious south Florida mosquitoes. Lt. Col. John W. Nocita, the 8/15's commanding officer, explained that the new facilities contributed to mission effectiveness because "the time previously devoted to the raising and lowering of tent sides to conform to the vagaries of Florida rains can now be utilized to further the air

defense mission of the battalion."[12] Unfortunately, troops not assigned to the HHB still suffered at their respective field locations.

While looking for permanent locations for the HAWK and Nike installations, the Army spent a great deal of time and money locating sites that would not upset residents, real estate developers, and naturalists. In Florida, the Army saved money by placing the sites in areas already owned or controlled by the government. Having built such facilities all over the country, the Army was aware of the propensity of some real- estate agents to raise heir prices and demand as many taxpayer dollars as possible. In fact, the underground magazines common at most CONUS Nike sites were the result of a desire to save money on land- acquisition costs by using less of the expensive suburban property required by the missile sites.[13] In Florida, however, the high water table precluded the use of underground magazines and thus the sites required more space for their aboveground magazines. In south Florida, with its high prices, tourist market, and "skilled" real estate developers, this could pose problems. The army tried its best to avoid the excesses of the south Florida real- estate market. Battery A was relocated inside Everglades NP on

---

11. "$600,000 Being Expended to Improve Site Conditions in Florida Defenses," *Argus*, August 1963, 1-2.
12. "Florida HAWK Unit Leaves Field Tent," *Argus*, August 1963.
13. The air defenses had to form a ring around the target they protected. This meant that, in the case of cities, they were often located in expensive suburban areas in close proximity to people's homes.

FIGURE 14. Completed HM-95 Krome Avenue Integrated Fire Control Area (IFC), February 1952. All other south Florida Nike IFCs were similar.

land once owned by the Iori farming operation. After Iori went bankrupt, the land was transferred from the USDA directly to the Army. Battery D and Battery B were similarly located on undeveloped and inexpensive land on the outskirts of Miami and in Key Largo. The Army ran out of luck when it came to Battery C. Army efforts to build Battery C in Carol City ran afoul of a local real- estate developer who made the Army pay dearly for its preferred tactical location. This would be the most expensive tract purchased by ARADCOM in the region, costing more than $800,000.[14]

Construction proceeded quickly and, for the most part, the Army completed the permanent sites on schedule. The completion of construction greatly relieved local commanders, who could then alleviate some of their morale problems as well as their own misgivings about potential problems related to delays in site completion. At one point, some commanders worried that the battalion's canine guard dogs would arrive before contractors completed the permanent sites. They had nightmares about housing dozens of military guard dogs in their own backyards. Luckily for the

would- be dog boarders, ARADCOM delayed the canine shipments until the sites were ready.

There would be other problems for the canine members of the Nike battalions. The region's climate and pests tormented the military dogs. Like their human handlers, the military guard dogs assigned to each launch area suffered greatly from the mosquitoes. Walking the perimeter with a German shepherd at night in the Everglades in June or July had to have been one of the worst duties at any south Florida missile site—soldiers sometimes remarked that they would rather forget their weapon than their can of insect repellant. In addition to suffering from the mosquitoes, the canine guards also faced other hazards unique among their brethren in ARADCOM. Guard dogs at south Florida missile sites frequently died from *Leptospirosis*, an infection caused by an organism in the local ground water. Again, HM- 03 Carol City stands out as the most "civilized" of all the south Florida batteries—it was the only south Florida battery whose canines escaped the ravages of this disease.[15]

---

14. Problems in acquisition and costs related to site construction are discussed in Osato and Straup, *ARADCOM's Florida Defenses*, 65-87.

FIGURE 15. Completed HM-95 Krome Avenue Lauch Area (LA) site. The site is now the home of the Immigration and Naturalization Service's Krome Avenue Processing Center. All other south Florida Launch Areas were similar.

Throughout the United States, the original 1950s-era air defense sites were unimproved and rather "rough" around the edges. The suburban location of many of the newer CONUS missile sites demanded, however, that they blend in as much as possible and not be eyesores. The tactical demands of the missile systems meant that they had to be located near the targets they defended. This requirement necessitated their location in suburban neighborhoods. Planners implemented site-beautification plans by landscaping the sites in a manner designed to be more aesthetically pleasing to neighbors. ARADCOM troops often participated in such projects in order to mollify the civilians who lived nearby. Beautification of the sites would not be such a big issue in Florida where the troops typically served at isolated locations around a metropolitan area that was not nearly as developed as it is today.

Most Homestead-Miami defense missile troops worked in locations that contributed to their morale problems. Again, Battery C was atypical in the Homestead-Miami defense; its soldiers alone had access to nearby amenities such as recreational facilities and restaurants. For the missile troops serving at the other batteries, even the ability of the soldiers at Battery C to pick up a hamburger at a local fast-food restaurant was an unimaginable luxury. Key West HAWK troops were not so isolated, but they faced other problems such as the costs involved in being stationed in a tourist locale with tourist prices. It should be remembered that

the 1960s Army was a draft Army with poorly paid soldiers.

Because of the need for highly trained technicians at the missile sites, and the knowledge that assignment to a CONUS missile unit was a way to avoid service in Vietnam, soldiers from a wide variety of diverse backgrounds served with the air defense units in south Florida. Some soldiers were fresh from college and collegiate athletic competition. Among the ARADCOM troops in south Florida were a record-holding pole vaulter and an Olympic-caliber swimmer. Specialist 4 (Sp4) Cruz Barrios, a switchboard operator at the 47th Brigade headquarters, had an even more unusual background. Barrios had been a member of a New York City-based unicycle-riding basketball team that traveled with the Ringling Brothers circus. Barrios frequently rode his unicycle to work in uniform, carrying packages in one hand and "smartly saluting with the other."[16]

FIGURE 16. Canine guards also faced challenges posed by the Florida climate. HM-03 Carol City Launch Area.

---

15. Osato and Straup, *ARADCOM's Florida Defenses*; McCormick, telephone interview with author. McCormick asserted that the canines were eventually pulled from the south Florida sites for this reason, although several LAs inspected for this report still have extant kennel facilities.

16. "'I'm the best there is,' says Sp4 Barrios," *Argus*, May 1970, 15.

FIGURE 17. Soldiers at C/2/52 Carol City landscape the Integrated Fire Control Area.

The soldiers of the south Florida missile batteries moved into their new facilities in 1965. These new locations featured large battery buildings at each of the IFC sites. These buildings housed the battery dormitory, mess hall, and administrative offices. More senior personnel lived two to a room, while junior enlisted people lived in a large dormitory bay. Most of the battery's 146 personnel lived at the IFC site unless they were senior staff members, officers, or married and living off- post. While the IFC battery buildings were much more comfortable than a squad tent in a tomato field, they provided limited opportunities for rest and recreation (R&R). At first, the battery buildings had only a small PX. A day room was available for some recreational activities; it usually featured a television as well as a small library. Food at the sites was typical G.I., "[certainly not] gourmet type, but usually pretty good."[17] Barracks life at the south Florida units frequently assumed the contours of military life familiar to service members everywhere. Card playing in the day room, beer drinking in the battery PX, and bull sessions throughout the area were the rule of the day.

For real R&R, troops lucky enough to have transportation would head into Miami and hit the many bars, clubs, and hangouts frequented by college students. Some of the troops met their spouses in this manner. A night on the town followed by a drive back to an isolated missile site, however, could pose unique challenges for the soldiers. In the case of Nike site HM- 69 in Everglades NP, troops applied special paint lines to the access road so that those who drank a bit too much might better navigate their way back to the barracks while under the influence.[18] Drunken revelers from A/2/52 sometimes caused serious problems for Everglades NP staff. On one occasion in January 1966, two drunken soldiers almost hit a vehicle head- on at the park's main entrance. The vehicle in question belonged to a park visitor selected to be honored as Everglades NP's one millionth guest.[19] Park staff discovered many wrecked vehicles in the borrow pit adjacent to the HM- 69 Launch Area. Drunken missile troops that crashed their vehicles on the way back to their duty location sometimes dumped them into the pit.

17. Krenek, e-mail to author.
18. Walter Meshaka, Everglades NP Museum Curator, oral interview with author, Everglades NP, May 1999. Troops often painted other things on buildings and roads, "FTA"—"F**k The Army"—seems to have been particularly popular, and can still be found at some south Florida missile facilities.
19. *Superintendent's Monthly Narrative Reports* (Everglades NP: Department of the Interior, January 1966).

Humans were not the only creatures living at the south Florida missile sites with a taste for the occasional alcoholic beverage. Many of the missile batteries of south Florida adopted their own mascots, which then lived with the soldiers at the respective missile sites. Various animals served in these capacities and were even given honorary Army ranks. The soldiers of D/2/52 chose a dog as their mascot. Known as Sp4 "Boo- How"—the name means "no good" in Chinese—the dog survived on a steady diet of sausages and beer provided by soldiers relaxing at the battery PX. In fact, the Boo-How developed quite a taste for what might be considered the typical soldier's "diet." On at least one occasion, Boo- How drank so much beer that she passed out in the battery commander's bunk. The mascot of D/2/52 soon went on the wagon, however, and with the help of D/2/52 1st Sergeant Alfred Meana, met some more respectable companions. A few months later, the battery adopted Sp4 Boo- How's litter of seven puppies. Clearly thriving in her sobriety and motherhood, the battalion commander soon promoted Sp4 to the rank of sergeant.[20]

Other batteries had different mascots. HAWK missile troops at Battery A/8/15 built and landscaped a pond in their battery area in order to house their alligator mascot known as "Alphagator" or "Al" for short. Key West defense HAWK troops kept a real hawk for their mascot. Known as "Charlie the gold bricking hawk," many press stories about the HAWK batteries of the Keys featured the bird. Unfortunately, the original Charlie did not survive long in his Key West location. He was killed during a hurricane.

Despite the isolation of their duty locations, off-duty missile troops participated in a wide variety of recreational activities and hobbies. Soldiers took advantage of their location and utilized the ample natural resources of south Florida by boating, fishing, hunting, and scuba diving. Many participated in even more unique activities. Some of the soldiers could not get enough of rockets and missiles while at work. While the defenders never fired a real Nike Hercules in south Florida, two soldiers of A/2/52 built and launched models of

FIGURE 18. Key West HAWK troops proudly proclaim their unique status.

Army and NASA rockets during their off- duty hours.[21] HHB/6/65 soldiers in Key West developed their own space- saving version of Ping- Pong by building miniature Ping- Pong tables that could be set up and used almost anywhere. Known as "minipong," this game demonstrated the ingenuity of soldiers seeking morale- boosting recreational opportunities while living on limited salaries in expensive tourist locales.[22]

In the 1970s, the Army provided more amenities for soldiers in south Florida as the transition toward the all- volunteer force demanded that soldiers receive fringe benefits comparable to those afforded civilian workers. The Army considerably upgraded battery recreational facilities and programs. They now showed movies three to five nights a week, and they installed hobby shops featuring wood- working shops, automotive repair tools, and photography equipment. The soldiers also moved into better accommodations. The Army replaced open squad bays with more private dorm rooms that the troops could decorate and personalize according to their own tastes.

In an ongoing effort to combat the possibility of bored soldiers finding trouble by fighting, drinking, and using drugs at the lonely missile outposts, the Army installed state- of- the- art weight lifting machines at each Nike site. At a cost of over $2,000 each, these machines allowed for "constructive off-duty recreation [and] better health" for soldiers serving in isolated locations.[23] Missile troops could participate in tennis and basketball at each IFC site

20. "Boo-How Stops Drinking for Family," *Argus*, July 1968, 25.
21. "Missilemen Launch own Honest John," *South Dade News Leader*, 26 October 1971, 3.
22. "Minipong Gets a Start at Key West," *Argus*, February 1971, 20.
23. "31st Bde. Buys Four Mini-Gyms for Batteries," *Argus*, April 1970, 27.

FIGURE 19. Soldiers of D/2/52 Krome Avenue work out at the Battery Integrated Fire Control Area building.

on the battery's own courts. In the summer, members of the battery often played softball. At the battalion level, missile troops participated in competition against the other batteries in golf, flag football, and basketball.

Soldiers also watched sanctioned entertainment provided by official Army show troupes. These shows, designed to boost the morale of soldiers stationed in war zones and remote areas—and to keep soldiers away from bars, prostitutes, and other problems—were a familiar part of Army life for missile troops. While celebrities like Bob Hope were still an important component of any USO show, the Army updated its entertainment in the early 1970s in an effort to become more "hip." Official shows took on a decidedly more psychedelic air. Lamé shirts, miniskirts, go- go boots, and giant smiling flower props demonstrate the shifting styles of the "Age of Aquarius." Changes in official entertainment illustrate the impact of popular culture on Army life. Off- duty time was not all fun and games. The air defense troops of south Florida assisted the local community wherever, whenever, and however possible. The Army frequently interacted with other military, government, and civilian agencies. Missile troops helped rangers in Everglades NP fight forest fires. Blood drives for the wounded in Vietnam and the local community, camps and tours for disadvantaged youth in south Florida, and other community- relations projects helped ensure that the Army maintained good rapport with its civilian neighbors. Nike commanders had to make special efforts in such projects because they had learned that while most citizens believed in the need for air

defenses and liked the idea of protection from Soviet bomber forces, most suburbanites did not relish the idea of living next to a missile site. Commanders conceived many projects with an eye toward providing positive public- relations benefits for the missile sites.

The soldiers of A/2/52 worked with a division of the Youth Conservation Corps (YCC) within Everglades NP on a pilot project designed to help preserve and maintain federal lands and waters. Under the direction of the U.S. Department of Agriculture and the Department of the Interior, A/2/52 helped members of the YCC build trash- collection points in the park, plant trees, and work in greenhouses. The missile battery provided housing and dining facilities for the youngsters while the National Park Service paid for their meals. This interagency cooperation provided valuable services to the park and helped the Army secure positive press for the Everglades Nike site.[24]

While performing their Army duties, the south Florida defenders demonstrated a high degree of competency with their weapons systems and a propensity to do well during inspections and exercises. south Florida's proximity to Cuba meant that HAWK and Nike troops would receive almost no warning of enemy attack. This shortened reaction time meant that the troops had to be on a high state of alert at all times. Flight time from Cuba to Miami via supersonic jet bomber was very short. Perhaps because of this need for highly honed vigilance, south Florida troops frequently outperformed other ARADCOM missile batteries.

For a time, south Florida missile troops were some of the best in ARADCOM. The soldiers of A/2/52 Everglades NP performed their jobs very well in the mid- to- late 1960s. They performed so well on major inspections like the operational- readiness inspection (ORE), command maintenance- management inspection (CMMI), short- notice annual practice (SNAP), and technical- proficiency inspection (TPI) that they won the ARADCOM "E" award for four years in a row from 1966 to 1969. This feat had never before been accomplished in ARADCOM. In recognition of their accomplishments, the soldiers of A/2/52 were allowed to attach the "E" award streamer permanently to the Battery A guidon. This "E"

---

24. "Homestead-Miami Missilemen help in YCC Project," *Argus*, October 1972, 13.

FIGURE 20. Army troupe performs at A/2/52 Everglades National Park, August 1972.

award streamer illustrated the fact that the Nike soldiers of A/2/52 managed to sustain a high level of performance over a very long period of time despite the inherent hardships presented by duty in the Everglades. A/2/52 was not the only outstanding unit among the missile troops of south Florida. HAWK units were also frequently represented among ARADCOM's elite "E" award winners. In 1969, HAWK crews of A/8/15 and D/8/15 also won the award. In annual year- end contests like the ARADCOM battle for the commander's trophy— presented each year to the overall best battery in ARADCOM—the Florida Nike and Hawk units often competed against each other for top positions in their respective weapons systems.[25]

Unfortunately, a scandal of major proportions, played out across the front pages of some of the nation's biggest newspapers, damaging the reputation of the south Florida units in the early 1970s. Known locally as "the Royal Palm Affair," this scandal involved drugs and lapses in the storage and security of the 2/52 ADA's nuclear weapons. In 1971, word leaked out that at least some of the honors earned by the 2/52 ADA may not have been properly or fairly achieved. Four soldiers formerly stationed at the battalion from 1968- 1970 went to the press with stories that tarnished the well- known record of success and achievement of the battalion. In a series of articles in the *Daily Oklahoman* and the *New York Times* newspapers in February 1971,

former 2/52 ADA battalion members Lt. Earl M. Bricker III, SSgt. George E. Reder Jr., Lt. Casey J. Sauers, and Capt. Alan C. Frazier accused the Army of covering up serious violations of accepted standards and procedures at the Florida defense sites. To achieve Nike Hercules battery officer certification, officers had to demonstrate their knowledge and familiarity with the weapon system through a series of tests. For promotions to higher ranks, enlisted personnel had to prove their knowledge of the Army's bureaucratic procedures and regulations. Bricker and others made charges that indicated a widespread resort to cheating by the officers and enlisted men of 2/52 trying to qualify for duty and promotions. The four former members of 2/52 charged that officers gained access to exams before their tests and that other officers coached them on the correct answers. They also charged that the officers gave enlisted soldiers answers to questions on their promotion exams.

These were all serious charges. But the four whistle blowers also stated that the officers and enlisted personnel of 2/52 violated site security and operational regulations on a regular basis. Many of these violations concerned the battalion's inventory of nuclear weapons and its nuclear defense mission. According to the four men, on two occasions in 1970 D battery failed to inventory its emergency war order codes properly and thus might have been unable to authenticate a valid message to launch

25. "A/2/52 Wins Third ARADCOM 'E' Award," *Argus*, November 1968; "Homestead-Miami Unit Sets Record with 4th 'E' Award," *Argus*, November 1969, 5.

FIGURE 21. Everglades National Park Ranger, Army Officer, and Youth Conservation Corps members.

To make matters even worse, the four whistle blowers accused the Army of attempting to cover up the scandal. The Army denied all of these charges and declared that it had already investigated the charges in June 1970 and found that "only one of the allegations [was substantiated]. A Lieutenant had made an unauthorized copy of written examination material. He was officially reprimanded. All battery control officers were reexamined with revised test material, which effectively negated any possible compromise of the original examinations."[26] Many of the officers accused of cheating in the scandal were eventually promoted and/or given Army decorations for outstanding service. The whistle blowers faced repercussions for coming forward with the information, and received poor performance reports damaging to their careers.[27] Memory of the scandal quickly faded, however, and the south Florida troops continued their service for almost a decade.

nuclear weapons. Nuclear warheads, said the whistle blowers, went without their scheduled maintenance checks and could have posed a serious safety hazard. Officers at some locations had a habit of disappearing from their appointed duty posts at "hot" batteries and thus often violated the two-officer policy rule requiring two officers to be present in order to maintain proper control of nuclear weapons.

More bad publicity came to the Florida units because the cheating, safety, and security scandal followed a large drug investigation that found evidence of widespread drug abuse by the soldiers of 2/52. The drug investigation resulted in numerous Article 15's, court- martials, and less-than- honorable discharges. Approximately thirty soldiers were disciplined in the investigation. The drug scandal, in combination with the cheating scandal, added to the perception that something was wrong at the Florida air defenses.

Troops in south Florida served in a unique capacity within ARADCOM by virtue of the fact that their threat was often much more real than that faced by other batteries across the U.S. They operated the only defense integrating HAWK and Nike batteries. They fulfilled unique mobility requirements given to no other state- side Nike batteries. They had a unique complement of weapons, including the ATBM version of the Hercules which could shoot down tactical ballistic missiles. They could use their missiles and their mobility to fulfill a surface- to-surface mission if necessary. This meant that they could actually strike targets on the ground and in the air. They also were unique in being deployed under "duress" during the height of the Cuban missile crisis and Cold War tensions. The soldiers of 2/52 ADA received a Presidential Unit Citation for their actions during the crisis. This was one of the few times that a unit received this award for completing a deterrence mission during the Cold War—essentially, they got a medal for *not* doing their job.[28] The south Florida missile troops served in unique facilities built without the underground

26. "Army Says Charges Fully Investigated," *South Dade News Leader*, 19 April 1972, 1.
27. For full coverage of the scandal see the above-mentioned series of articles in *The Daily Oklahoman*, February 1971, as well as the following: "Army Says Charges Fully Investigated," *South Dade News Leader*, 19 April 1972, 1; "Army: Nike-Test Cheating was Probed," *Miami Herald*, 19 April 1972, b2; "Army, Congress Didn't Press Missile Probe, Officer Says," *Miami Herald*, 18 April 1972, a5; "Congress Failed to Look into Cheating," *Homestead News Leader*, 17 April 1972, 1; "Unit Cited for Violations," *Army Times*, 3 May 1972, 4; "Ex-Officers Accuse Army on Nuclear Base Security," *New York Times*, 20 April 1972, 3.
28. Bob Wright, Chief of Records at the Army Center for Military History, Washington, D.C., asserts that this is highly unusual.

magazines and other underground facilities typical of CONUS Nike sites.

The switch from bombers to missiles as the preferred method of delivering nuclear destruction in the 1960s and 1970s sounded the death knell for ARADCOM and the CONUS air defense batteries. Escalating costs related to the war in Vietnam, as well as the failure of the Soviet bomber threat to materialize, led to the dissolution of ARADCOM. Once again, however, the Florida units stood out amongst their fellow defenders. While the Army shut down all other CONUS missile defenses in 1974, Florida air defenses stayed active for another five years because of the unique situation in south Florida. After the disbandment of ARADCOM, the Army transferred the Florida units to the U.S. Army Forces Command (FORSCOM) where they would serve until their own retirement. Not until 1979, when planners decided that Florida defenses could offer nothing to the national security of the nation, did the Florida units finally abandon their positions.[29]

Some of Florida's former missile sites still play important roles in the everyday life and history of the region. The former Battery D/2/52 site at Krome Avenue served as a refugee-processing center during the Mariel boat lift in 1980. Both the IFC and LA of the site housed Cuban refugees. The former LA of the site serves in this capacity today. The Krome Avenue facility is frequently a focal point in the Miami Cuban community's battles against Castro and in their efforts to ensure that U.S. policy makers retain the Cold War's hard-line stance against communist Cuba. The Battery A/2/52 IFC area in Everglades NP serves as a research center for the park's scientific staff. The three missile storage barns at HM-69 are currently used by the National Park Service to shelter NPS boats and equipment when hurricanes threaten the area. The eye of Hurricane Andrew passed directly over the facility in 1992, and the missile storage barns suffered almost no damage from that storm. Developers razed Battery C/2/52's IFC and replaced it with a housing development.

FIGURE 22. "E" Award being attached to the A/2/52 unit flag.

The remains of south Florida's air defense missile sites stand as visible reminders of the Cold War that, because of the region's proximity to Cuba and its large population of Cuban exiles, still rages even at a time when the rest of the nation is willing, ready, and able to move on. The region's air defense sites also have relevance on the national scene. At a time when the U.S. is once again weighing the costs associated with the design, construction, and deployment of defensive missile systems and the strategic ramifications of such programs, the history of the nation's earlier air defenses and the stories of the troops that served there should receive greater attention. Nike sites were built based on a set of assumptions put forth in NSC-68 and held at the forefront of "classic" cold warrior thinking. Yet, these assumptions, at least in the case of those that drove the construction of the nation's Nike air defenses, never came to pass. Officials installed the Nikes to protect the nation from a massive fleet of Soviet bombers. The Soviets never built bombers in any great numbers; they relied on ICBMs for the majority of their nuclear strike capability. Thus, the largest defensive building program in the U.S. since the Civil War countered a threat that never materialized. While this situation was, of course, a good thing, it should always be remembered when considering the history of the Cold War, the south Florida missile defenses, and any future construction of similar systems.

29. Kirkpatrick, "The Second Battalion."

Appendix Two: List of Acronyms

AADCP .... Army Air Defense Command Post

ABAR .... Alternative Battery Acquisition Radar

ADA .... Air Defense Artillery

AFB .... Air Force Base

ARADCOM .... Army Air Defense Command

ARRB .... Assassination Records Review Board

ATBM .... Anti- Tactical Ballistic Missile

CANF .... Cuban American National Foundation

CFC .... Cuban Freedom Committee

CIA .... Central Intelligence Agency

CINC .... Commander in Chief

CINCLANT .... Commander in Chief, Atlantic Fleet

CIS .... Commonwealth of Independent States

CMH .... Center for Military History

CONUS .... Continental United States

CRC .... Cuban Revolutionary Council

DEW .... Distant Early Warning

EAA .... Everglades Agricultural Area

E&E .... Escape and Evasion

Ex- Com .... Executive Committee, National Security Council

FBI .... Federal Bureau of Investigation

FBIS .... Foreign Broadcast Intercept Service

FCC .... Federal Communications Commission

FDR .... Franklin Delano Roosevelt

FLIC .... Florida Legislative Investigation Committee

FORSCOM .... Forces Command

FRD .... Democratic Revolutionary Front

FRUS .... Foreign Relations of the United States

GI .... Government Issue

GOC .... Ground Observer Corps

HAWK .... Homing All the Way Killer

HERC . . . . Nike Hercules missile

HHB . . . . Headquarters and Headquarters Battery

HIPAR. . . . . High Power Acquisition Radar

HM . . . . Homestead- Miami

HQ. . . . . Headquarters

HSCA . . . . House Select Committee on Assassination

HUAC. . . . . House Un- American Activities Committee

ICBM . . . . Intercontinental Ballistic Missile

IFC. . . . . Integrated Fire Control Area

INS. . . . . Immigration and Naturalization Service

Interpen . . . . Intercontinental Penetration Force

IR . . . . Infrared

IRBM . . . . Intermediate Range Ballistic Missile

KW. . . . . Key West

LA . . . . Launch Area

LIC. . . . . Low Intensity Conflict

LOPAR . . . . Low Power Acquisition Radar

M- 26. . . . . 26th of July Movement

MHI. . . . . Military History Institute

MIA. . . . . Missing in Action; Miami International Airport

MIRV . . . . Multiple Independent Reentry Vehicle

MRR . . . . Movement for Revolutionary Recovery

NARA . . . . National Archives and Records Administration

NAS. . . . . Naval Air Station

NASA . . . . National Aeronautics and Space Administration

NATO . . . . North Atlantic Treaty Organization

NP . . . . National Park; National Preserve

NSA. . . . . National Security Agency

NSC- 68 . . . . National Security Council planning document 68

OPLAN. . . . . Operations Plan

OSS . . . . Office of Strategic Services

PX . . . . Post Exchange

R&R . . . . Rest and Recreation

SAC .... Strategic Air Command

SAM .... Surface to Air Missile

SAT .... Southern Air Transport

SDI .... Strategic Defense Initiative

SIGINT .... Signal Intelligence

SOF .... Soldier of Fortune

SRB .... Solid Rocket Booster

TAC .... Tactical Air Command

UN .... United Nations

USACE .... United States Army Corps of Engineers

USAF .... United States Air Force

USAFSS .... United States Air Force Security Service

USARLANT .... United States Army Atlantic Command

USCGS .... United States Coast and Geodetic Survey

USIA .... United States Information Agency

Bibliography

ARCHIVAL SOURCES

Everglades National Park Museum and Archives, Everglades National Park, Florida.

National Archives and Records Administration I, Suitland, Maryland.

National Archives and Records Administration II, College Park, Maryland.

National Security Archive, George Washington University, Washington, D.C.

Naval Historical Center, Washington Navy Yard, Washington, D.C.

Richter Library, Cuban Exile Collection and Archives, University of Miami, Coral Gables, Florida.

Smathers Library, Florida History Collection, University of Florida.

U.S. Army Center for Military History, Fort Myer, Washington, D.C.

U.S. Army Corps of Engineers, Headquarters, Office of History, Washington, D.C.

U.S. Army Military History Institute, Carlisle Barracks, Pennsylvania.

BOOKS

Agee, Philip. *Inside the Company: CIA Diary.* New York: Bantam, 1976.

Allison, Graham. *Essence of Decision: Explaining the Cuban Missile Crisis.* 2d ed., Boston: Little Brown, 1999.

Allman, T. D. *Miami: City of the Future.* New York: Atlantic Monthly, 1987.

Attwood, William. *The Twilight Struggle: Tales of the Cold War.* New York: Harper & Row, 1987.

Ayers, Bradley Earl. *The War That Never Was: An Insider's Account of CIA Covert Operations Against Cuba.* Indianapolis: Bobbs- Merrill, 1976.

Balseiro, Jose- Agustin. *The Hispanic Presence in Florida: Yesterday and Today, 1513- 1973.* Miami: E. A. Seemann, 1977.

Beck, Melvin. *Secret Contenders: The Myth of Cold War Counterintelligence.* New York: Sheridan Square, 1984.

Benjamin, Jules R. *The United States and the Origins of the Cuban Revolution: An Empire of Liberty in an Age of National Liberation.* Princeton: Princeton University Press, 1990.

Beschloss, Michael R. *At the Highest Levels: The Inside Story of the End of the Cold War.* Boston: Little, Brown, 1993.

_____. *Mayday, The U- 2 Affair: The Untold Story of the Greatest US- USSR Spy Scandal.* New York: Harper and Row, 1986.

Blight, James G., and David Welch. *On the Brink: Americans and Soviets Reexamine the Cuban Missile Crisis.* New York: Hill and Wang, 1989.

Blight, James G., Bruce J. Allyn, and David Welch. *Cuba on the Brink: Castro, the Missile Crisis, and the Soviet Collapse.* Lanham, Maryland: University Press of America, 2002.

Bonsal, Philip W. *Cuba, Castro, and the United States.* Pittsburgh: University of Pittsburgh Press, 1971.

Brands, H. W. *The Devil We Knew: Americans and the Cold War.* New York: Oxford University Press, 1993.

Bretos, Miguel A. *Cuba & Florida: Exploration of an Historic Connection, 1539- 1991.* Miami: Historical Association of Southern Florida, 1991.

Castillo, Celerino. *Powderburns: Cocaine, Contras & the Drug War.* Oakville, Ontario: Sundial, 1994.

Cockburn, Leslie. *Out of Control.* New York: Atlantic Monthly, 1987.

Corn, David. *Blond Ghost: Ted Shackley and the CIA's Crusades.* New York: Simon and Schuster, 1994.

Cortada, James N. *U.S. Foreign Policy in the Caribbean, Cuba, and Central America.* New York: Praeger, 1985.

Crispell, Brian Lewis. *Testing the Limits: George Armistead Smathers and Cold War America.* Athens: University of Georgia Press, 1999.

Critchlow, James. *Radio Hole- in- the- Head/Radio Liberty: An Insider's Story of Cold War Broadcasting.* Washington, D.C.: American University Press, 1995.

Croucher, Sheila L. *Imagining Miami: Ethnic Politics in a Postmodern World*. Charlottesville, Virginia: University Press of Virginia, 1997.

Cullather, Nicholas. *Operation PBSUCCESS: The United States and Guatemala 1952- 1954*. Langley, Virginia: U.S. Central Intelligence Agency, 1997.

Didion, Joan. *Miami*. New York: Simon and Schuster, 1987.

Dorschner, John and Roberto Fabricio. *The Winds of December: The Cuban Revolution 1958*. New York: Coward, McCann & Geoghegan, 1980.

Engelhardt, Tom. *The End of Victory Culture: Cold War America and the Disillusioning of a Generation*. New York: Basic Books, 1995.

Escalante Font, Fabian. *Cuba, La Guerra Secreta de la CIA. The Secret War: CIA Covert Operations Against Cuba, 1959- 62*. Melbourne, Florida: Ocean Press, 1995.

Evans, John E. *Time for Florida: A Report On the Administration of Farris Bryant, Governor 1961- 1965*. Tallahassee: n.p., 1965.

Fagen, M. D., ed. *A History of Engineering and Science in the Bell System: National Service in War and Peace (1925- 1975)*. New York: Bell Telephone Laboratories, 1978.

Ferrer, Edward B. *Operation Puma: The Air Battle of the Bay of Pigs*. Miami: International Aviation Consultants, 1982.

Fischer, Beth A. *The Reagan Reversal: Foreign Policy and the End of the Cold War*. Columbia: University of Missouri Press, 1997.

Fitzgerald, Frances. *Way Out There in the Blue: Reagan, Star Wars, and the End of the Cold War*. New York: Simon and Schuster, 2000.

Frederick, Howard H. *Cuban- American Radio Wars: Ideology in International Telecommunications*. Norwood, New Jersey: Ablex Pub. Corporation, 1986.

Fursenko, Aleksandr, and Timothy Naftali. *"One Hell of a Gamble": Khruschev, Castro, and Kennedy 1958- 1964*. New York: W.W. Norton, 1997.

Gaddis, John Lewis. *The Long Peace: Inquiries into the History of the Cold War*. New York: Oxford University Press, 1987.

_____. *We Now Know: Rethinking Cold War History*. New York: Oxford University Press, 1997.

Gambone, Michael D. *Eisenhower, Somoza, and the Cold War in Nicaragua, 1953- 1961*. Westport, Connecticut: Praeger, 1997.

García, María Cristina. *Havana USA: Cuban Exiles and Cuban Americans in South Florida, 1959- 1994*. Berkeley: University of California Press, 1996.

Garvin, Glenn. *Everybody Had His Own Gringo: The CIA & the Contras*. Riverside, New Jersey: Brassey's Book Orders, 1992.

Gibson, James William. *The Perfect War: Technowar in Vietnam*. Boston: Atlantic Monthly Press, 1986.

Gosse, Van. *Where the Boys Are: Cuba, Cold War America and the Making of a New Left*. London: Verso, 1993.

Green, David. *The Containment of Latin America: A History of the Myths and Realities of the Good Neighbor Policy*. Chicago: Quadrangle Books, 1971.

Gutman, Roy. *Banana Diplomacy: The Making of American Policy in Nicaragua*. New York: Simon and Schuster, 1988.

Haynes, John Earl. *Red Scare or Red Menace?: American Communism and Anticommunism in the Cold War Era*. Chicago: Ivan R. Dee, 1996.

Henriksen, Margot A. *Dr. Strangelove's America: Society and Culture in the Atomic Age*. Berkeley: University of California Press, 1997.

Heston, Thomas J. *Sweet Subsidy: The Economic and Diplomatic Effects of the U.S. Sugar Acts, 1934- 1974*. New York: Garland, 1987.

Higgins, Trumbull. *The Perfect Failure: Kennedy, Eisenhower, and the CIA at the Bay of Pigs*. New York: Norton, 1987.

Hinckle, Warren A., and William W. Turner. *The Fish is Red: The Story of the Secret War Against Castro*. New York: Harper & Row, 1981.

Hixson, Walter. *George Kennan: Cold War Iconoclast*. New York: Columbia University Press, 1989.

Hunt, E. Howard. *Give Us this Day*. New Rochelle, New York: Arlington House, 1973.

Immerman, Richard H. *The CIA in Guatemala: The Foreign Policy of Intervention*. Austin: University of Texas Press, 1982.

Johnson, Haynes. *The Bay of Pigs: The Leaders' Story of Brigade 2506*. New York: W.W. Norton, 1964.

_____. *Sleepwalking Through History: America in the Reagan Years*. New York: Doubleday, 1991.

Jordan, David C. *Revolutionary Cuba and the End of the Cold War*. Lanham, Maryland: University Press of America, 1993.

Kennedy, Robert F. *Thirteen Days: A Memoir of the Cuban Missile Crisis*. New York: W.W. Norton, 1969.

Kirkpatrick, Jeane J. *Dictatorships and Double Standards: Rationalism and Reason in Politics*. New York: Simon and Schuster, 1982.

Kirkpatrick, Lyman B. *The Real CIA.* New York: Macmillan, 1968.

Kornbluh, Peter. *Bay of Pigs Declassified: The Secret CIA Report on the Invasion of Cuba.* New York: The New Press, 1998.

Kornbluh, Peter, and James G. Blight. *Politics of Illusion: The Bay of Pigs Invasion Reexamined.* Boulder, Colordao: Lynne Rienner, 1997.

Kornbluh, Peter, and Malcolm Byrne. *The Iran- Contra Scandal: The Declassified History.* New York: New Press, 1993.

LaFeber, Walter. *America, Russia, and the Cold War, 1945- 1992.* New York: McGraw- Hill, 1993.

Langley, Lester D. *The United States, Cuba, and the Cold War: American Failure or Communist Conspiracy?* Lexington, Massachusetts : D.C. Heath, 1970.

Lebow, Richard Ned, and Janice Gross Stein. *We All Lost the Cold War.* Princeton: Princeton University Press, 1994.

Leffler, Melvyn P. *A Preponderance of Power: National Security, the Truman Administration, and the Cold War.* Stanford: Stanford University Press, 1992.

_____. *The Specter of Communism: The United States and the Origins of the Cold War, 1917- 1953.* New York: Hill and Wang, 1994.

Leynes, Jennifer Brown. *Biscayne National Park Historic Resource Study.* Atlanta: National Park Service, Southeast Region, 1998.

Light, Robert E. *Cuba versus CIA.* New York: Marzani & Munsell, 1961.

Linenthal, Edward T., and Tom Englehardt, eds. *History Wars: The Enola Gay and other Battles for the American Past.* New York: Metropolitan Books, 1996.

Marchetti, Victor and John D. Marks. *The CIA and the Cult of Intelligence.* New York: Knopf, 1974.

Marshall, Jonathan. *The Iran- Contra Connection: Secret Teams and Covert Operations in the Reagan Era.* Boston: South End Press, 1987.

Masud- Piloto, Felix Roberto. *From Welcomed Exiles to Illegal Immigrants: Cuban Migration to the U.S., 1959- 1995.* Lanham, Maryland: Rowman & Littlefield, 1996.

May, Elaine Tyler. *Homeward Bound: American Families in the Cold War Era.* New York: Basic Books, 1988.

May, Ernest R., ed. *American Cold War Strategy: Interpreting NSC- 68.* New York: St. Martin's, 1993.

May, Ernest R., and Philip D. Zelikow. *The Kennedy Tapes: Inside the White House During the Cuban Missile Crisis.* Cambridge, Massachusetts: Belknap Press, 1997.

May, Lary. *Recasting America: Culture and Politics in the Age of Cold War.* Chicago: University of Chicago Press, 1989.

McCormick, Thomas J. *America's Half- Century: United States Foreign Policy in the Cold War and After.* Baltimore: Johns Hopkins University Press, 1995.

McGehee, Ralph W. *Deadly Deceits: My 25 Years in the CIA.* New York: Sheridan Square, 1983.

Mesa- Lago, Carmelo. *Cuba After the Cold War.* Pittsburgh: University of Pittsburgh Press, 1993.

Morgan, Mark L., and Mark A. Berhow. *Rings of Supersonic Steel: Air Defenses of the United States Army 1950- 1979.* San Pedro, California: Fort MacArthur Military Press, 1996.

Morgan, Mark. *Nike Quick Look III: Bomarc/AF Talos.* Fort Worth: Aeromk, 1990.

Nash, Philip. *The Other Missiles of October: Eisenhower, Kennedy, and the Jupiters 1957- 1963.* Chapel Hill: University of North Carolina Press, 1997.

Nathan, James. *The Cuban Missile Crisis Revisited.* New York: St. Martin's, 1992.

Ninkovich, Frank A. *U.S. Information Policy and Cultural Diplomacy.* New York: Foreign Policy Association, 1996.

Oakes, Guy. *The Imaginary War: Civil Defense and American Cold War Culture.* New York: Oxford University Press, 1994.

Operation Zapata: The "Ultrasensitive" Report and Testimony of the Board of Inquiry on the Bay of Pigs. Frederick, Maryland: University Publications of America, 1981.

Paige, John C. *Historic Resource Study for Everglades National Park.* Washington, D.C.: National Park Service, U.S. Dept. of the Interior, 1986.

Pardo- Maurer, R. *The Contras, 1980- 1989: A Special Kind of Politics.* New York: Praeger, 1990.

Parkinson, F. *Latin America, the Cold War, & the World Powers 1945- 1973: A Study in Diplomatic History.* Beverly Hills: Sage Publications, 1974.

Paterson, Thomas G. *Contesting Castro: The United States and the Triumph of the Cuban Revolution.* Oxford: Oxford University Press, 1994.

_____, ed. *Kennedy's Quest for Victory: American Foreign Policy, 1961- 1963.* New York: Oxford University Press, 1989.

_____. *On Every Front: The Making and Unmaking of the Cold War.* 2d ed., New York: W.W. Norton, 1996.

Pérez, Louis A., Jr. *Cuba and the United States: Ties of Singular Intimacy.* Athens: University of Georgia Press, 1990.

_____. *Essays on Cuban History: Historiography and Research.* Gainesville: University Press of Florida, 1995.

Persons, Albert C. *Bay of Pigs: A Firsthand Account of the Mission by a U.S. Pilot in Support of the Cuban Invasion Force in 1961.* Jefferson, North Carolina: McFarland, 1990.

Pessen, Edward. *Losing Our Souls: The American Experience in the Cold War.* Chicago: I.R. Dee, 1993.

Portes, Alejandro, and Alex Stepick. *City on the Edge: The Transformation of Miami.* Berkeley: University of California Press, 1993.

Prados, John. *Presidents' Secret Wars: CIA and Pentagon Covert Operations from World War II through the Persian Gulf.* Chicago: I.R. Dee, 1996.

Rabe, Stephen G. *Eisenhower and Latin America: The Foreign Policy of Anti- Communism.* Chapel Hill: University of North Carolina Press, 1988.

_____. *The Most Dangerous Area in the World: John F. Kennedy Confronts Communist Revolution in Latin America.* Chapel Hill: University of North Carolina Press, 1999.

Reporting on Cuba: Literacy Campaign, Bay of Pigs (Playa Giron), October Crisis, *Hurricane "Flora",* Guantanamo Base, Fighting the Bandits, Sugar Harvest. Havana: Book Institute, 1967.

Rieff, David. *The Exile: Cuba in the Heart of Miami.* New York: Simon & Schuster, 1993.

_____. *Going to Miami: Exiles, Tourists, and Refugees in the New America.* Boston: Little, Brown, and Company, 1987.

Rodriguez, Felix I., and John Weisman. *Shadow Warrior: The CIA Hero of a Hundred Unknown Battles.* New York: Simon & Schuster, 1989.

Schaffel, Kenneth. *The Emerging Shield: The Air Force and the Evolution of Continental Air Defense 1945- 1960.* Washington, D.C.: Office of Air Force History, 1991.

Schiffren, Andre, ed. *The Cold War and the University: Toward an Intellectual History of the Postwar Years.* New York: New Press, 1997.

Schlesinger, Stephen, and Stephen Kinzer. *Bitter Fruit: The Untold Story of the American Coup in Guatemala.* Garden City, New York: Doubleday, 1982.

Schmitz, David F. *Thank God They're On Our Side: The United States and Right Wing Dictatorships, 1921- 1965.* Chapel Hill: University of North Carolina Press, 1999.

Scott, Peter Dale. *Cocaine Politics: Drugs, Armies, and the CIA in Central America.* Berkeley: University of California Press, 1998.

Sherry, Michael S. *The Rise of American Air Power: The Creation of Armageddon.* New Haven: Yale University Press, 1987.

Snyder, Alvin A. *Warriors of Disinformation: American Propaganda, Soviet Lies, and the Winning of the Cold War.* New York: Arcade Publishing, 1995.

Triay, Victor Andres. *Fleeing Castro: Operation Pedro Pan and the Cuban Children's Program.* Gainesville: University Press of Florida, 1998.

Utz, Curtis A. *Cordon of Steel: The U.S. Navy and the Cuban Missile Crisis.* Washington, D.C.: Naval Historical Center, 1993.

Welch, Richard E. *Response to Revolution: The United States and the Cuban Revolution, 1959- 1961.* Chapel Hill: University of North Carolina Press, 1985.

Whitacre, Christine, ed. *Last Line of Defense: Nike Missile Sites in Illinois.* Denver: National Park Service, Rocky Mountain System Support Office, 1996.

Whitfield, Stephen J. *The Culture of the Cold War.* Baltimore: Johns Hopkins University Press, 1991.

Woodward, Bob. *Veil: The Secret Wars of the CIA, 1981- 1987.* New York: Simon and Schuster, 1987.

Wyden, Peter. *Bay of Pigs: The Untold Story.* New York: Simon and Schuster, 1980.

Yergin, Daniel. *Shattered Peace: The Origins of the Cold War and the National Security State.* Boston: Houghton Mifflin, 1977.

DOCUMENTS AND MANUSCRIPTS

Bright, Christopher J. "Ack, Track, Smack: The Army's Nuclear Antiaircraft Missiles, Eisenhower, and Continental Defense." Paper presented as part of the panel "The Cold War and its Implications: Locally, Nationally and Internationally" at the Second Los Alamos International History Conference, Los Alamos, NM, August 1998.

_____. "*Still Other* Missiles of October: The Army's Nike-Hercules, Predelegation, and the Cuban Missile Crisis." Paper presented at the George Washington University Graduate Student Cold War Conference, Washington, D.C., 28 April 2000.

Cuban- American National Foundation. *U.S. Radio Broadcasting to Cuba: Policy Implications.* Washington, D.C.: Cuban- American National Foundation, 1982.

Elliston, Jon. *Psy War on Cuba: The Declassified History of U.S. Anti- Castro Propaganda.* New York: Ocean Press, 1999.

Florida State Department of Education. *A Resource Unit: Americanism vs. Communism.* Tallahassee: Dept. of Education, 1962.

Hatheway, Roger, and Stephen Van Wormer. *Historical Cultural Resources Survey and Evaluation of the Nike Missile Sites in the Angeles National Forest, Los Angeles County, California.* San Diego: Westec Services, 1987.

Hinds, James R. "History of the 2d Missile Battalion [1965]." 2/52/ADA Organizational History Files, Carlisle Barracks, MHI. Photocopy.

Keefer, Edward C., Charles S. Sampson, and Louis J. Smith, eds. *Foreign Relations of the United States 1961-1963: Volume XI—Cuban Missile Crisis and Aftermath.* Washington, D.C.: Department of State, 1996.

Kesaris, Paul, and Robert Lester. *CIA Research Reports: Latin America: 1946- 1976.* Frederick, MD: University Publications of America, Inc., 1982.

Kirkpatrick, Charles Edward. "The Second Battalion. 52nd Air Defense Artillery 1958- 1983, [1983]." 2/52/ADA Organizational History Files, Carlisle Barracks, MHI. Photocopy.

Kugler, Richard. *The U.S. Army's Role in the Cuban Crisis, 1962.* Office of the Chief of Military History, Washington, D.C., 1967. TOP SECRET declassified.

Lonnquest, John C. *To Defend and Deter: The Legacy of the United States Cold War Missile Program.* Champaign: U.S. Army Construction Engineering Research Laboratories, 1996.

Martin, Jean, and Geraldine Rice. *ARADCOM in the Cuban Crisis, September- December 1962.* Colorado Springs: Headquarters U.S. Army Air Defense Command, 1963.

_____. *History of ARADCOM January- December 1963, Book I, The Florida Units.* Colorado Springs: Headquarters U.S. Army Air Defense Command, 1963.

Martini, John A., and Stephen Haller. *What We Have We Shall Defend: An Interim History and Preservation Plan for Nike Site SF- 88L, Fort Barry, California.* San Francisco: National Park Service, 1998.

McAuliffe, Mary S., ed. *CIA Documents on the Cuban Missile Crisis, 1962.* Washington, D.C.: Central Intelligence Agency, 1992.

McLean, David R. *Excerpts from History: Western Hemisphere Division, 1946- 1965.* Langley, Virginia: Central Intelligence Agency History Office, 1973.

McMaster, B.N., et al, eds. *Historical Overview of the Nike Missile System.* Gainesville, Florida: Environmental Science and Engineering, Inc., 1984.

McMullen, Richard F. *The Fighter Interceptor Force 1962-1964.* Colorado Springs: Headquarters Air Defense Command, 1964. SECRET declassified.

Moenk, Jean R. *USCONARC Participation in the Cuban Crisis 1962.* Ft. Monroe: Headquarters U.S. Continental Army Command, 1964. TOP SECRET declassified.

Newman, T. Stell. *Biscayne National Monument Historical Studies Plan—Preliminary.* Denver: National Park Service, U.S. Department of the Interior, 1975.

Osato, Timothy J., and Sherryl Straup. *ARADCOM'S Florida Defenses in the Aftermath of the Cuban Missile Crisis 1963- 1968.* Colorado Springs: Headquarters U.S. Army Air Defense Command, 1968. SECRET declassified.

Paterson, Thomas G. *The United States and Castro's Cuba, 1950s- 1970s: The Paterson Collection.* Wilmington, Delaware: Scholarly Resources Inc., 1999.

Radio Broadcasting to Cuba Advisory Board. *Report by the Advisory Board for Radio Broadcasting to Cuba.* Washington, D.C.: The Board, 1986.

Research Institute for Cuba and the Caribbean. *The Cuban Immigration, 1959- 1966, and its Impact on Miami- Dade County, Florida.* Coral Gables, Florida: Center for Advanced International Studies, University of Miami, 1967.

Smith, Louis J., ed. *Foreign Relations of the United States 1961- 1963, Volume X, Cuba, 1961- 1962.* Washington, D.C.: Department of State, 1997.

Thompson, Thomas N. *USAFSS Performance During the Cuban Crisis Volume III The Aftermath: Permanent Operations.* N.p.: Headquarters U.S. Air Force Security Service, 1964. TOP SECRET declassified.

U.S. Army. "Battery D, Second Battalion, 52nd Air Defense Artillery Welcome Guide and Fact Booklet." 2/52/ADA Organizational History Files, Carlisle Barracks, MHI. Photocopy.

_____. *Congressional Fact Paper Draft—Cuba Threat and Army Plans.* Washington D.C.: Headquarters U.S. Army, 1962.

U.S. Army Air Defense Command. *U.S. Army Air Defense Command Annual Historical Summary.* Colorado Springs: Headquarters U.S. Army Air Defense Command, 1966. SECRET declassified.

U.S. Central Intelligence Agency. *Inspector General's Survey of the Cuban Operation and Associated Documents.* Washington, D.C.: Central Intelligence Agency, 1997.

U.S. Department of Defense. *Coming in from the Cold: Military Heritage in the Cold War.* Washington, D.C.: Dept. of Defense, 1994.

U.S. House Committee on Foreign Affairs. Subcommittee on International Operations. Foreign Policy Implications of TV Marti: Hearing Before the Subcommittees on *International Operations and on Western Hemisphere Affairs of the Committee on*

Foreign Affairs, House of Representatives. 100th Cong., 2d sess., 1988.

U.S. Navy Headquarters Atlantic Command. *CINCLANT Historical Account of the Cuban Crisis- 1963*. Norfolk, Virginia: Headquarters Atlantic Command, 1963.

Van Voorhies, Christine, and Michael Russo. *USAF Cultural Resources Servicewide Overview Project: 482 TFW Air Force Reserve Command, Homestead Air Reserve Base, Dade County, Florida*. Atlanta: National Park Service, Southeastern Region, 1995.

Winkler, David F. *Searching the Skies: The Legacy of the United States Cold War Defense Radar Program*. Langley AFB, Virginia: Headquarters Air Combat Command, 1997.

White, Mark J., ed. *The Kennedys and Cuba: The Declassified Documentary History*. Chicago: Ivan R. Dee, 1999.

INTERVIEWS

Abreu, Carlo. Interview by author, Brigade 2506 Museum, Miami, Florida, May 1999.

Bender, Donald. E- mail to author, August 1999.

Halsey, Bud. E- mail to author, July 1999.

Krenek, Richard. E- mail to author, October 1999.

McCormick, Richard H., Col. U.S. Army (ret.). Telephone conversation with author, October 1999.

Reder, George. E- mail to author, October 1999.

Smathers, George A. Interview by Donald A. Ritchie. *George A. Smathers: United States Senator from Florida, 1951- 1969: Oral History Interviews, August 1 to October 24, 1989*. Washington, D.C.: Senate Historical Office, 1991.

JOURNALS AND JOURNAL ARTICLES

Aguirre, Benigno E. "The Differential Migration of the Cuban Social Races," *Latin American Research Review* 11 (1976): 103- 124.

Bright, Christopher John. "Nike Defends Washington: Antiaircraft Missiles in Fairfax County, Virginia, during the Cold War, 1954- 1974." *Virginia Magazine of History and Biography* 105 (Summer 1997): 317- 346.

Cole, Merle T. "W- 25: The Davidsonville Site and Maryland Air Defense, 1950- 1974." *Maryland Historical Magazine* 80 (1985): 240- 260.

Gleijeses, Piero. "Ships in the Night: the CIA, the White House and the Bay of Pigs." *Journal of Latin American Studies* 27 (February 1995): 1- 42.

Horowitz, Irving Louis. 'The Cuba Lobby Then and Now." *ORBIS* 42 (Fall 1998): 553- 64.

Rabe, Stephen G. "The Caribbean Triangle: Betancourt, Castro, and Trujillo and U.S. Foreign Policy, 1958-1963." *Diplomatic History* 20 (Winter 1996): 55- 78.

_____. "John F. Kennedy and Latin America: The 'Thorough, Accurate, and Reliable Record' (Almost)." *Diplomatic History* 23 (Summer 1999): 539- 552.

Rieff, David. "From Exiles to Immigrants." *Foreign Affairs* 74 (July- August 1995): 76- 90.

Walker, J. Samuel. "The Decision to Use the Bomb: A Historiographical Update." *Diplomatic History* 14 (Winter 1990): 97- 114.

MAGAZINE ARTICLES

Balmaseda, Liz. "Miami's 'Little Managua': The Contra Rebels Run Their War from South Florida." *Newsweek* 107 (26 May 1986): 36- 38.

Berman, Phyllis. "The Fanjuls of Palm Beach: The Family with a Sweet Tooth." *Forbes* 145 (14 May 1990): 56- 62.

Branch, Taylor. "The Kennedy Vendetta: Our Secret War on Cuba." *Harper's Magazine* (August 1975).

"The Hothead Irregulars." *Newsweek* 99 (22 March 1982): 24- 26.

"Inside Camp Cuba- Nicaragua." *Time* 119 (8 February 1982): 34.

Lovler, Ronnie. "Training for the Counterrevolution: Cuban Guerrillas in Florida." *The Nation* 233 (26 September 1981): 265- 269.

Moeller, Stephen. "Vigilant and Invincible." *ADA Magazine* (May- June 1995).

Portes, Alejandro. "Morning in Miami: A New Era in Cuban- American Politics." *The American Prospect* 38 (May- June 1998).

Thomas, Evan. "Bobby Kennedy's War on Castro." *Washington Monthly* 27 (December 1995): 24- 31.

_____. "On the Trail of the Truth: One Woman's Mission to Find Out About Her Father Forces the CIA to Come Clean About the Bay of Pigs." *Newsweek* 131 (11 May 1998): 37.

NEWSPAPERS AND NEWSPAPER ARTICLES

Amlong, William R. "How the CIA Operated in Dade." *Miami Herald* (9 March 1975).

ARADCOM Argus

Army Times

Defender (Homestead- Miami, Key West Missile Defense Command Newspaper)

Fighter Forum (31s TFW, Homestead AFB, TAC, USAF)

Ft. Lauderdale News

Homestead News Leader

Kelly, Jim. "The Fidel Fixation." *Miami New Times* (17 April 1997).

Key West Citizen

Miami Herald

Miami News

Miami New Times

New York Times

News Leader and Cutler Ridge Perrine Post

South Dade News Leader

Wall Street Journal

THESES AND DISSERTATIONS

Clark, Juan M. "The Exodus From Revolutionary Cuba 1959-1974: A Sociological Analysis." Ph.D. diss., University of Florida, 1975.

Horne, Jeremy. "Americanism Versus Communism: The Institutionalization of an Ideology." Ph.D. diss., University of Florida, 1988.

Schnur, James Anthony. "Cold Warriors in the Hot Sunshine: the Johns Committee's Assault on Civil Liberties in Florida, 1956-1965." M.A. thesis, University of South Florida, 1995.

Sistrunk, Walter Everett. "The Teaching of Americanism Versus Communism in Florida Secondary Schools." Ed.D. diss., University of Florida, 1966.

Stark, Bonnie. "McCarthyism in Florida: Charley Johns and the Florida Legislative Investigation Committee, July 1956 to July 1965." M.A. thesis, University of South Florida, 1985.

WEB SITES

Bender, Donald E. "Nike Missiles and Missile Sites." <http://alpha.fdu.edu/~bender/nike.html>.

_____. "Nike Missile System Overview." <http://alpha.fdu.edu/~bender/nikeview.html>.

Gencorp. "Aerojet History." <http://www.aerojet.com/About_Aerojet/history/1950>.

National Security Archive. "Chile." <http://www.gwu.edu/~nsarchiv/latin_america/chile.html>.

_____. "Cuban Missile Crisis." <http://www.gwu.edu/~nsarchiv/nsa/cuba_mis_cri/cuba_mis_cri.html>.

North American Air Defense Command (NORAD). "Chronology of Radar Defense and Surveillance." <http://www.spacecom.af.mil/norad/maschron.html>.

Primary Source Media. "World Government Documents Archive: Declassified Documents Reference System—U.S." <http://www.ddrs.psmedia.com/index.html>.

Thelen, Edward. "Edward Thelen's Nike Missile Web Page." <http://www.nike-tech.org>.

Winslow, Gordon, et al. "South Florida Research Group." <http://www.cuban-exile.com>.

Word, David. "The Early Warning Connection." <http://www.creativexposure.com/earlywng/contacts_and_links.htm>.

Index

As the nation's principal conservation agency, the Department of the Interior has responsibility for most of our nationally owned public lands and natural resources. This includes fostering sound use of our land and water resources; protecting our fish, wildlife, and biological diversity; preserving the environmental and cultural values of our national parks and historical places; and providing for the enjoyment of life through outdoor recreation. The department assesses our energy and mineral resources and works to ensure that their development is in the best interests of all our people by encouraging stewardship and citizen participation in their care. The department also has a major responsibility for American Indian reservation communities and for people who live in island territories under U.S. administration.

NPS D- 433 January 1997